The Eucharist in the New Testament and the Early Church

Eugene LaVerdiere, S.S.S.

The Eucharist in the New Testament and the Early Church

A PUEBLO BOOK

The Liturgical Press   Collegeville, Minnesota

A Pueblo Book published by The Liturgical Press

Cover design by Frank Kacmarcik. Eucharistic fish (2nd century), Catacomb of St. Callisto.

Library of Congress Cataloging-in-Publication Data

LaVerdiere, Eugene.
    The Eucharist in the New Testament and the early church /
Eugene LaVerdiere.
        p.   cm.
    "A Pueblo book."
    Includes bibliographical references and index.
    ISBN 0-8146-6152-1
    1. Lord's Supper—History—Early church, ca. 30–600.   2. Bible.
N.T.—Criticism, interpretation, etc.   I. Title.
BV823.L33   1996
234'.163—dc20   96-19721
                                                           CIP

To Mom and Dad
Gladys and Laurier LaVerdiere
With Love and Gratitude

Contents

List of Tables

Preface

"When you assemble as a Church . . ." (RSV). The words are from St. Paul, writing to the Corinthians (1 Cor 11:18).[1] For Paul, the expression, "to assemble as a Church," referred to the nature and purpose of the assembly at which the Church celebrated the Eucharist.

There is no separating the Eucharist from the assembly celebrating it. Nor is there separating the assembly from the Church it represents. As Alexander Schmemann put it, "the very word 'church' — *ekklesia* — means 'a gathering' or 'an assembly' and to 'assemble as a church' meant, in the minds of the early Christians, to constitute a gathering whose purpose is to realize the Church."[2]

In his book, *The Eucharist: Sacrament of the Kingdom,* Schmemann, an Orthodox theologian, drew on the Eucharistic experience of both East and West. His reflections on the Eucharist never lose sight of what he called "an obvious, undoubted triunity of the *assembly,* the *eucharist* and the *Church,* to which the whole early tradition of the Church, following St. Paul, unanimously testifies."[3]

The same "triunity" — the assembly, the Eucharist and the Church — guided me in this study of *The Eucharist in the New Testament and the Early Church.* The Eucharist is the sacrament of the assembly, the sacrament of the Church. From the very beginning, there was no separating the three.

Nor is there separating references to the Eucharist from the letter, gospel, or other work in which they appear.[4] First Corinthians, for example, or Mark's Gospel both constitute the literary context for references to the Eucharist and reflect the ecclesial context which called for the letter or gospel.[5]

The study covers approximately one hundred years of early Christian writing, starting with Paul's First Letter to the Corinthians, written in A.D. 56, the third year of Nero's principate (54–68). Paul's appeal to tradition, putting us in touch with the previous twenty-five years of Eucharistic history, allows us to reach back all the way to "the Lord Jesus, on the night he was handed over" (1 Cor 11:23). And that is where the study begins.

After exploring the Eucharist in 1 Corinthians, the Gospels of Mark, Matthew, and Luke, the Book of Acts, the Gospel of John, the *Didache*, and the letters of Ignatius of Antioch, the study ends with Justin Martyr and his *Dialogue with Trypho*, written *circa* 155 during the reign of Antoninus Pius (138–161). Until Justin, Christians wrote of the Eucharist for people who also were Christians and knew the Eucharist from experience. Justin was the first, so far as we know, who described it for people who were not Christians and had no personal experience of the Eucharist.

The eleven chapters in this book were previously published as a special series commemorating the first one hundred years (1895–1995) of *Emmanuel* magazine, a magazine devoted to Eucharistic spirituality.[6] Each of the articles has been revised for publication in the present book. I am deeply grateful to *Emmanuel's* editor, Anthony Schueller, S.S.S., for encouraging me to publish the articles in book form. Collaborating in the capacity of senior editor with Father Schueller, the associate editors, and all who work at *Emmanuel*, has been an inspiration and a joy.

I am also grateful to The Liturgical Press, which invited me to publish the series in its valued Pueblo collection. As always, the editors at The Liturgical Press have been very helpful. My secretary, Mary Maloney, has also been more than helpful, poring over each draft, as only one could whose work is Eucharistic ministry.

I am grateful also to my teachers, Ernest Lussier, S.S.S., Herve Thibault, S.S.S., Joseph Nearon, S.S.S., and Francis Costa, S.S.S., at St. Joseph Seminary in Cleveland. All four have now gone home to God. As priests and religious they dedicated their lives to the Eucharist, the sacrament of the kingdom of God. They now dine in the fullness of God's kingdom.

My greatest teachers, of course, have been my parents, Gladys and Laurier LaVerdiere, who generously handed on what they themselves received, my sister, Sister Claudette LaVerdiere, M.M., currently president of the Maryknoll Sisters, my brother Gary LaVerdiere, S.S.S., manager of *Emmanuel* magazine, and Peter LaVerdiere, my youngest brother, who saved the honor of the family, blessed us with a sister-in-law, Cheryl, and three nephews, Jason, Charles, and Kevin.

In the words of St. Paul, "I give thanks to my God at every remembrance of you, praying always with joy in my every prayer for all of you, because of your partnership for the gospel from the first day until now" (Phil 1:3-5).

Eugene LaVerdiere, S.S.S.
February 5, 1995
Baptism of St. Peter Julian Eymard

NOTES

1. The translation, "when you assemble as a Church" *(synerchomenon hymon en ekklesia)* is from the RSV. Other translations, such as "when you come together as a church" (NRSV), "when you all come together in your assembly" (NJB), and "when you meet as a church" (RNAB), either fail to evoke the assembly for the Lord's Supper or misread the expression, *en ekklesia* (as a Church).

2. Alexander Schmemann, *The Eucharist: Sacrament of the Kingdom*, trans. Paul Kachur (Crestwood, New York: St. Vladimir's Seminary Press, 1988) 11.

3. Ibid.

4. Modern studies and syntheses of the Eucharist in the New Testament, while very helpful, have tended to isolate Eucharistic references from the totality of a work's message and from the assembly with which the references were associated. For studies available in English, see J. Delorme and others, *The Eucharist in the New Testament: A Symposium,* trans. E. M. Stuart (Baltimore: Helicon Press, 1965); Xavier Leon-Dufour, S.J., *Sharing the Eucharistic Bread: The Witness of the New Testament,* trans. Matthew J. O'Connell (New York: Paulist Press, 1987); Jerome Kodell, *The Eucharist in the New Testament.* Zacchaeus Studies: New Testament (Collegeville: The Liturgical Press, 1988). For the Eucharist in other early Christian writings, see Willy Rordorf and others, *The Eucharist of the Early Christians,* trans. Matthew J. O'Connell (New York: Pueblo Publishing Company, 1978).

5. By taking both the literary and the ecclesial context into consideration, we may avoid facile reconstructions of the origins and development of the Eucharist. For a discussion of the issues involved, see David N. Power, *The Eucharistic Mystery: Revitalizing the Tradition* (New York: Crossroad, 1992) 23–41. Reflecting on the difficulties presented by the New Testament data, Power notes, "What emerges is an awareness of the pluralism in Eucharistic thought and practice reflected in a diversity of texts coming from different communities. Access to the events of the Last Supper and to early Christian commemoration of the pasch is had only through the diverse interpretations of the New Testament books" (23).

6. Chapters 1 and 3 to 11 appeared in issues of *Emmanuel* from January/February to December 1994. Chapter 2 appeared in the January/February 1995 issue.

1

Before Ever There Was a Name:
Our Daily Bread

How did people refer to the Eucharist
before it had a name?
What did the Eucharist look like
in the very beginnings, before the
development of rites and formulas?
In search of answers, we have two
major points of reference:
the passion and resurrection of Jesus
and the Eucharistic tradition of Antioch.
The first is a point of departure.
What does it imply?
The second is a point of arrival.
What does it presuppose?

The Eucharist. That is what we call it. We also call it "the Mass."
Some call it "the liturgy," others "Holy Communion."

Names matter. They say or ought to say what something is. They
also say what something means to us. Sometimes what they mean to
us falls short of the reality.[1] That is why some names are better than
others.

While the name "Eucharist" is not found in the New Testament, the
verb "to give thanks" *(eucharistein)*, which gave rise to it, was part of
the Eucharistic tradition almost from the beginning (see 1 Cor 11:23-
25). The name "Eucharist" first appears in a collection of early Christian
writings known as "the Apostolic Fathers."[2] The oldest attestation is

in the *Didache* (9:1) in the heading for a set of blessings for community meals, "Regarding the Eucharist" *(Peri de tes eucharistias).*[3] The *Didache*'s reference to "the Eucharist" assumes the name was already well known, at least in the community of the *Didache.*[4]

One of the earliest names for the Eucharist is "the breaking of the bread" *(he klasis tou artou),* which appears both in Luke's Gospel (24:35) and in the Acts of the Apostles (2:42). Like the name "Eucharist," it is related to very early Eucharistic texts, which refer to Jesus' gesture of breaking bread for his disciples (see 1 Cor 11:24). The name emphasizes the quality of sharing among the early Christians.

The very oldest name we have for the Eucharist is "the Lord's Supper" *(to kyriakon deipnon).* That is what the early Christians called it in the early 50s of the first century. We know this from Paul's First Letter to the Corinthians: "When you meet in a place, then, it is not to eat *the Lord's Supper,* for in eating, each one goes ahead with his own supper and one goes hungry while another gets drunk" (1 Cor 11:20-21). Attitudes and behavior at Corinth made a mockery of the Lord's Supper.

The way Paul refers to the Lord's Supper presumes that everybody in the community knew the Eucharist by that name and were aware of its demands. The name, "the Lord's Supper," must therefore have been around for some time, perhaps even from the early 40s, a mere ten or fifteen years after Jesus' passion and resurrection. From the First Letter to the Corinthians, we know that Paul received the tradition of the Lord's Supper "from the Lord" and that he handed it on as part of the gospel (1 Cor 11:23). The name, "the Lord's Supper," is closely associated with the same liturgical tradition and can be traced back to the Church of Antioch, which formed Paul and sent him on mission.

The Eucharist, of course, was even older than that. It went back to meals in the apostolic community shortly after the events of the passion and resurrection, when these events were still extremely fresh in memory. But what did the Eucharist look like in those early days between the passion and resurrection of Jesus and the year 40 or so, when Christians first called it the Lord's Supper? And how did they refer to it or talk about it before calling it the Lord's Supper?

It is not easy to talk about the Eucharist before ever it had a name. It is like talking about Christians before they received the name "Christian." "It was in Antioch," Acts tells us, "that the disciples were first called Christians" (Acts 11:26).[5] It is not easy, but it is not impossible. I suggest one of the ways the early Christians referred to the Eucharist was as "our *epiousios* bread," an expression that made its way into the earliest tradition of the Lord's Prayer. We translate "our *epiousios* bread" as "our daily bread," although the word *epiousios* is not really translatable, but we shall come to that.

In the Beginning

The origin of the Eucharist is inseparable from Jesus' passion and resurrection. The Eucharist presupposes that Jesus gave his life for others. He gave it for his disciples, for the crowds who came to hear him, even for those who sought and brought about his death. As the Son of Man, *the* human being, he gave his life for all human beings. As Paul wrote to the Church at Rome: "Indeed, only with difficulty does one die for a just person, though perhaps for a good person one might even find courage to die. But God proves his love for us in that while we were still sinners Christ died for us" (Rom 5:7-8).

From the point of view of the Eucharist, what is significant is not simply the fact that Jesus suffered and died, but that he suffered for others and gave his life that all might live. The Eucharist presupposes that Jesus suffered and died with the same spirit that moved him in his ministry throughout his life. Jesus died as he lived. In giving his life, Jesus overflowed with God's love for all human beings. As John put it, Jesus died "that they may all be one, as you, Father are in me and I in you" (John 17:21). It would take many decades to put it like that, but the reality was there from the beginning.

From the very beginning, the Eucharist also presupposed that God raised Jesus to new life and that he appeared to the disciples shortly after his resurrection, while they were still in shock over his death but had not dispersed. Like his passion and death, Jesus' resurrection was a salvific and life-giving event, and his appearances as risen Lord were transforming events.

The Eucharist presupposes that Jesus offered his life in the passion-resurrection. Its beginnings coincide with the experience of Jesus continuing to offer his life as risen Lord. The Eucharist is inseparable from Jesus' passion, death and resurrection. It is also inseparable from Jesus' first appearances to the disciples. It is as Christ, who died and was raised, that Jesus is present in the Eucharist. It is also as risen Lord. The Eucharist is both the memorial of Christ's passion-resurrection and "the Lord's Supper."

Ophthe, "He Made Himself Seen"

The oldest term we have for Jesus' post-resurrection appearances to the disciples is *ophthe,* an aorist passive form of the Greek verb, "to see" *(horao).* *Ophthe* is usually translated, "he appeared," but is more accurately, even if awkwardly, rendered, "he made himself seen." The advantage of this rather convoluted expression, "he made himself seen," is that it conveys both the act of Christ appearing and the seeing activity of those who saw him, along with the appearance's transforming effects upon the disciples.

Jesus' disciples were not able to see him unless he somehow made himself be seen by them. Recall how the disciples of Emmaus were prevented from recognizing him (Luke 24:16) until "he took bread, said the blessing, broke it, and gave it to them" (Luke 24:30-31). Recall also how Mary Magdalene thought the person speaking to her was the gardener until he called her by name (John 20:14-16). There is more to an appearance than meets the eye.

The verb form *ophthe* had an extraordinary background in the Septuagint, where it refers exclusively to appearances of God, of the angel of the Lord and of the glory of God. For example, *ophthe* is the term Genesis used to describe how God appeared to Abraham as he sat in the entrance of his tent by the terebinth of Mamre (Gen 18:1). It is also the term Exodus used to describe how an angel of the Lord appeared to Moses in fire flaming from a bush without consuming it (Exod 3:2).

Christians adopted the term at a very early time to speak of Christ's appearance to the disciples. *Ophthe* is the term used in what may well be our oldest Christian creed. We find it in 1 Corinthians when Paul reminded the Christians

"that Christ died for our sins in accordance with the scriptures;
that he was buried;
that he was raised on the third day in accordance with the scriptures;
that he appeared *(ophthe)* to Kephas then to the Twelve" (1 Cor 15:3b-5).

Paul handed on this creed to the Corinthians in the year 51, but, along with the liturgical tradition for the Lord's Supper, he had received it much earlier, most likely during his Christian formative years at Antioch. When the early Christians said Christ "appeared" *(ophthe),* they associated the event with Old Testament experiences of the glory of God or the angel of the Lord, as when God appeared to Abraham and to Moses.

The Eucharist began in Jerusalem in one of those appearances of Jesus, not long after the resurrection when the disciples were gathered for a meal. As Luke indicates, the community of disciples stayed together after Jesus' crucifixion and death (Luke 24:33), devoting themselves to prayer (Acts 1:13-14). Jesus had taught them how to pray, and they had the example of Jesus' personal prayer (see Luke 11:2b-4; Matt 6:9-13). It is hard to imagine what else could have kept them together.

The First Appearances of the Risen Lord

Jesus' first appearance was to Simon. The event was reported by the community welcoming the disciples of Emmaus: "The Lord has truly been raised and has appeared *(ophthe)* to Simon!" (Luke 24:34). This first appearance was included in the creed Paul quoted to the Corinthians: "He appeared *(ophthe)* to Kephas, then to the Twelve" (1 Cor 15:5), to the Church in its apostolic head and in its foundations.

The New Testament also speaks of several appearances in the context of a meal with the disciples and the whole community (Luke 24:13-35, 36-49; John 21:1-14).[6] Acts refers to Jesus' appearances as "eating together" *(synalizomai)* with the apostles (Acts 1:4).[7] It is in appearances such as these, when the Lord Jesus appeared to the disciples and they recognized him in their midst, that the Eucharist began.

The beginnings of the Eucharist were both simple and awesome. They were simple in that the community of disciples were ordinary men and women who gathered for an ordinary meal. They were awesome in that the personal presence and appearance of Christ transformed the community of disciples into a new people, men and women who shared in the risen life of Christ and transformed their meal into what would eventually be called, "the Lord's Supper."[8] Those very early Eucharistic meals were certainly eaten in memory of Jesus but without the standardized forms and formulas that would later be inseparable from the Lord's Supper of the Church.

So long as the memory of Jesus and what he did the night he was handed over (see 1 Cor 11:23) remained vivid, the very fact of coming together for dinner was enough to evoke it. There was no need to recall Jesus' presence and say explicitly what he did.

In the beginning, the Eucharistic meals were not at all festive. Still taken up with the events of Jesus' passion and death, the disciples did not anticipate the appearance of Jesus at their meal. The menu for those first meals after Christ's death must have been extremely simple, varying according to what was easily available. One item, however, was always included. Every meal included bread, the staple food, not only for Palestinian Jews but for the whole Mediterranean world. So basic was bread for a meal that people often referred to having a meal simply as "eating bread."[9] Bread was their principal element of nourishment. Dipped into various sauces (Mark 14:20) and taken with other food such as fish (John 6:9), three small flat loaves provided adults an ample meal (Luke 11:5-6).

What distinguished the early Eucharistic meals was the sharing of the disciples, who had been called together and formed by Jesus over many months as he pursued his mission. The disciples had a history together and with Jesus, and that history must have influenced the way they continued to take meals together. Acts describes the community as including those making up the Eleven,[10] "together with some women, and Mary the mother of Jesus, and his brothers" (Acts 1:14).[11] Among the women were Mary Magdalene and the others who accompanied her to the tomb (Luke 24:10).[12]

These disciples already had a lot to share. The appearance of Jesus as the risen Lord brought them together as never before, inviting them to remember their days with Jesus of Nazareth and seeing Jesus' life with them in an entirely new light. In a way, they were the same community Jesus called, formed and associated with his mission. But they were also a new community transformed by the events of Christ's passion and resurrection.

Jesus' appearances were very mysterious, stretching human image-making possibilities to the limits, as did the appearances of God, the angel of the Lord and the glory of God in the Old Testament. How does one begin to describe an appearance of God? For the risen Lord, however, the early Christians had the finest possible image, that of the historical Jesus during the months and years he spent with them.

Jesus was the human sacrament of God in history. For the early Church, Jesus would also be the historical sacrament of the risen Lord among them. For the risen Lord's prayer before God, they had the image and experience of Jesus at prayer (see Luke 11:1). For the risen Lord's presence to them at meals, they had the image of Jesus at table with them in the course of his ministry.[13] Of all the meals Jesus shared with them, the most memorable was the most recent, the one Jesus shared with them the night he was handed over. The Last Supper gave them the images needed to express the deepest implications of their meals with Christ the risen Lord.

The early Christians spoke of their post-Easter meals with Jesus with constant reference to the Last Supper. If there was no separating the resurrection from the passion, neither was there separating the Lord's Supper from the Last Supper. They saw the Lord's Supper and the Last Supper as one. It is not surprising that Christians soon presented the Lord's Supper as actually unfolding at the Last Supper, as we see already in the tradition Paul handed on to the Corinthians: "the Lord Jesus, on the night he was handed over, took bread, and, after he had given thanks, broke it and said, 'This is my body that is for you. Do this in remembrance of me'" (1 Cor 11:23-25). This is how the memorial of Christ's passion and resurrection was to be celebrated, uniting the last meal of Jesus' historical life and the first of his risen life. And this is how the story would be told in the Gospels.

Our Bread, Our Meal

We have an idea what the Eucharist looked like in those earliest days before the development of an ordered structure with liturgical formulas and a special ritual. But how did early Christians refer to it? I suggest they spoke of it as "our daily bread," an expression found in both the Lukan and the Matthean versions of the Lord's Prayer.[14] The key element in the Greek expression for "our daily bread" (*ho artos hemon ho epiousios)* is the adjective *epiousios,* usually translated into English as "daily." But before examining *epiousios* as part of the early Christian vocabulary for Eucharist, we need to explore the even simpler expression, "our bread."

Since bread was so basic for a meal, and since the word "bread" was often used to refer to the entire meal, to eat bread together was to have a meal together. A meal was not something taken individually but with others, such as a family or community. The word "bread," consequently evoked the family or community event, the people gathered and sharing the meal, far more than the food they shared. If so, it seems safe to assume that the simplest and most ordinary way for Christians to refer to their Eucharistic meal together was to speak of "our bread," that is, "our meal."

The expression indicated that there was something special about their bread or meal, something that characterized it and distinguished it from the meals, "the bread," taken by other people, something that made it different from meals they themselves might take while away from the community. Only those who took part in their meal could know what that something special was, let alone appreciate it. This was not something easily described for someone who never experienced it. It depended on how the early Christians viewed themselves and on their sense of identity as a community.

Above all, what distinguished "our bread" was the presence and experience of the risen Lord among them, filling those who had suffered so much grief with a joy they had never known. Luke gives an inkling of this joy in the words of the disciples of Emmaus after they recognized the risen Lord: "Were not our hearts burning [within us] while he spoke to us on the way and opened the scriptures to us?" (Luke 24:32). There was also the participants' sense of who they were as a community with a common history in Jesus' ministry, in the events of the passion and resurrection and in the early reports of the Lord's appearance to Simon. Each of their meals with the risen Lord added to that history in common.

As new members became part of the community, the older members shared their community's story with them, making them part of that "our" in "our bread." Those who experienced "our bread" knew how extraordinary it was and what the expression meant. Those who were not part of the community and did not experience "our bread" had no inkling. No amount of guessing would have helped. For outsiders, associating "our bread" with the *ophthe* of divine manifestations in the Old Testament would have seemed preposterous.

Our Daily *(Epiousios)* Bread

The expression, "our bread," enabled the early Christians to indicate or point to their special meal experience, but it did not really say what "our bread" was. It would take a name to do that, a name like "the Lord's Supper," but it would be a good decade before Christians arrived at such a name. It stands to reason that those who experienced "our bread" would have wanted to describe so extraordinary a meal experience and speak of it more amply. For this, they needed some additional language that would at least evoke the experience. The word they came up with was *epiousios,* an adjective. "Our bread" was "our *epiousios* bread." Not that the word was already part of their lexicon. For their meal experience with the risen Lord, they coined a new word.[15]

The word *epiousios* was nowhere to be found in ancient Greek literature, not even in the thousands of papyri which have contributed so much to our knowledge of the Hellenistic vernacular in the first century. In the New Testament, the term appears exclusively in the two traditional texts of the Lord's Prayer. In all of early Christian literature outside the New Testament, it appears only in the *Didache* (8:2), which quite closely reproduces the Matthean tradition of the Lord's Prayer, and in Greek patristic works which quote or comment on the Lord's Prayer. Because of this limited usage, we lack the contexts needed for arriving at a precise definition and an adequate translation.

People have tried other avenues in search of a translation, pouring over the way the various ancient languages rendered *epiousios*, or trying to derive the meaning through the word's etymology or by analogy with similar words. None of these efforts have been conclusive. Our English translation, "daily," is due to the authority of liturgical tradition, which preserved the Old Latin version's *panis quotidianus*.[16]

Why then did the early Christians use such an undefinable and untranslatable word? As often happens, the correct answer may be the most obvious. An adequate definition or translation may have been very far from their mind. Coining a new word presupposes a new reality, a new experience, or at least a new way of viewing something. Meals in which the risen Lord appeared and was present to the disciples were a new reality with a totally new experience, which could not have been foreseen. Such a new reality called for a new word, hence *epiousios*, evoking something to do with the very substance or being of things, but without placing the Eucharist in any existing category.

Epiousios is a proper adjective for Eucharist.[17] To know what it means, one must know what it means to celebrate Eucharist. Beyond that, it points to the meal that is different from all other meals and provides a unique word to describe it.

The fact that the word was not used elsewhere in the New Testament, even in relation to the Eucharist, is not so surprising. The word *epiousios* was useful only within the community of believers. It said absolutely nothing to someone outside the community. For that, the rapidly growing community needed a name for Eucharist, a name like "the Lord's Supper." With such a name, *epiousios* was no longer needed or useful, and so it fell into disuse, to be preserved only in the traditions of the Lord's Prayer.

It may even be that early translations, such as the Old Latin *quotidianus* (daily) and Jerome's *supersubstantialis* (supersubstantial) were not intended as real translations. They may simply have served to point to the Eucharist, as did the Greek adjective *epiousios*. As such, "our daily bread," may have evoked exactly the same reality and experience as "our *epiousios* bread" without attempting to translate it.

"Our *epiousios* bread" is the bread or meal that is absolutely characteristic of us as Christians. Were I to attempt a translation that would evoke our characteristic Christian meal today, I would suggest "our Eucharistic bread." To know what the term meant at so early a date, however, we would have to reflect on early Christian experience of Eucharist before ever there was a name, as we have just done.

Without future developments in the New Testament, which has a rich theology of the Eucharist, reflection on the very first weeks and years after Jesus' passion and resurrection would not prove very satisfying. But in view of those later developments, it helps us appreciate a name such as "the Lord's Supper" and the extraordinary theology of the early liturgical formula Paul quoted in 1 Corinthians 11:23-25. It also enables us to separate what is absolutely basic about the Eucharist from everything that is secondary.

NOTES

1. "The Liturgy," for example, refers to far more than the Eucharist. It needs to be specified, as when we refer to "The Liturgy of the Eucharist." "Holy Communion," on the other hand, says too little. It needs to be related to the Eucharistic prayer in which the assembly unites itself with Christ's offering of himself in a supreme act of thanksgiving.

2. The title, "Apostolic Fathers," which refers to the earliest Christian writings after the New Testament, was introduced by scholars in the seventeenth century, when Jean Cotelier gathered the writings of Barnabas, Clement of Rome, Ignatius of Antioch, Polycarp of Smyrna, and Hermas under the title *Patres aevi apostolici* (2 vols., 1672). In modern times, the collection also includes the *Didache*. See Johannes Quasten, *Patrology* (Westminster, Maryland: The Newman Press, 1950) 1:40-42.

3. The title is followed by the instruction, "Give thanks *(eucharistesate)* as follows." For the Greek text I have relied on Jean-Paul Audet, *La Didache. Instructions des Apotres* (Paris: J. Gabalda, 1958) 226–243.

4. For the date of various parts of the *Didache*, see below, chapter 9.

5. Years before Luke-Acts was written, Paul stressed that those who were baptized into Christ were neither Jew nor Greek (Gal 3:26-27). Rather, they were "of Christ" (*Christou*, Gal 3:29), a designation still in use at the time of Mark (*circa* A.D. 70). The designation appears in Jesus' teaching to the Twelve: "Anyone who gives you a cup of water to drink because you belong to Christ (more literally, because you are of Christ, in Greek, *Christou*), amen, I say to you, will surely not lose his reward" (Mark 9:41). It would take a few years before those who were "of Christ" would receive the name "Christians" *(Christianoi)*.

6. The fact that these stories associate Jesus' appearances with meals is itself very significant. Stories such as these presuppose considerable development in the

Christian community but are based on meal experiences preserved in very early tradition.

7. The verb *synalizomai*, literally, having salt *(alas)* together *(syn)*, means "coming together for a meal." Translations such as "meeting with them" (RNAB) and "while staying with them" (NRSV) are too vague. "While at table with them" (NJB) is better.

8. The expression, "the Lord's Supper" *(to kyriakon deipnon)*, refers to the Lord Jesus with an adjective, *kyriakos*. It consequently describes the Eucharist not so much as a supper offered by the Lord or presided over by him but as a supper to which all are invited and at which all partake as one, qualities flowing directly from Jesus' identity as risen Lord. The same adjective, *kyriakos*, appears in the expression "the Lord's Day" *(he kyriake hemera*, Rev 1:10).

9. Compare Mark 6:31, "People were coming and going in great numbers, and they had no opportunity even to eat *(phagein)*," and Mark 3:20, "Again [the] crowd gathered, making it impossible for them even to eat," more literally, "to eat bread" *(arton phagein)*.

10. After Judas' betrayal, the Twelve were reduced to Eleven, including Peter (Acts 1:13).

11. The term "brothers" *(adelphoi)* refers to Jesus' "brothers and sisters." Luke's Gospel spoke of Jesus' "mother and his brothers" in 8:19-21, a passage whose parallel in Mark 3:31-34 uses the masculine plural, "brothers" *(adelphoi)*, to speak of Jesus' "brothers and sisters" (Mark 3:35; 6:3). Very likely, "the brothers and sisters" refer to extended family and perhaps even townspeople associated with Jesus from his earliest years.

12. These are the women who followed Jesus from Galilee (Luke 23:49; see 8:1-3) and were present at his burial (Luke 23:55).

13. Luke's Gospel includes ten stories of Jesus at table with disciples and others (5:27-39; 7:36-50; 9:10-17; 10:38-42; 11:37-54; 14:1-24; 19:1-10; 22:14-38; 24:13-35, 36-53). On these meals, see E. LaVerdiere, *Dining in the Kingdom of God* (Chicago: Liturgy Training Publications, 1994).

14. The expression also appears in the *Didache* (8:2), whose text of the Lord's Prayer is very close to that of Matthew.

15. Referring to a Greek papyrus in which *epiousios* was used, Arndt and Gingrich *(A Greek-English Lexicon of the New Testament and Other Early Christian Literature)* conclude against Origen *(De Orat.* 27, 7) that the term could not have been coined by the evangelists (Chicago: The University of Chicago Press, 1957), *epiousios*, 296. The papyrus to which they referred, however, was from the fifth century A.D., several centuries after the term *epiousios* was used in the early traditions of the Lord's Prayer (see Joseph Fitzmyer, *The Gospel According to Luke X–XXIV*, The Anchor Bible 28A (Garden City, New York: Doubleday & Company, Inc., 1985) 904.

16. See Eugene LaVerdiere, "Give Us Each Day Our Daily Bread," *Bread from Heaven*, ed. Paul Bernier (New York: Paulist Press, 1977) 19–33. The chapter appeared as an article in *Emmanuel* 82 (February 1976) 72–79.

17. Another proper adjective for the Eucharist is *kyriakos* as used in the expression *to kyriakon deipnon.* The Eucharist is "our *epiousios* bread (meal)" and "the *kyriakos* supper."

2

Telling What Happened:
The Genesis of a Liturgical Narrative

When the early Christians
first assembled for the Eucharist,
they surely told stories of Jesus.
But what stories did they tell?
Did they tell what Jesus
did and said at the Last Supper?
Or did they tell stories of
Jesus' passion and resurrection?
What can be said about the origins
of our liturgical narratives?
What difference do they make
for the Eucharistic liturgy?

Every time we celebrate the Eucharist, we tell the story of how it began. All over the world, in cities, large and small, in towns and villages, in great cathedrals, parish churches and little chapels, wherever we celebrate the Eucharist, we tell what Jesus did "on the night he was handed over" (1 Cor 11:23b). We tell the story of the Last Supper.

It is a very old tradition. People have been telling the story of the Last Supper from earliest Christian times, announcing the gospel, catechizing and celebrating the Eucharist. We know it from Saint Paul, introducing a liturgical tradition for the Church at Corinth: "For I received from the Lord, what I also handed on to you" (1 Cor 11:23a). Like the traditional baptismal creed in 1 Corinthians 15:3-5, the liturgical tradition and its story of the Last Supper come to us from the formative days of the Church at Antioch.

A Eucharistic Story

Christians may disagree about the story's meaning and purpose, but no one challenges its importance. For Catholics and many others, it says not only what Jesus did but what we do, or ought to do, when we celebrate the Eucharist. It says what the Lord Jesus does in and through us as often as we eat this bread and drink the cup, announcing the death of the Lord until he comes (see 1 Cor 11:26).

The story connects our celebration of the Eucharist with the Last Supper Jesus took with his disciples the night before he died. It shows how we fulfill his command: "Do this in remembrance of me" (1 Cor 11:24, 25; Luke 22:19).

The story has few parallels. A baptismal story comes to mind in which Jesus commands the disciples to go and make disciples of all nations, "baptizing them in the name of the Father, and of the Son, and of the holy Spirit" (Matt 28:19). But there is a difference. While Jesus personally celebrated meals, including the Last Supper, with his disciples, he himself did not baptize (see John 4:2).

Granted, however, that the story is very important, why do we tell it every time we celebrate the Eucharist? Why cannot we celebrate the Eucharist without telling how it began? Why cannot we celebrate the Eucharist like baptism, doing what Jesus commanded but without telling the story of its origins?

Christian common sense tells us the story of the Last Supper does make a difference, a very great one. But what precise difference does it make? Is telling the story of the Last Supper of the very essence of the Eucharist?[1]

Granted also that the story is among our oldest Christian traditions, does this mean it was told from the very beginning when the apostolic community first gathered for a meal and Jesus appeared to them? It seems more likely the conversation would have focused on Jesus himself, his presence as risen Lord, and how his presence affected them personally.

Did Christians begin telling the story of the Last Supper shortly after that, in those first weeks and months after Jesus' resurrection, when they referred to the Eucharist as "our meal," "our bread," and eventually "our *epiousios* bread"? Probably not. They more likely told stories of Jesus' passion, death and resurrection and what these events meant for their life and mission.

Only later, though not much later, judging from 1 Corinthians 11:23-25, did they focus on the Last Supper and tell its story in the celebration of the Eucharist. Having a traditional story about the beginning does not mean the story itself was told in the beginning. That helps account for the way the Eucharist was celebrated in the community of the *Didache,* which refers to the Eucharist and includes blessing prayers for the Eucharist but never so much as mentions Jesus' Last Supper.[2]

When finally the early Christians told the story of the Last Supper in their celebration of the Eucharist, they presented it as very closely related to Jesus' passion and resurrection. Without the passion and resurrection, there would have been no Last Supper.

They also presented the Last Supper as an anticipation of the Eucharist. Without the Eucharist, there would have been no reason to tell stories of the Last Supper. From the very start, the story of the Last Supper was thus a Eucharistic story. Presupposing the Eucharist and the Eucharist's relationship to Christ's passion and resurrection, the story presented the Last Supper both as the Lord's Supper and as the memorial of Christ's passion and resurrection.

According to this historical reconstruction, at the very beginning, in their celebration of the Eucharist, the early Christians spoke of Jesus' appearance and presence to them. Very soon, they also told stories of Jesus' passion and resurrection. Only later did they concentrate on the Last Supper and what Jesus did and said "the night he was handed over."

What motivated this change of focus? What moved the early Christians to begin telling the story of the Last Supper in their celebration of the Eucharist? Why did they continue to do so, even including it in their Eucharistic prayer? What function did the story serve?

From these questions we get a greater appreciation of the story of the Last Supper as told in our Eucharistic prayers. Their answers, however, would give an even greater appreciation. It is true that we lack precise historical information about Christianity's earliest days. Everything in the New Testament is told in light of later developments. But we do have a clear point of departure *(terminus a quo)* in Jesus' resurrection. We also have a point of arrival *(terminus ad quem)* in some very early traditions, including that of the Lord's Supper as presented in 1 Corinthians 11:23-25.

What happened between these two points may be hypothetical, but is not without basis. What effect did Jesus' resurrection have on the early Christians? What do the resurrection appearances imply? What do the traditions concerning the Eucharist and life in the Christian community presuppose?

The New Testament provides a window into the past. Its Gospels, epistles and other writings may present the beginnings through the lens of a later time and context, but they do say something about the beginnings. They also describe early community situations analogous in many ways to those in the very first community. At the very beginning, an early Christian community's response to the gospel message was quite similar to the first disciples' response to the risen Lord. Later changes in the community's response were also similar to changes in the response of the first disciples.

The following reflections on the genesis of a liturgical narrative proceed in four steps.

- They begin with some basic observations on the story of the Last Supper, "the institution narrative," as it is called, and its relationship to the Eucharistic prayer.
- They continue with reflections on the story both as a liturgical story, told as part of the Eucharistic liturgy, and as an ordinary gospel story, told as part of a gospel narrative.
- They then consider what it was like in the very beginnings, when there must have been some kind of Eucharistic prayer, but without the story of the Last Supper.
- Finally, they examine historical situations in the actual celebration of the Lord's Supper that invited, indeed required that the story of the Last Supper be told. With that, we should be in a good position to grasp the story's function in our celebration of the Eucharist.

In the Eucharistic Prayer

A look at today's Eucharistic prayers suggests that, from a literary point of view, the story of the Last Supper is out of place. At the prayer's most solemn moment, after praising God and invoking God's Spirit, we interrupt the prayer to tell what Jesus did and said at the Last Supper. Then, after proclaiming the mystery of faith, we resume with the prayer. Or so it seems.

For example, with Eucharistic Prayer II we address God in the second person: "Lord, *you* are holy indeed, the fountain of all holiness." Continuing in the same second person we then invoke God's Spirit:

"Let *your* Spirit come upon these gifts to make them holy, so that they may become for us the body and blood of our Lord, Jesus Christ."

In literary terms, what we say is in the form of a prayer. We declare God holy, using the present indicative, in this case the eternal-present indicative: "Lord, *you* are holy indeed, the fountain of all holiness." We then look to the future, using the imperative, focusing God's eternal-present on our present moment and the Eucharistic offerings.

Then, after mentioning "the body and blood of our Lord, Jesus Christ," we put aside the second person of direct address and continue in the third person. We tell what Christ did and said at the Last Supper: "Before he was given up to death, a death he freely accepted, he took bread and gave you thanks. . . ."

In literary terms, what we say is in the form of a story in third-person narrative. Using the indicative past tense, we tell what Jesus did and said nearly two thousand years ago, at a critical moment in history. In doing that, we actualize what Jesus did and said, make it ours, and bring it to bear on the present.

After proclaiming the mystery of faith, we return to the second person of direct address: "In memory of his death and resurrection, we offer *you*, Father, this life-giving bread, this saving cup." And so we continue until the great "Amen!"

In literary terms, what we say is once again in the form of a prayer. Beginning with the present indicative, we renew our offering and give thanks. Looking to the future and using the imperative, we then ask the Lord to remember and have mercy.

The story of the Last Supper is obviously different in form from the prayer in which it was inserted. It is possible we have never noticed this seeming anomaly.

Not that we take the story for granted. The Last Supper and its story, telling what Jesus did and said there, is as awesome for us as it was for the disciples the night the Supper was held. The Last Supper anticipates and interprets the passion and resurrection of Jesus. It is hard to imagine the passion without it.

What we may take for granted is telling the story as part of a Eucharistic prayer. It is one thing to tell the story of what Jesus did and said at the Last Supper. It is another to tell it in the midst of a Eucharistic prayer at the Lord's Supper.

The narrative interruption, however, is only apparent. Liturgy is not literature. A Eucharistic prayer must be examined from a liturgical point of view, not just from a literary or rhetorical point of view.[3]

Eucharistic prayers, including Eucharistic Prayer II, are prayers of thanksgiving. So was the prayer of Jesus at the Last Supper. Before breaking bread, Jesus gave thanks (1 Cor 11:24). That is what the word "Eucharist" means, "giving thanks." Celebrating the Eucharist is above all an act of thanksgiving. Like all acts of thanksgiving, it is for something that was done for us. Remembering what was done, we are grateful.[4]

Our prayer of gratitude is spoken in the present. What Jesus did is part of the past. What links the two is remembering. Remembering, an act of memory, is the spark of thanksgiving. There is no thanksgiving, including Eucharistic thanksgiving, without remembering.

Thanking and Remembering

As an act of thanksgiving, the Eucharist begins with remembering. That is why the two are so closely linked in the Eucharistic prayers, where we give thanks for God's gracious gifts in creation and in history. To do that we spell out what God has done for us. We say why we are grateful, unless somehow the reason is so clear it does not need to be expressed. That is the way it is with biblical expressions of thanksgiving.[5] That is the way it is with every expression of gratitude.

Telling the story of what Jesus did and said at the Last Supper, we bring to mind the special grounds we have for thanking God in the Eucharist. To do what Jesus did in memory of him, to celebrate and proclaim the death of the Lord, we need first to remember what he did.[6]

But does remembering what Jesus did at the Last Supper require that it be spelled out every time? How was it with the first disciples in the weeks and months right after the passion-resurrection? To give thanks they needed to remember. But to remember, did they need to be reminded each and every time? In particular, did they have to tell the story of what Jesus did and said when the events were still very fresh in memory?

There is no denying that we need to remember, as the early Christians needed to remember. But what is it we need to remember? The question still remains. What was it the first Christians needed to remember? Was it the Last Supper, or was it Christ's passion and resurrection?

In the Eucharist, Christians have always needed to remember Christ's passion and resurrection. Christians need to remember in order to do what Jesus did in remembrance of him, announcing the death of the Lord until he comes (1 Cor 11:26). Why then do Eucharistic prayers tell the story of the Last Supper instead of the passion-resurrection?

That, quite early on, the first Christians remembered and told a story of the Last Supper is obvious. They told it as a gospel story, closely related to that of the passion-resurrection. That is how the Last Supper has come down to us in the Gospels. They also told it when they celebrated the Eucharist. That is how it became part of our liturgical tradition. But does that mean they told the story of the Last Supper from the very beginning? When they did tell it, the most normal context would have been the celebration of the Eucharist. But did they do it as part of their Eucharistic prayer?

Such questions are challenging and enlightening, like those asking how Christians referred to the Eucharist before it had a name. In that case, they helped us see why the Eucharist was eventually given a name, the needs to which the name responded and the functions it served. The same is true for the narrative of the Last Supper.

Reflection on the very beginnings helps us see how the Last Supper was related to the passion-resurrection, both in early tradition and in the gospel narratives. It also helps us see why the story was told in the celebration of the Eucharist, as well as the needs to which it responded, and the functions it served.

It ought to help us see why to this day, every time we celebrate the Eucharist, we tell the story of how it began and what difference it makes.

Gospel Narrative, Liturgical Narrative

What is the difference between a liturgical and a literary narrative of the Last Supper? The most basic difference is one we have already noted. The liturgical narrative is told in the context of a Eucharistic prayer. The literary narrative is read in a variety of contexts, including the liturgy of the word, meditative reading such as *lectio divina*, and catechesis, always, however, with reference to its literary context in First Corinthians or the Synoptic Gospels.

In some ways, telling the story in the celebration of the Eucharist is like telling it as part of the gospel, in particular of the passion-resurrection. The Eucharist is the gospel in action, proclaiming Jesus' passion and resurrection, as Paul wrote to the Corinthians: "For as often as you eat this bread and drink the cup, you proclaim the death of the Lord until he comes" (1 Cor 11:26).

Liturgical narratives, however, are also very different from literary or rhetorical narratives. The liturgical telling of the Last Supper is done in a symbolic setting, where acts, gestures and ritual are more important than words. Outside the liturgy, the gospel of the Last Supper takes place in a literary or rhetorical setting, where words and verbal communication are uppermost.

As told in the Eucharistic liturgy, the story of the Last Supper is very short, much shorter than in the Synoptic Gospels, where the story also includes the preparations for the Supper (Mark 14:12-16; Matt 26:17-19; Luke 22:7-13) and the announcement of Judas' betrayal (Mark 14:17-21; Matt 26:20-25). In Luke the Last Supper is presented as a formal supper at which Jesus gave a farewell discourse (Luke 22:14-38).

With several other stories, such as Jesus' prayer at Gethsemane, the story of the Last Supper in the Synoptic Gospels forms a kind of prologue for the story of the passion-resurrection.[7] At the beginning of each Gospel, a prologue announces the Gospel's principal themes. The Last Supper does the same for the passion-resurrection, as told in the Synoptic Gospels. In John's Gospel it not only announces but develops the principal themes of the passion-resurrection at great length.

A Gospel prologue is the entire Gospel in miniature. As such, it relies a great deal on symbolic language and imagery. That is how, in the Matthean and Lukan prologues, the story of Jesus' conception and birth refers to his entire life and mission, including his death and resurrection.[8]

As a prologue, the story of the Last Supper is the story of the passion-resurrection in miniature. And for that, it too uses symbolic language and imagery. That is why, in the Synoptic Gospels, the story of the Last Supper, referring to Jesus' climactic prepassion meal, draws on the liturgical tradition of the Lord's Supper, so rich with images and symbolic language.

In some ways, then, the story of the Last Supper in the Gospels (Mark 14:12-26; Matt 26:17-30; Luke 22:7-38) is like the other stories in the Gospels. It tells what happened at a given point in Jesus' life. It tells what he did and said to his disciples and how they reacted to him. At the same time, however, the story is quite different from other Gospel stories. At its climactic and most solemn moment, it quotes from a liturgical formula, told not in ordinary gospel language but in solemn liturgical language.

The story of the Supper's preparation is gospel narrative. So is the part of the Supper in which Jesus announced that one of the Twelve would betray him. The part of the Supper, however, in which Jesus "took bread, said the blessing, broke it, and gave it to them" (Mark 14:22-25; Matt 26:26-29; Luke 22:19-20) is formal liturgical narrative.

Originally intended for liturgical prayer, Mark introduced the liturgical narrative into his story of "the beginning of the gospel of Jesus Christ [the Son of God]" (Mark 1:1), adapting it to the overall purpose of his Gospel. Following suit, Matthew and Luke introduced it into their account of the gospel, adapting it for their own purposes.

Liturgical gospel narrative is also different from literary gospel narrative in that it makes full sense only in a liturgical setting as part of a liturgical act. St. Paul referred to that setting as when Christians assemble as a Church (1 Cor 11:18). He referred to the liturgical act as eating the Lord's Supper (1 Cor 11:20) and he quoted the liturgical narrative in relation to the Eucharistic liturgy at Corinth.

The liturgical narrative also makes full sense only as part of Eucharistic prayer. That is the way it was even with the liturgical text Paul presented in 1 Corinthians 11:23-25. Jesus broke bread, pronounced it his body, and took the cup, pronounced it the new covenant in his blood, once he had given thanks.

To fulfill his command, "Do this in remembrance of me, the early Christians had to do the same. Their Eucharistic action, including telling the story of what Jesus did, required that they too give thanks. Like Jesus, they gave thanks in deed, by breaking bread and taking the cup, and in word, praising God in thanksgiving.

In its proper context, that of liturgical prayer, the story of the Last Supper expresses both the historical and the present grounds for giving thanks, telling what Jesus did "on the night he was handed over" and what we do, making the event present, every time we celebrate Eucharist.

When the narrative is told outside the liturgical context, as in the story of Jesus' passion-resurrection, it evokes the liturgical setting and the liturgical act. It invites seeing the passion-resurrection through the lens of liturgical, Eucharistic experience. Indirectly, it also associates the liturgical celebration of the Eucharist with the passion-resurrection.

In the Beginning

To tell the story of the Last Supper, the Synoptic Gospels relied on liturgical traditions of the Last Supper. These liturgical traditions, however, were themselves based on a pre-liturgical, extremely early, historical tradition of the event.[9]

Paul's story of what Jesus did and said at the Last Supper (1 Cor 11:23-25) tells about the very beginnings of the Eucharist. As a liturgical formula, the story also tells what Christians repeated every time they assembled "as a church" (1 Cor 11:18) at "the table of the Lord" (cf. 1 Cor 10:21) "to eat the Lord's Supper" (1 Cor 11:20).

As a narrative, the story told of a very significant meal which took place at a particular moment in history. The story is about "the Lord Jesus on the night he was handed over" (1 Cor 11:23).

As a liturgical formula, the story linked the unique historical event of the Last Supper with the repeated liturgical event of the Lord's Supper. "On the night he was handed over" the Lord Jesus commanded those at the Last Supper to do what he did in remembrance of him. And that is what they did every time they celebrated the Lord's Supper.

The link between the Christian Lord's Supper and Jesus' Last Supper is also indicated in the formula's introduction, which refers not merely to Jesus but to "the Lord Jesus," Jesus as risen Lord, "on the night he was handed over." The account's point of view in presenting the Last Supper is thus that of the Lord's Supper. At the time of the Last Supper, Jesus' passion and resurrection may have been imminent, but were still in the future. At the time of the Last Supper, Jesus was not yet handed over. Calling Jesus "the Lord" reflects the faith of the early Church celebrating the Lord's Supper after the resurrection.

Attributing the Last Supper to "the Lord Jesus" suggests that what the earliest Christians remembered at the Lord's Supper was first the appearance of the risen Lord to the first disciples, together with the event of the resurrection. Their celebration of the Lord's Supper was dominated by the experience of the risen Lord, giving rise to Eucharistic expressions such as "drinking the cup of the Lord" *(poterion kyriou pinein)*, "partaking of the table of the Lord" *(trapezes kyriou metechein)*, (1 Cor 10:21) and "the Lord's Supper" *(to kyriakon deipnon)* (1 Cor 11:20).

The formula's reference to "the night he was handed over" situates the Supper historically in relation to Jesus' passion. The Synoptic Gospels do the same by telling the story of the Last Supper as part of the whole story of the passion-resurrection. Since they showed how the Supper took place in fact "on the night he was handed over," there was no need for them to say it.

In every case, the Lord's Supper, while celebrated in the joyous atmosphere of Jesus' resurrection, was related directly to the passion. Indeed, the two events were inseparable.

The resurrection was not an ordinary hopeful event in a series of hopeful events. For the disciples, whose hope collapsed with Jesus' passion and death, it marked a renewal of hope, transforming their former hope into one beyond anything they could have anticipated. Their Christian hope was inversely proportional to the loss they had experienced in the passion.

It was very important to situate the Supper historically, but the formula did much more. It interpreted the passion theologically according to the Scriptures (see 1 Cor 15:3-5), presenting Christ's passion in relation to the incomparable Song of the Suffering Servant in Isaiah 52:13–53:12. As in the case of the Suffering Servant, what appeared to be meaningless and cause for despair was in reality very meaningful and cause for great hope.

The expression, "he was handed over," does not refer to the plotting of the chief priests and others or to Judas' betrayal but to God. The Supper took place on the night Jesus was handed over by God. There is no understanding Jesus' death apart from the relationship between God and Jesus. The same is emphasized in our Eucharistic Prayer II, which situates the Supper "before he (our Lord, Jesus Christ) was given up to death," adding, "a death he freely accepted."

The Pauline formula does not say how Jesus was handed over. That story would be told in the Gospel accounts of the passion-resurrection. In the words of Jesus, however, it does say why he was handed over: "This is my body that is for you" (1 Cor 11:24).

Situating the Lord's Supper "on the night he (the Lord Jesus) was handed over," suggests that what the early Christians remembered at the Lord's Supper was his passion and death, together with his resurrection. The Lord's Supper was thus dominated by the experience of the passion as well as of the risen Lord, giving rise to expressions describing the Eucharist as "a participation in the blood of Christ *(koinonia tou haimatos tou Christou)*" and "a participation in the body of Christ *(koinonia tou somatos tou Christou)*" (1 Cor 10:16), and declaring the Eucharistic cup "the new covenant in my blood *(he kaine diatheke en to emo haimati)*" (1 Cor 11:25).

In the very beginning, it would seem, then, that what the early Christians remembered in the Eucharist was Jesus' passion and resurrection, with each giving meaning to the other. Only later, even if not much later, did they remember the Last Supper.

The earliest celebrations and experiences of the Eucharist were thus associated with the passion-resurrection of the Lord Jesus, not with the many meals Jesus took with them during his earthly ministry. Only later, in conjunction with the Last Supper, did they associate these other meals with the Lord's Supper.[10]

The Lord's Supper

As Paul indicates in 1 Corinthians 11:23-25, it did not take very long before the early Christians began telling the story of the Last Supper at the Lord's Supper, even as they gave thanks as Jesus himself gave thanks. Instead of focusing directly on the passion and resurrection, they told the story of Jesus' Last Supper as their symbolic (sacramental) expression.

The dynamism for such a change did not come from the Last Supper and what Jesus actually did and said there, however important these were, but from the Christian experience of the Lord's Supper. It is not so much that the historical experience of the Last Supper demanded there be a Lord's Supper. Rather, it is the Christian, Eucharistic experience of the Lord's Supper that brought the Last Supper to mind. Consequently, it is not the Lord's Supper that was patterned on Jesus' Last Supper, but the story of the Last Supper which was patterned on the Lord's Supper.

The story of the Last Supper was written in light of the community's Eucharistic experience and what later would be called "the Lord's Supper." The way its story was told responded to concrete pastoral needs, which may well have been related to those Paul addressed in 1 Corinthians.

At first, the Lord's Supper was celebrated in an atmosphere of hope, joy, and freedom, all flowing from Jesus' resurrection and his presence to the community as risen Lord. Was this not "the cup of the Lord"? Was this not "the table of the Lord"? This was "the Lord's Supper"!

As we see from Paul's letters, however, beginning with the earliest, the meaning and implications of Jesus' resurrection were not immediately clear. According to Jewish expectations, especially among the Pharisees, the resurrection was to be at the consummation of history.

Here was Jesus' resurrection in the midst of history. How then did Jesus' resurrection affect the course of history?

What did the resurrection of Jesus imply regarding the lives of those who placed their belief in him? What did Jesus' presence among them as risen Lord imply concerning their relationships to one another, their moral behavior and ordinary activities such as work? Since Jesus was risen and living in their midst, were they now beyond or above such preoccupations? What meant their new freedom in Christ?

The early Christians had to face all those issues and, no doubt, many more that had a serious bearing on their assembly for the Lord's Supper. It seems quite clear that the problems in the Church at Corinth stemmed in large part from an exaggerated sense of each one's personal freedom. Many showed little concern for the gospel's demands regarding everyday life in history for Christians who indeed enjoyed new life in Christ but were not yet risen with Christ.

In light of Jesus' resurrection, the past mattered little, the present could hardly be more meaningful, and everything was hopeful. Jesus' resurrection inaugurated a new creation, a new covenant. In the risen Lord, everything was made new. It must have been quite exhilarating to celebrate the Eucharist in such an atmosphere.

Throwing off the weight of sin, personal and corporate, and freed from old divisions, everyone looked to the future. In the company of the risen Lord, that future looked very short, no matter how many the years. At the table of the Lord, they celebrated Jesus' resurrection and their share in his risen life. Soon they would be with him in glory at the table of heavenly fulfillment.

So it must have been in those first days and weeks after Jesus' resurrection. In light of the resurrection, the pain of his passion seemed insignificant. In light of their new life, the challenges of the past were no longer a concern. At the Lord's Supper, they were all one, brothers and sisters at the table of the Lord.

But, as months turned into years, the honeymoon ended, the first fervor waned, the new began to fade, old divisions reappeared and the sins of the past reasserted themselves. They were indeed free, but then they were not. All was new but the old remained very close. They really were saved. But what did that mean? The challenges of living as Christians in a world that continued as if nothing had happened were no longer so simple as they once seemed.

The Last Supper

We can appreciate the immediate impact of Jesus' resurrection on the early Christians, also the effect of Jesus' presence among them as risen Lord, however mysterious, and how it must have been at the meals they shared at the table of the Lord. We can also appreciate why, when difficulties mounted and problems seemed overwhelming, they reflected on the passion in search of understanding.

But that still does not say why they turned to the story of the Last Supper and included its story in their Eucharistic prayer. I suggest that what led them to do this were the many problems they encountered not just in general areas of life but in the actual celebration of the Eucharist.

Some of those problems may have been like those Paul dealt with in his Second Letter to the Thessalonians. It seems that some at Thessalonica felt that their new freedom in Christ, the risen Lord, exempted them from ordinary, human preoccupations such as work. Idleness, however, did not keep them from eating freely at the community meal. It also gave them a lot of time to meddle in the affairs of others and cause trouble in the community.

The issue was important enough for Paul to address it directly. Indeed, the problem had existed from the community's very beginning: "In fact, when we were with you, we instructed you that if anyone was unwilling to work, neither should that one eat. We hear that some are conducting themselves among you in a disorderly way, by not keeping busy but minding the business of others. Such people we instruct and urge in the Lord Jesus Christ to work quietly and to eat their own food" (2 Thess 3:10-12).

Paul's response presupposes that the Thessalonian community took meals in common.[11] At least some of those meals, as in the Corinthian community, were Eucharistic meals. If idleness weighed heavily on community life in general, it must have been especially troublesome at the Lord's Supper, which was celebrated on the first day of the week. Unlike the Sabbath, the first day of the week was not observed as a day of rest but as the first day of the new creation.[12]

There were many other problems, of course, as we learn from the First Letter to the Corinthians. There were factions in the community (1 Cor 1:10-17), serious enough to cripple the community, so serious they made a mockery of the Lord's Supper (1 Cor 11:17-34). It was extremely difficult for people of extremely diverse backgrounds to live as one in Christ and to assemble as one at the table of the Lord of all.

Paul's Letter to the Galatians refers to a very different kind of problem when he, Kephas, Barnabas, and some Christians from Jerusalem were at a community meal in Antioch. Ordinarily, the Christians who were of Jewish background ate with those of Gentile background. But when some came from Jerusalem, Kephas and the others who were of Jewish background, including even Barnabas, withdrew from the others, intending to take their meal apart. Challenging their hypocrisy, Paul defended the truth of the gospel (Gal 2:11-15). Paul does not refer to that meal as the Lord's Supper. It does seem, however, that the community, in terms familiar from 1 Corinthians, had assembled "as a Church" *(en ekklesia)* and "in one place" *(epi to auto)*. If so, these would be strong indications that the community had indeed assembled for the Lord's Supper (see 1 Cor 11:18-20).[13]

I suggest that it was to counter problems similar to those that arose in the early Pauline communities, celebrating the Lord's Supper, that the early Christians began telling the story of Jesus' Last Supper. It was not so much to anchor the Lord's Supper historically that they told what "the Lord Jesus" did "on the night he was handed over." It was rather to spell out the implications of Christ's passion and resurrection for the celebration of the Lord's Supper.

Telling the story of what Jesus did and said at the Last Supper was extremely challenging and prophetic. The early Christians may not have forgotten what Jesus did and said at the Last Supper with his disciples, but in a relatively short time they no longer attended to what it demanded of them in their celebration of the Lord's Supper. They needed to be reminded, as Christians everywhere have needed to be reminded through the centuries down to our own.

Telling the story of the Last Supper ensures that our celebration of the Lord's Supper is also the memorial of Christ's passion and resurrection. Stories of the risen Lord make no sense apart from stories of the passion and resurrection. Neither does the Lord's Supper, the gospel in action, make sense apart from the memorial of Christ's passion and resurrection.

And that is why every time we celebrate the Eucharist, we tell the story of how it began. There is no other way to ensure the Eucharist's integrity. The story tells not only what Jesus did and said on the night he was handed over but what we do, or ought to do, when we celebrate the Eucharist. Indeed, it says what the Lord Jesus does in and through us as often as we eat this bread and drink the cup, announcing his death until he comes!

NOTES

1. Much the same issue was raised by Terrance W. Klein, "Institution Narratives at the Crossroads," *Worship* 67 (September 1993) 407–418; see especially 416–418.

2. See *Didache* 9, 10, 14.

3. Beginning with his dissertation, *La struttura letteraria della preghiera eucaristica: Saggio sulla genesi letteraria di una forma* — toda *veterotestamentaria, beraka guidaica, anafora cristiana;* Analecta Biblica 92 (Rome: Biblical Institute, 1981), the work of C. Giraudo, S.J., provides a point of reference for much of today's scholarly reflection on the relationship between the narrative of the Last Supper and Eucharistic prayer. See also his "Le recit de l'institution dans la priere eucharistique a-t-il des antecedents?" *Nouvelle Revue Theologique* 106 (1984) 513–536. While Giraudo's contribution is extremely valuable, it is also limited by his exclusively literary approach to liturgical narrative (see Thomas J. Talley, "The Literary Structure of Eucharistic Prayer," *Worship* 58 (September 1984) 404–420; his review of Giraudo's work begins on p. 408.

4. Giraudo referred to the narrative insertion as an "embolism," a term derived from the Greek verb *emballo,* meaning "to throw into," "to insert," and the Greek noun *embolon,* meaning "graft" as when a branch is grafted on a tree. "Jusqu'ici nous avons parle d'un corps etranger accueilli et greffe sur le formulaire de priere pour des raisons theologiques. Si nous voulons preciser davantage, par une denomination technique, la modalite de son insertion et par consequent la specificite de la figure literaire qui en resulte, nous dirons que le lieu theologique de la demande est insere dans le formulaire par maniere d'*embolisme,* terme forme du grec *embolon* (greffe) et designant dans notre cas une greffe litteraire" (Giraudo, *Op. Cit.,* 521).

5. For biblical expressions of thanksgiving, consider the many psalms of thanksgiving, which recall a moment or period of distress as well as God's deliverance in the past as the basis for thanking God in the present (e.g. Psalms 9, 18, 21, 30, 31). A similar pattern can be found in Paul's letters, most of which include a thanksgiving unit after the opening salutation (e.g., 1 Cor 1:4-9; Phil 1:3-8).

6. While remembering what Jesus did is closely related to doing what he did in memory *(anamnesis)* of him, the two are not the same. Remembering is a condition for thanksgiving. Doing in memory of him is an expression of thanksgiving. The relationship between the two is similar to that between an eyewitness *(autoptes,* Luke 1:2) and a witness *(martys,* Luke 24:48). In remembering what Jesus did and being an eyewitness, the beneficiary is the one who remembers or personally saw. In doing what Jesus did in memory of him and in witnessing, the intended beneficiary is someone else. For the background and meaning of *anamnesis,* see Fritz Chenderlin, S.J., "Do This as My Memorial," *Analecta Biblica* 99 (Rome: Biblical Institute Press, 1982).

7. The stories forming the various prologues include the plotting of the chief priests and scribes (Mark 14:1-2; Luke 22:1-2) or elders (Matt 26:1-5), Judas' offer to betray Jesus to them (Mark 14:10-11; Matt 26:14-16; Luke 22:3-6), the anointing of Jesus at Bethany (Mark 14:3-9; Matt 26:6-13), the announcement of Peter's denial (Mark 14:27-31; Matt 26:31-35; see Luke 22:31-34), and the prayer of Jesus at Gethsemane (Mark 14:32-42; Matt 26:36-46; Luke 22:39-46).

8. See especially Raymond Brown, *The Birth of the Messiah,* New Updated Edition (New York: Doubleday, 1993).

9. Joachim Jeremias, *The Eucharistic Words of Jesus*, trans. Norman Perrin from the 3rd edition (1960) with the author's revisions to July 1964 (Philadelphia: Fortress Press, 1966) 191–193. After sifting and analyzing the data, Jeremias concluded firmly: *"at the beginning there stands not liturgy, but historical account"* (192).

10. Some recent research on the origins of the liturgical formula for the Lord's Supper stresses the formula's continuity with early Jewish prayer forms and with very little reference to Christ's passion and resurrection. See, for example, the otherwise fine articles of Thomas Talley and Terrance Klein, to which I have already referred. Klein's comments on a passage in Dom Gregory Dix's *The Shape of the Liturgy,* 2nd ed. (London: A and C Black Limited, 1945; reprint, New York: The Seabury Press, 1982) 55, illustrate the point.

"Dix's great insight was to recognize the persuasive Jewish *Sitz-im-Leben* of the earliest Christian Eucharists. The command of Jesus did not refer to the repetition of a sacral fellowship meal. This could be presumed as fundamental to Jewish religious practice. In other words, Jesus did not have to institute a meal, because the meal was already there. What Jesus did was to invest this meal with a new anamnetic character.

"It seems as though Dix's insight has been largely overlooked in the discussion involving the role of the institution narrative. The recent advances in understanding that narrative as an embolism now make it possible to suggest that perhaps this embolism, which has as its purpose the grounding of anamnesis in concrete historical remembrance, only became necessary when the original Jewish *Sitz-im-Leben* of the festal meal receded into the background" (*Op. Cit.,* 413–414).

11. The fact that the community took their meals in common suggests either that 2 Thessalonians was written at an early date, not long after 1 Thessalonians, or that its author, while writing much later, meant to evoke an early setting. In either case, the letter provides evidence that the Church at Thessalonica assembled for a communal meal for some time after its establishment.

12. See Eugene LaVerdiere, "The Origins of Sunday in the New Testament," *Sunday Morning: A Time for Worship,* ed. Mark Searle (Collegeville: The Liturgical Press, 1982) 11–27.

13. The incident occurred in A.D. 49 or 50, shortly after an important general assembly held in Jerusalem (Gal 2:1-10; Acts 15:1-29). Reporting on the assembly, the Book of Acts adds that "Paul and Barnabas remained in Antioch, teaching and proclaiming with many others the word of the Lord (Acts 15:35).

3

Proclaiming the Death of the Lord:
The Eucharist in the Letters of Paul

Paul knew the formative power of
tradition. In letters written between
A.D. 51 and 62, he drew on baptismal and
Eucharistic traditions and showed their
implications for a Christian community.
When problems arose at Corinth,
Paul reminded the community of the
tradition he handed on to them.
1 Corinthians 11:23-25 is an
eloquent witness to the prophetic
power of Eucharistic tradition.

The Eucharist is a tradition. Every time we celebrate the Eucharist,
we repeat the words of a liturgical formula, itself traditional, saying
what Christ did "on the night he was handed over." Taking bread and
giving thanks, breaking bread and sharing it, and also a cup, we do
what Christ did in remembrance of him. This was his command.[1] And
this is our tradition. For nearly two thousand years it has been our
tradition.

Like names and liturgical formulas, traditions matter. They express
and reinforce a community's identity. Traditions announce who we
are or who we are meant to be, in this case, the body of Christ and a
new covenant in Christ's blood.

Sometimes traditions can be a problem, as when they become too
rigid and stifle a community's vitality. In Mark's community, adher-
ing to "the tradition of the elders" would have prevented it from

reaching out to the Gentiles (7:1-15).[2] Traditions may also develop too quickly, severing a community from its moorings. At Corinth, for example, the basic tradition concerning freedom in Christ led to unwarranted individualism, threatening the unity, if not the very existence, of the community. But usually, traditions are a great blessing, defining and facilitating the flow of a community's life and energy, as the embankment does for a river.

The Eucharistic tradition of Christ's Last Supper has come down to us through the New Testament in four different forms, each with its own traditional formula, showing discreet but significant adaptations to the life setting of a particular community as well as the hand of a New Testament author. Two of the traditional formulas, 1 Corinthians 11:23-25 and Luke 22:19-20, are developments of the Eucharistic tradition of Antioch. The other two, Mark 14:22-25 and Matthew 26:26-29, are developments of a Palestinian tradition.

The oldest form of the Eucharistic tradition is the one Paul referred to, quoting 1 Corinthians 11:23-25:

"The Lord Jesus, on the night when he was betrayed
took bread, and after he had given thanks, broke it and said,
   'This is my body that is for you.
   Do this in remembrance of me.'
In the same way also, the cup, after supper, saying,
   'This cup is the new covenant in my blood.
   Do this, as often as you drink it, in remembrance of me.'"

This tradition is important, not only for its antiquity, but for its place in Paul's mission and ministry as a proclaimer of the gospel. Paul knew the power of a tradition. In 1 Corinthians, he summoned that power prophetically, challenging the Church at Corinth to be faithful to what he handed on to them and they themselves received.

The Tradition

The traditional formula Paul quoted in 1 Corinthians 11:23-25 presupposes that at its origins the Lord's Supper was celebrated as a full meal. This is clear from Paul's reference to "after supper." Paul's message in 1 Corinthians 11:17-22 also presupposes that the Lord's Supper continued to be celebrated as a full meal in the Church at Corinth.

The Eucharistic meal was divided into two parts, the supper itself and the cup taken after supper. The meal thus had the format of a symposium, in which the meal proper was followed by a dialogue, discourse, or entertainment over wine.

The supper was introduced by a formula declaring that the bread broken was the body of the Lord Jesus and commanding the assembly to do what the Lord Jesus had done in remembrance of him (1 Cor 11:23-24). The cup after supper was introduced by a similar formula declaring that the cup was the new covenant in Christ's blood, and, at least as Paul presented it, repeating the command that the assembly do this in remembrance of him (1 Cor 11:25).

The Eucharistic formula, therefore, actually consisted of two formulas spoken at different moments in the Lord's Supper. Recalling the two formulas, Paul brought them together in a single rhetorical statement (1 Cor 11:23-25), summarized the second formula by referring to the first, and most likely added, "Do this, as often as you drink it, in remembrance of me."

Paul's modification of the cup formula placed the emphasis on the meaning of the cup and Jesus' command. Paul thus adapted the Eucharistic formula in response to the situation at Corinth, where the Christians very much needed to be reminded that what they were celebrating was the new covenant in Christ's blood. Adding further emphasis, Paul also reminded them of Christ's command that they drink the cup as he drank it, making clear that it was his memorial.

Handing on the Tradition

"For I received from the Lord what I also handed on to you" (1 Cor 11:23). That is how Paul introduced the tradition, presenting himself as a link in the chain of Eucharistic tradition. He received *(paralambano)* the tradition of Eucharist in the early 40s while in the community at Antioch.[3] He handed it on *(paradidomi)* to the Corinthians in the year 51 when first proclaiming the gospel to them. Like Paul, the Corinthians also were to become a link in the chain of Eucharistic tradition, handing on to others what Paul handed on to them. Several years later, *circa* 54, Paul reminded them of this in 1 Corinthians.

To hand on the tradition, the community at Corinth first had to appropriate it, be faithful to it and reappropriate it, over and over again, making it a vital and integral element in the community's commitment to be with Christ, the Lord Jesus. For this, they had to make the actions and words of Christ their own. Like the Lord Jesus, they had to take bread, give thanks and break it so that they too could say, "This is my body that is for you." Like the Lord Jesus, they had to do the same with the cup, saying, "This cup is the new covenant in my blood." That is how they would fulfill his command to do this in remembrance of him and proclaim his death until he came.

The Eucharistic tradition was part of Paul's gospel to all the Churches, and it influenced every one of his letters. Since the letters were to be read in the liturgical assembly, Paul wrote them with that setting in mind. He adapted greetings, blessings, prayers, and hymns from the liturgical assembly and used them in his letters, giving the letters a unique, apostolic, and Eucharistic form. The letters also have a strong homiletic tone, suggesting that in writing them Paul imagined himself personally addressing the Eucharistic assembly. Indeed, some portions of Paul's letters may be adaptations of homilies in which he addressed the same issues.[4]

For Paul's most explicit teaching concerning the Eucharist, however, we turn to his First Letter to the Corinthians, where he actually quoted the community's traditional, Eucharistic formula (1 Cor 11:23-25) and dealt with two sets of problems which had important implications for celebrating and living the Eucharist.

One set of problems stemmed from the pagan, religious environment from which the community came and with which it remained surrounded (1 Cor 8:1–11:1). Most of the Christians of Corinth were of Gentile background. They had once taken part in the worship of idols and in religious banquets associated with them, just as those of Jewish background had participated in the synagogue. As converts to Christ, they had turned away from idol worship but still had to deal with the many ambiguities of living in an urban environment where pagan temples, images, cults, public processions and festivals shaped the culture and marked every aspect of life.

What did the Eucharist demand of them? Could they eat meat that was offered to idols? Could they take part in pagan banquets, separating the social and cultural from the religious aspects of such banquets? In sorting out the various issues, Paul turned to the Old Testament for events paralleling baptism and the Eucharist in search of historical precedents. He also focused on the community's Eucharistic *koinonia*, common-union (1 Cor 10:1-22) and its implications for members exercising their freedom in Christ. Some were interpreting their Christian freedom in a very individualistic manner, with no consideration for others in the community (see 1 Cor 9:1-27; 10:23–11:1).

The second set of problems stemmed from the social environment from which the Christians came and to which they still belonged (1 Cor 11:2–14:40). Some of the members were men, some were women. Did this difference affect their roles in the liturgical assembly (see 1 Cor 11:3-16)? Some members of the community were slaves, others free. Some members were rich, while other members were poor (see 1 Cor 11:17-34). Did these differences among them affect their positions in the assembly? As Christians, all were born anew as children of God, and all were one in Christ (Gal 3:26-28). But did their rebirth and oneness in Christ do away with all genetic, sexual, and social differences among them?

What behavior was appropriate in the liturgical assembly? Did the Christians' new identity as Christians leave them free to disregard the commonly accepted norms for public behavior in the Corinthian setting? What did the Eucharist demand of them? While sorting out these issues, Paul developed the social implications of the community's participation in the Lord's Supper (1 Cor 11:17-34). It is in this section he quoted the traditional liturgical account of what Jesus did "on the night he was handed over" (1 Cor 11:23-25). Again, a main problem was the distorted view some had regarding the exercise of their freedom in Christ (see 1 Cor 11:3-16; 12:1–14:40).

In order to celebrate the Eucharist as the Lord's Supper, to do in remembrance of the Lord Jesus what he did on the night he was handed over, the community had to deal with these many issues and with the problems they were experiencing. It was not just a matter of getting away with the maximum permissible and doing the minimum required, but of proclaiming the death of the Lord until he came. It was a matter of handing on the gospel of the Eucharist, proclaiming "the death of the Lord until he comes" (1 Cor 11:26).

The Eucharist was a central element in Paul's Gospel. Paul referred to the Eucharist when he first preached at Corinth: "When I came to you, brothers,[5] proclaiming the mystery of God" (1 Cor 2:1). The Eucharist was part of God's mystery, revealed in Jesus Christ, the suffering servant of the Lord, handed over by God (1 Cor 11:23a; see Isa 52:13–53:12) and giving his life as saving nourishment for all (1 Cor 11:23b-25). As Christians handing on the gospel of the Eucharist, the community took part in that same "mystery of God" and proclaimed it to others.

The gospel of the Eucharist was part of Paul's "message of the cross," a humanly foolish message for those who demanded "signs" or looked for "wisdom." But for those who believed, the gospel of Christ crucified revealed "the power of God and the wisdom of God" (1 Cor 1:18-24). As Christians handing on the gospel of the Eucharist, the community made Paul's "message of the cross" their own. Like Paul, they proclaimed "Christ crucified" every time they celebrated the Eucharist and they revealed "the power and the wisdom of God."

When Paul first came to Corinth, he did not preach the gospel of the Eucharist "with persuasive [words of] wisdom, but with a demonstration of spirit and power" (1 Cor 2:4). Nor did he do so in 1 Corinthians, avoiding "the wisdom of human eloquence, so that the cross of Christ might not be emptied of its meaning" (1 Cor 1:17). In his letter, Paul was now calling the community to the same simple and direct proclamation of the gospel of the Eucharist. Without it, they could not claim genuine fidelity to the traditions he handed on to them and they themselves received.

The Attraction of Paganism

Paul wrote 1 Corinthians from Ephesus (see 1 Cor 16:8) after receiving word from Chloe's people about divisions and rivalries in the community (1 Cor 1:11)[6] along with a letter with various practical questions on Christian living.[7] The letter may have been hand-delivered by a small delegation from Corinth, made up of Stephanas, Fortunatus, and Achaicus (1 Cor 16:17). The household of Stephanas had been the first to be converted not only in Corinth but in all of Achaia, of which Corinth was the capital. Paul expected this household to provide leadership for the community, providing a core around which all the Christians of Corinth would gather (1 Cor 16:15-16).

In their letter, the Corinthians affirmed their fidelity in maintaining the traditions as Paul handed them on to them, and Paul commended them for doing that (1 Cor 11:2). In affirming their fidelity, however, they also referred to problems they were experiencing in the community. Concerning these, Paul received further and more specific information from Chloe's people and the delegation that brought the letter from Corinth.

In one of their questions, the community asked about the eating of meat that was offered to idols (1 Cor 8:1). The same question came up at the apostolic assembly in Jerusalem (Acts 15:20). On that occasion, "the apostles and presbyters, in agreement with the whole church," sent a letter to Antioch (Acts 15:22) with this solemnly worded decision: "It is the decision of the holy Spirit and of us not to place on you any burden beyond these necessities, namely, to abstain from meat sacrificed to idols, from blood, from meats of strangled animals, and from unlawful marriage" (Acts 15:28-29). In his response (1 Cor 8:1–11:1) Paul was more nuanced, dealing concretely with different cases, distinguishing the various aspects of the question and showing their implications for the celebration of the Eucharist (1 Cor 10:1-22).

People rarely ate meat in the ancient world, doing so mainly during religious festivals when the meat of sacrificial victims became available in the market. It was one thing to buy such meat and eat it at home, or even at the home of unbelievers for whom it had no religious meaning (1 Cor 10:25-29). It was another thing to participate in public temple banquets where meat offered to idols was served. Held in temple dining rooms, of which many have been excavated in Corinth and its environs,[8] religious banquets played an important role in the cultural life of the city, especially during religious festivals and the biennial Isthmian games, which were associated with the temple of Poseidon and for which people came from the whole Aegean region and well beyond.[9] For recent converts from paganism, such festivals and games, together with their banquets, remained very attractive.[10]

Some members of the Christian community were appealing to the special knowledge (*gnosis*) and freedom they had in Christ to justify eating meat that was offered to idols. As Christians, they knew that "there is no idol in the world" and that "there is no God but one." Since idols were really nothing, why could Christians not eat meat that was sacrificed to idols (1 Cor 8:4)? Further, since idol worship had no objective, religious value, what prevented Christians from reclining and dining with others in the temple of an idol (1 Cor 8:10)?

The question of eating meat offered to idols might not have been a major issue, except that not all in the community looked on idols in the same way. For some, idols were harmless images, whose worship meant nothing. For them, eating meat offered to idols had no religious implications. For others, however, idols represented demonic presences, whose worship was all too real. For them, sharing in pagan religious banquets meant sharing in the table of demons.

Those who were sure in their new knowledge might easily lead the others to do what may not have been wrong in itself but for them was seriously wrong. The issue, therefore, was not so much the fact of eating meat that had been offered to idols or even participating in temple banquets. It was that of scandalizing those who were "weak," and would be drawn into eating meat offered to idols out of solidarity with those who were "strong."

In his response, Paul exhorted those who felt "strong" not to be overconfident. They might well have a hidden weakness. Being baptized and participating in the Eucharist did not guarantee anyone's salvation. Like their ancestors in the exodus, they might again desire evil things (1 Cor 10:6), slip back into idolatry (1 Cor 10:7), indulge in immorality (1 Cor 10:8), test Christ (1 Cor 10:9), not to mention grumble about restrictions on their freedom (1 Cor 10:10), all of which were serious matters. Those who thought they were "standing secure should take care not to fall" (1 Cor 10:12). For their baptism and the Eucharist to be personally salvific, Christians had to live according to their baptismal and Eucharistic commitments.

In any case, leading the "weak" to participate in what they considered the table of demons was leading them into what for them was idolatry and had absolutely to be avoided. Christians who participated at the table of the Lord could not participate at the table of demons. At the table of the Lord, everyone, whether "weak" or "strong," joined in solidarity, committing themselves to the Lord Jesus and to one another in Christ. The "strong" enjoyed freedom in Christ but with due regard for their common-union *(koinonia)* with the others and the mission of the community (1 Cor 10:23-24, 28-29). Like Paul, they had to freely limit the exercise of their freedom out of concern for the community and its universal mission (1 Cor 9:1-27; 10:32-33).

In making his point, Paul drew a parallel between the baptism and Eucharist of Christians and the exodus experience of their ancestors, who "were all under the cloud and all passed through the sea." Using a reverse typology, Paul viewed the Israelite story through a Christian lens and presented it in transparently Christian terms, speaking of the Israelites as being "baptized into Moses in the cloud and in the sea," and as eating "the same spiritual food" and drinking "the same spiritual drink." None of this, however, kept God from striking down those who turned to idolatry and indulged in immorality (1 Cor 10:1-5).

Spelling out his warning in biblical terms, Paul witnessed to the beginnings and early development of a Christian typology for baptism and Eucharist. The cloud and the passing through the Red Sea were seen as literary and theological symbols of baptism. The manna and the water from the rock were seen as literary and theological symbols of Eucharist. Unlike the Synoptic Gospels and to a lesser extent John, Paul may not have connected the Eucharist with the Passover, but he did associate it with the closely related theme of the exodus.

From Paul's presentation, we see how baptism and Eucharist were very closely related in both life and theology. We see too how Paul reflected on gospel realities and challenges in light of the Old Testament, where baptism and Eucharist had a prehistory.

In his response, Paul also provided the early Church with important theological and pastoral vocabulary, describing the Eucharist as a "spiritual food" and a "spiritual drink" (1 Cor 10:3), "the cup of blessing that we bless" and "the bread that we break," "participation *(koinonia)* in the blood of Christ" and "participation *(koinonia)* in the body of Christ" (1 Cor 10:16), "the cup of the Lord" and "the table of the Lord" (1 Cor 10:21).

Men and Women in the Assembly

One of the problems that arose at Corinth had to do with women veiling their heads and men wearing their hair long. Should women have their heads veiled when they prayed or prophesied in the assembly? From today's standpoint, the issue seems extremely minor. But as often happens, something quite minor becomes a flashpoint for deeper and more significant matters. Things as simple as clothing, even a particular piece of clothing such as a headcovering, and things as simple as long hair easily become symbolic, focusing emotion, anger, and deep resentment.[11]

From Paul's response, we learn many things about the early Christian assembly. We note, first of all, that praying and prophesying in the assembly were not limited to men. Paul assumes that women as well as men were not only allowed but expected to pray and prophesy in the assembly. Those who prophesy address the assembly, building up its members, encouraging them, and providing solace. Someone who prophesies builds up the Church (1 Cor 14:3-4). Prophesying in the early Christian assembly, as well as praying, were part of what we would describe as liturgical ministries of the word. The spiritual gifts, the various ministries and the works of God, of which Paul speaks in 1 Corinthians 12:4-11, knew no discrimination.

The issue in the Christian community was not whether women, like men, could pray and prophesy in the assembly, but whether they had to have their heads covered to perform these ministries. In first-century Corinth, women were expected to have their heads covered. To do otherwise was to project masculine or unfeminine behavior. By the same token, men were expected to have their hair cut short. Wearing their hair long projected effeminate, unmasculine attitudes. Some members of the community had concluded from their new freedom in Christ that such social and cultural norms no longer applied to them (see 1 Cor 9:1-27; 10:23-33). In essence, the issue involved the blurring of sexual differences, something not uncommon in first-century Corinth.[12]

It is true that for those who were baptized into Christ, "there is neither slave nor free person, there is not male and female," and that all are "one in Christ Jesus" (Gal 3:28). Everyone can be a Christian and assume those roles in the assembly that express their new Christian identity.

But the statement from Galatians is about those whom the gospel invited to be Christians, not about abolishing the difference between those who accepted the invitation. One did not have to be a Jew or first become one in order to become a Christian. Nor, of course, did a Jew have to become a Gentile. Christianity transcended the difference between Jew and Gentile.

That is why those who were Gentiles (uncircumcised) should not be circumcised, and those who were Jews (circumcised) should not be uncircumcised (1 Cor 7:18-19). In this respect, "everyone should remain in the state in which he (or she) was called" (1 Cor 7:20). The outward difference between Jew and Gentile remained, but among those who were "of Christ" (*Christou*, Gal 3:29), it no longer mattered. In Christ, being Jewish or being Greek was of no consideration.

For the same reason, one did not have to be a free person to become a Christian. Nor did one have to become a slave, at least not in the ordinary sense.[13] But becoming a Christian did not alter someone's social status as slave or free. Oneness in Christ made a big difference in their attitudes toward one another. "For the slave called in the Lord is a freed person in the Lord, just as a free person who has been called is a slave of Christ" (1 Cor 7:22). But as with those of Jewish or Gentile origin, "everyone should continue before God in the state in which he (or she) was called" (1 Cor 7:24).[14]

The same applied to being male and female. Both men and women were called to be one in Christ, and so to pray and prophesy in the same assembly. Their becoming Christian did not flow from human generation, from the relationship between male and female.[15] Nor did it depend on their being a man or a woman. The expression "male and female" *(arsen kai thely)* refers to Genesis: "God created man in his image; in the divine image he created him; male and female he created them" (Gen 1:27).

The passage from Genesis emphasizes the radical unity of the human race, using the term "man" (LXX, *anthropos*) to include both man and woman. As persons, created in the image of God, man and woman are equal. At the same time, the passage states the difference between the sexes, enabling them to act in the image of God. Blessed by God, they are to be fertile and multiply (Gen 1:28).

As Christians the man and woman not only maintain their human equality but achieve a new equality and unity in Christ. As human beings, be they Jew or Gentile, slave or free person, they also continue their procreative mission. Being Christian, however, is a matter not of human generation but of grace. That is why "there is not male and female," so far as being "children of God in Christ Jesus" (Gal 3:26).[16]

Oneness in Christ, therefore, did not abolish the distinction between male and female. Nor did it allow either to set aside the behavior that was appropriate for each. In their behavior and in their outward appearance, men and women should respect the order and manifest the identity given them from their creation at birth (1 Cor 11:7-12).

In reading the passage, it is very important to keep Paul's main point in mind: while recognizing the oneness of men and women, in Adam and in Christ (see Rom 5:12-21), let women be women and let men be men. Both men and women are indeed one in Christ. As such, they are also heirs according to the promise made to Abraham (Gal 3:29). Formerly, only men (sons) could be heirs, and in that context, the term "son" applied only to males. In baptism, however, women also become heirs. To express the equality of men and women as Abraham's heirs in Christ, Paul extends the term "sons" and gives it a Christian, inclusive meaning: "For through faith you are all children *(huioi)* of God in Christ Jesus" (Gal 3:26).[17]

It is easy to become distracted from Paul's main point by the three arguments he adduced in its favor, the first from social propriety (1 Cor 11:3-6), the second from creation (1 Cor 11:7-12), and the third from sexual identity (1 Cor 11:13-15). The arguments may be significant in themselves, but they have no direct bearing on the roles of men and women in the Christian assembly.

At the Lord's Supper

Among the problems in the community, some, such as eating meat that had been offered to idols, involved behavior and relationships outside the Christian assembly and the Lord's Supper (1 Cor 8:1–11:1).

These problems were related to the religious and cultural environment of a pagan city like Corinth.

Other problems, such as the behavior and appearance of men and women, involved attitudes, problems, and behavior in the assembly itself (1 Cor 11:2-16). These problems reflected the moral climate of a cosmopolitan city like Corinth.

Still other problems involved attitudes, behavior, and relationships in the assembly's central and defining event, the Lord's Supper (1 Cor 11:17-34). These problems reflected the social and economic environment of a city like Corinth. Like the previous problems, those in the Lord's Supper reflected a distorted, individualistic sense of Christian freedom, incompatible with the Eucharistic assembly and the Lord's Supper.

The Christian community at Corinth suffered from many kinds of divisions. There were the factions referred to at the beginning of the letter, with some claiming allegiance to Paul, others to Apollos, some to Kephas and still others to Christ (1 Cor 1:11-12). There were also those who thought of themselves as enlightened and secure in the faith and ignored others viewed as weak (1 Cor 8:1-13). Divisive, too, were those of variant sexual orientation who ostentatiously displayed their difference even in the exercise of their ministry (1 Cor 10:3-16).

In a context where freedom in Christ became a warrant for individualistic self-expression and factionalism, these divisions surely had an impact on the community's assembly as Church *(en ekklesia)*[18] and the Lord's Supper. As if these divisions were not enough for a small community,[19] further divisions arose from differences in economic class and social status among the members. There were wealthy people in the community, and there were poor. Some in the community were free, while others were slaves. These last differences had a great impact on the Lord's Supper itself.

When the early Christians assembled as a Church *(en ekklesia)*, they met in a home that was large enough to welcome the whole community. Concretely, this meant they met in a wealthy home, one with several rooms arranged around a central open court. But even a wealthy home did not have a dining room to accommodate the entire Christian community. There were those who ate in the dining room, the principal reception room in the house. And there were those who ate in adjoining rooms or in the open courtyard, depending on the architectural style of the house.

A wealthy home in Corinth also had a separate dining room or area for slaves. In a wealthy Jewish or Gentile home, slaves did not eat in the main dining room along with free people, nor did they eat reclining. They sat, as did women and minors. Reclining was a mark and expression of freedom, reserved for free adult males.

All such distinctions and restrictions should have disappeared at the Lord's Supper *(to kuriakon deipnon,* 1 Cor 11:20), which was inspired by the values of Christ's universal lordship and reflected its image. But they did not. Paul said in his letter that the Lord's Supper in Corinth was no more than each one's private supper *(to idion deipnon),* with participants disregarding one another, each one going ahead with his or her own supper, and with one going hungry while another was getting drunk (1 Cor 11:21).

It is easy to understand how this could come about, given the currents of freedom and individualism in a community with rich and poor, slave and free, all meeting in a wealthy member's home. In principle, the poor should have had equal access with the rich to the dining room, and the slaves with free members; but they obviously did not have this equal access. While the wine flowed freely in the main dining room, the food served in other rooms, where slaves, the poor and some others were eating, proved rather meager. In such a setting, each one had to look for himself or herself. Those who did not went without.

To address this situation, Paul quoted the liturgical tradition which they not only received, but in turn passed it on to others (1 Cor 11:23-25). The Lord's Supper was to be a meal of generous self-giving showing the unity possible in Christ, a common-union *(koinonia)* of people from very disparate backgrounds. The Lord's Supper should have shown what it meant to be one as God's children *(huioi)* in Christ, where "there is neither Jew nor Greek, there is neither slave nor free person, there is not male and female" (Gal 3:28). In terms of the situation at Corinth, we should add, "there is neither rich nor poor."

In the Lord's Supper, the community was to do what Jesus did, giving his life for them and for all. They were to be the body of Christ in the world, proclaiming by the gift of their own life in Christ — and Christ's life in them — the death of the Lord until his coming (1 Cor 11:26). The Lord's Supper was to be one great resounding *Marana tha* ("O Lord, come!") (1 Cor 16:22). Proclaiming the death of the Lord was a proclamation of the gospel, announcing life and salvation.

Proclaiming the death of the Lord was not just a matter of words. It was a matter of deeds. Eating "this bread" and drinking "this cup" meant taking bread, giving thanks, and breaking the bread as Jesus did. The command, "Do this in remembrance of me," called for something to be done, not just spoken. In the same way, "This is my body which is for you" declared what is being done. Jesus' Eucharistic words are meant to be active, creative, and effective words. They are also prophetic words. Spoken in the assembly for the Lord's Supper, their challenge is clear.

When the Christians ate "this bread" and drank "this cup," they did what he commanded them to do "in remembrance *(anamnesis)* of me" (1 Cor 11:24, 25). They witnessed to his presence, making his voice and gestures theirs, announcing, "This is my body that is for you," and "This cup is the new covenant in my blood." When they did do what he did "in remembrance of him," the words of the Lord Jesus resounded, calling for a response. This was indeed his body! And this cup was indeed a new covenant in his blood!

At Corinth, the words and the gestures had become empty because the Corinthian community no longer did what Jesus did. Their Eucharist was no longer a remembrance of Christ's passion and resurrection, no longer expressed what he did "on the night he was handed over." As such, the community was no longer acting as a link in the chain of Eucharistic tradition, handing on to others what had been handed on to them. That is why Paul told them their supper was no longer "the Lord's Supper." And that is why he reminded them of the tradition, reminding them of what they believed and once did, hoping to stir the faith and love they had once shown. Without these, there could be no hope.

If their supper was no longer the Lord's Supper *(to kuriakon deipnon)* but each one's own individual supper *(to idion deipnon),* there was no point to their assembling in one place *(epi to auto).*[20] Better that they should eat and drink in their own homes (1 Cor 11:22). We recall that besides assembling for the Lord's Supper "in one place" or "in common" *(epi to auto),* Christians also assembled as smaller Church *(ekklesia)* communities in individual homes, such as that of Aquila and Prisca at Ephesus, to which Paul refers in 1 Corinthians 16:19 (see also Rom 16:3-4).

There were other problems in the community, related to those we have seen, problems in the exercise of gifts and ministries in the assembly (1 Cor 12:1–14:40). As in other parts of 1 Corinthians, Paul's biggest challenge was the maintaining of unity. With regard to gifts and ministries, therefore, as in other areas, he stressed how diversity did not imply opposition and division but complementarity.

Appealing for unity, Paul exhorted everyone to respect the body of Christ of which they were members. Freedom, the charisms, and the ministries were not meant for the good of the individual, but for building up the body, in which each member could and should find meaning and purpose. In the Eucharist, "my body that is for you," each member works in concert to build Christ's body, the Church.

It is in this context that Paul extols the primacy and eternal quality of love among all other virtues and gifts (1 Cor 13:1-13; see 8:1-2). It is love that moved Christ to offer his life for all. Love, too, that is needed for the Lord's Supper. It is love that moved Paul to hand on the tradition of what Jesus did the night he was handed over. It is out of love that the Corinthians received it and handed it on to others. Love is also what kept Paul from giving up on the Christian community at Corinth and moved him to write the first letter to the Corinthians. "Love never fails" (1 Cor 13:8).

NOTES

1. The earliest written witness for this tradition is 1 Corinthians, a good part of which concerns pastoral issues related to the Lord's Supper. For the tradition itself, see 1 Corinthians 11:23-25. For very helpful commentaries in English on 1 Corinthians, see Hans Conzelmann, *1 Corinthians*, ed. George W. MacRae, S.J., and trans. James W. Leitch, *Hermeneia* (Philadelphia: Fortress Press, 1975); and Jerome Murphy-O'Connor, O.P., *1 Corinthians*, New Testament Message 10 (Wilmington: Michael Glazier, 1979). For an excellent study of 1 Corinthians, see Margaret M. Mitchell, *Paul and the Rhetoric of Reconciliation, An Exegetical Investigation of the Language and Composition of 1 Corinthians* (Louisville: Westminster, 1991). For Paul's message concerning the Eucharist, see Xavier Leon-Dufour, S.J., *Sharing the Eucharistic Bread*, trans. Matthew J. O'Connell (New York: Paulist Press, 1987) 203–229.

2. Rigid adherence to tradition would be a basic problem in the community of the *Didache*, as I show in chapter 9.

3. The wording of the tradition came to Paul from the community at Antioch, but Paul's receiving it in faith was "from the Lord" (1 Cor 11:23).

4. Such a relationship to Paul's preaching would help account for some of the thematic and verbal parallels between letters such as Galatians and Romans.

5. The Greek plural *adelphoi,* which the Revised New American Bible translates as "brothers," is grammatically inclusive whenever it refers to women as well as men. Since the community at Corinth surely included women (see 1 Cor 11:3-16), the appropriate English translation for *adelphoi* is consequently not "brothers" but "brothers and sisters," as given in the New Revised Standard Version. Like many other languages, ancient and modern, Greek distinguishes regularly between gender, a matter of grammar, and sex, a matter of genetics, while English does not. As a result, English tends to confuse masculine and feminine with male and female.

6. Chloe may have been a merchant with business in both Ephesus and Corinth. Paul assumes that she and her people were known to the community at Corinth.

Like Crispus, Gaius and the household of Stephanas (see 1 Cor 1:14-16), they may also have been members.

7. Paul refers to five questions in all, introducing the first with the expression, "Now in regard to the matters about which you wrote" (*peri de hon egrapsate*, 1 Cor 7:1), and the four others with "Now in regard to" (*peri de*, 1 Cor 7:25; 8:1; 12:1; 16:1).

8. See Nancy Bookidis, "The Sanctuary of Demeter and Kore: An Archeological Approach to Ancient Religion," *American Journal of Archeology* 91 (1987) 480–481; James Wiseman, *Corinth and Rome I: 228 B.C.–A.D. 267*, Aufstieg und Niedergang der Romischen Welt, ed. *Temporini*, VII/1 (1979) 438–548; Nancy Bookidis and Joan Fisher, "The Sanctuary of Demeter and Kore in Corinth: Preliminary Report V," *Hesperia* 43 (1974) 267–307.

9. Just as the Isthmian games were associated with the sanctuary of Poseidon, the Olympic games were associated with that of Zeus, and the Delphic games with that of Apollo.

10. Comparable situations exist today in places such as India, Sri Lanka, and Thailand, where Hinduism or Buddhism are dominant cultural forces and there is no separating religion from culture. Wherever that is the case, Christians are constantly surrounded by the religious practices that contributed to their personal and ethnic identity but which they have left behind at baptism. The attraction is especially strong at festival times when a whole region or city is swept up in cultural and religious celebration. A foreign visitor experiences such festivals very differently from those who are native to the culture.

11. A good example of how volatile the question of women covering their heads can be is seen in traditional Muslim environments where women are required to wear the *chador*, the traditional, long black veil reaching to the ground, covering not only a woman's head but her whole person.

12. The problem applied not only to women but also to men, some of whom wore their hair long and had it done up in elaborate coiffures, affecting an unmasculine attitude. See Jerome Murphy-O'Connor, O.P., "Sex and Logic in 1 Corinthians 11:2-11," *Catholic Biblical Quarterly* 42 (October 1980) 482–500.

13. In the New Testament, beginning with the letters of Paul, the term "slave" (*doulos, doule*) was an important metaphor for those who followed Christ the Lord (*kurios*). For a study of the theme in 1 Corinthians 9 and the setting of slavery in the ancient world, see Dale B. Martin, *Slavery as Salvation* (New Haven: Yale University Press, 1990).

14. See S. Scott Bartchy, *First-Century Slavery and 1 Corinthians 7:21*, SBL Dissertation Series 11 (Missoula, Montana: The Society of Biblical Literature, 1973).

15. Note the difference in the wording of Galatians 3:28: "There is neither Jew nor *(oude)* Greek, there is neither slave nor *(oude)* free person," but then "there is not male and *(kai)* female."

16. The idea is well expressed in the prologue of St. John: "But to those who did accept him he gave power to become children *(tekna)* of God, to those who believe in his name, who were born not by natural generation nor by human choice nor by a man's decision but of God" (John 1:12-13).

17. Since for many an inclusive understanding of the term *huioi* ("sons") cannot be presumed, the RNAB translated it as "children." The Greek term for "children," in relation to their parents, not necessarily in relation to their age, would be *tekna* (singular *teknon*).

18. See Eugene LaVerdiere, "The Eucharist, Sacrament of the Transformation of the World," a presentation made at the 45th International Eucharistic Congress in Seville, Spain (June 6–13, 1993), which dealt with the meaning and implications of assembling specifically as Church, *Emmanuel* (September 1993) 378–385.

19. Today, the Corinthian community would be considered a small, grassroots, evangelical, and catechetical community, free of large institutional structures. It would also be considered extremely dysfunctional. Since the entire community was able to meet in one home, it must have counted somewhere from 50 to 100 members, no more.

20. The Greek idiomatic expression, *epi to auto* ("in one place") corresponds to *epi ton auton topon* ("in" or "at the same place"). It can also be translated into English by "in common" or "together." Besides 1 Corinthians 11:20, see 14:23 and Matthew 22:34, also with the verb "assemble" *(synerchomai)*, and Luke 17:35 and Acts 1:15; 2:1, with the verb "to be" *(eimi)*.

4

In the Following of Christ:
The Eucharist in Mark's Gospel

Not long after Paul's death, Mark wrote
"The beginning of the gospel of Jesus
Christ [the Son of God]" (Mark 1:1).
Steeped in baptismal and Eucharistic
tradition, Mark told the gospel of
Jesus in the form of a story.
The Eucharist is an integral part of
Mark's story. In Mark, following Christ
means joining him in the breaking of
the bread (1:14–8:21) and in drinking the
cup that he drank (8:22–16:8).

It was around the year A.D. 70, perhaps in the late 60s, when Mark
wrote "The Gospel According to Mark." The early Christians did not
call it that. They called it "According to Mark," in Greek, *kata Markon*.[1]

Mark himself, of course, did not refer to his Gospel as *kata Markon*.
He did not even refer to it as a gospel. For him it was "the beginning
of the gospel of Jesus Christ [the Son of God]" (Mark 1:1).

In "the beginning of the gospel," Mark told the story of Jesus, his
mission as the Christ, his ministry and his extraordinary teaching. He
also told the story of Jesus' disciples, who followed him from Galilee
to Jerusalem and the passion-resurrection. Telling the story of Jesus and
the disciples, Mark also told of the early Christians, and their mission
to Gentiles as well as Jews. Mark's story of Jesus and his disciples was
also the story of the Church.

Mark told the traditional story of the gospel in a new and creative way. From their baptismal catechesis, readers could recognize the individual stories, even small collections of them, the discourses also, especially the little ones, along with Jesus' parables and sayings. They also could see how all of these were transformed by their new context in Mark's story of "the beginning of the gospel." No one had ever told the story of Jesus, the disciples, and the early Church the way Mark told it.

Baptism and the Eucharist played a very important role in Mark's story of "the beginning of the gospel." Baptismal images put people in touch with the moment of their conversion, how they became followers and how eager they had been to tell the story. Eucharistic images and liturgical formulas evoked their early experiences of Eucharist and the enthusiasm with which they lived it as followers of Christ. With the baptismal and Eucharistic images Mark helped readers to connect "the beginning of the gospel" with how the gospel began for them.

Forty Years of History

When Mark referred to the Eucharist and told Eucharistic stories, the Eucharist already had forty years of history for him to draw on, beginning with the unforgettable night Jesus gathered his disciples for a Last Supper before being handed over.

After rising from the dead, Jesus appeared (*ophthe*)[2] to his followers as they shared a meal in his memory (*anamnesis*)[3] once, twice, three times, until the event became a tradition (*paradosis*).[4]

Soon the disciples found words to refer to the event and its tradition — at first, "our bread" (*ho artos hemon*), then "our daily (*ho epiousios*) bread."

Then came a story, telling the event in simple, direct, but very symbolic and theological language, the liturgical story of the Eucharist. Told every time the early Christians gathered for the Eucharist, the story itself became part of the tradition.

Like most stories, the story of the Eucharist was told as narrative, but it also included elements of drama. Ordinary narratives could be told in most any setting. Not so the Eucharistic narrative, which, like drama, needed a special setting. The setting for the story of the Eucharist was the Christian community assembled as a Church for the Lord's Supper.

The event, its memory, the tradition, the words referring to it, the story and its traditional telling, all were part of the mystery of the

Eucharist, proclaiming the gospel of God and forming the early Christians into a Church. Such an important mystery was bound to influence the way many other stories would be told, especially those of the meals Jesus shared with his disciples as part of his ministry. Well before Mark wrote the Gospel, the story of Jesus nourishing a vast crowd with very little bread was told as a Eucharistic story. The story is told no less than six times in the New Testament (Mark 6:34-44; 8:1-9; Matt 14:14-21; 15:32-38; Luke 9:10-17; John 6:1-13).

The Eucharist influenced all of Paul's letters, but it formally broke into Christian literature when Paul reminded the Christians of Corinth what the Lord Jesus did "on the night he was handed over," challenging them to really do what the Lord Jesus did: "The Lord Jesus, on the night he was handed over, took bread, and, after he had given thanks, broke it and said: 'This is my body that is for you. Do this in remembrance of me.' . . ." (1 Cor 11:23-25). Eucharistic fidelity meant doing what Jesus did in memory of him, celebrating the Lord's Supper in truth, and living the Eucharist as a Eucharistic people.

It was only a matter of time before the Eucharistic story was told as part of the larger Christian story. This was done in catechetical instructions, at informal gatherings and more formally in homilies. It is also what Mark did in his Gospel.

Mark was the first Christian writer to include the story of Eucharist in the greater story of Jesus. Many, no doubt, including Mark, had told the story of Eucharist as part of Jesus' story, especially the story of his passion-resurrection. The early Christian communities were not without their storytellers. So far as we know, however, Mark was the first to put the story in writing.

A Time of Crisis

Mark told the story of Eucharist because it was an important part of the gospel; but even more importantly, he told the story because the community was in a period of crisis. The Eucharist would help them see the implications of the gospel at an important juncture in their history.

Mark wrote his Gospel shortly after Nero's persecution of Christians at Rome.[5] He wrote in a time of war, during the First Jewish Revolt, when the Jews of Judea rebelled against Rome but were crushed by Rome's well-trained legions in a long and deadly conflict (A.D. 66–73). At the height of the war, Jerusalem itself was destroyed, along with the temple, and a good part of the population was reduced to slavery (A.D. 70).

The Christians of Jerusalem fled north into Galilee and regions beyond. News of the war spread quickly, evoking for both Jews and Christians lurid images of a destruction long before (587 B.C.), a destruction recorded by the prophets when Babylon's armies overwhelmed Jerusalem and deported many of Judea's people to Babylon. The Gospel may have been written before Jerusalem was actually destroyed. But when Mark put stylus to papyrus, the siege of Jerusalem was at least being prepared, if it had not already been laid, and the city was doomed.

In the community for which Mark wrote, reactions varied. There were those who wanted to return to Jewish traditions and practices; but this was a Christian community of Jewish origins which had been breaking bread with Christians of Gentile origins. Thus, returning to Jewish traditions and practices was no longer possible. Others in the community had lost all hope in history as the arena of salvation. With that they lost their sense of mission and Eucharist. Entirely focused on the Lord's imminent return, they saw history, indeed the whole created universe, coming to an end.

Fortunately, the community had its prophets — Christians like Mark, who remembered an earlier time when the community was in crisis, when Jesus was seized and put to death, leaving his disciples in disarray. The crisis, however, had passed. What seemed to be the end proved to be the beginning: "You seek Jesus of Nazareth, the crucified. He has been raised; he is not here . . . . But go and tell his disciples and Peter, 'He is going before you to Galilee; there you will see him, as he told you" (16:6-7). Mark's community needed to be reminded.

For Mark, the Christians were reliving Jesus' passion and resurrection. Had Jesus not asked them to deny themselves, take up their cross and follow him (8:34)? What they were experiencing was not the end but "the beginning of the gospel of Jesus Christ." Their Eucharist was part of that beginning, celebrating and proclaiming the call of Christ to follow him.

Mark told the story of Jesus and his followers so those living in the late 60s and early 70s, indeed in all future decades, including our own,[6] would recognize the pattern of his passion-resurrection, associating themselves with his community, drinking the cup that Jesus drank and offering their lives with him that all might live. From this Eucharistic offering flowed the mission of the Church. The situation may have seemed hopeless, but it was not the end. It was "the beginning of the gospel of Jesus Christ [the Son of God]," over and over again. Before the end came, the gospel had to be preached to all the nations (Mark 13:10).

The Eucharist in Mark's Gospel

Mark integrated the story of the Eucharist in the whole gospel story. Its high point came in Jesus' Last Supper (14:17-26) on the threshold of the passion-resurrection (14:1-16:8). But like the passion-resurrection, it was introduced early in the Gospel (2:13-17, 18-22), in a series of conflicts (2:1-3:6) ending in an alliance between Pharisees and Herodians bent on having Jesus put to death (3:6).[7]

Mark's Gospel can be divided into four parts: the title (1:1), the prologue (1:2-13), the body (1:14–16:8) and an appended alternative ending (16:9-20). The body of the Gospel can also be subdivided into two parts (1:14–8:21; 8:22–16:8).

TABLE I
An Outline of Mark's Gospel

I. Prefatory title		1:1
II. Prologue		1:2-13
III. Body		1:14–16:8
A. Part I. Who is Jesus?		1:14–8:21
Section 1. Jesus and the call of the disciples	1:14–3:6	
Section 2. Jesus and the constitution of the Twelve	3:7–6:6a	
Section 3. Jesus and the mission of the Twelve	6:6b–8:21	
Breaking the Bread for five thousand (6:34-44)		
Breaking the Bread for four thousand (8:1-9)		
B. Part II. What does it mean for Jesus to be the Christ?		8:22–16:8
Section 1. The following of Christ, the Son of Man	8:22–10:52	
Can you drink the cup that I drink? (10:35-45)		
Section 2. Jesus' coming in glory	11:1–13:37	
Section 3. Jesus' passion-resurrection	14:1–16:8	
The Last Supper (14:17-26)		
Take this cup away from me (14:32-42)		
IV. Epilogue		16:8-20

The first part of the body raises the question, "Who is Jesus?" and by implication, "What does it mean to be Jesus' disciples?" The part unfolds in three sections, showing how Jesus called disciples to follow him (1:14–3:6), constituted them as the Twelve (3:7–6:6a) and sent them on mission (6:6b–8:21). It ends with Jesus asking, "Do you still not understand?" (8:21).

The second part of the body raises a further question, "What does it mean for Jesus to be Christ?" and by implication, "What does it mean to be a follower of Christ?" The second part also unfolds in three large sections, showing how Jesus taught his disciples to follow Christ, the Son of Man (8:22–10:52), await his coming in glory (11:1–13:37), and join with him in the passion-resurrection (14:1–16:8). This second part ends with a report that the women "fled from the tomb," and "said nothing to anyone, for they were afraid" (16:8).

In both parts, the Eucharist, a symbolic event, plays an important role, both raising questions and responding to them. In this, Mark's purpose was not to give information on the origins and nature of the Eucharist. Presupposing these were known, he drew on Eucharistic imagery and quoted from liturgical formulas to present the gospel of Jesus more effectively and apply it to the life of the community.

Jesus, the gospel, and the Eucharist were not just a matter of history. In word and symbol, they belonged to the present. In "the beginning of the gospel," Mark drew on the community's current experience of the gospel and the Eucharist to illumine the past, and he brought the past, so illumined, to bear on the present. In the process, history, faith, literature, liturgy and theology blended into a new reality, the Gospel According to Mark.

Mark's story of the Eucharist, like other good stories, builds up to a climax, indeed two climaxes, one for each major part of the body. The first comes in the third section (6:6b–8:21), with two stories of Jesus breaking bread in the desert (6:34-44 and 8:1-10). This section is often referred to in Latin as the *sectio panis*, the "bread section" because of its many references to bread (6:7b–8:21). Biblically, the section evokes stories of God nourishing the people in the desert of the exodus.[8]

The second and even greater climax again comes in the third section, Jesus' passion-resurrection (14:1–16:8) with the story of the Last Supper and Lord's Supper (14:12-26). Biblically, this section evokes the Passover as celebrated yearly in the Jewish liturgical calendar. With Jesus' passion-resurrection, the Last Supper forms part of the climax events of the whole Gospel.

The Breaking of the Bread

The first part of Mark's Gospel focuses on the nature and scope of the Church (1:14–8:21). The Church is a people called by Christ for the sake of the kingdom of God (1:14–3:6), constituted as the Twelve of Christ, fulfilling the Twelve of Israel (3:7–6:6a), and sent on mission to Gentiles as well as Jews (6:6b–8:21). The kingdom of God is universal. Unlike the Twelve of Israel, set apart as a particular people to be God's own, the Twelve of Christ has a mission to gather all peoples into the kingdom of God.

In setting out the universal mission of the Church, Mark relies on Eucharistic imagery, in particular on two stories of Jesus' breaking bread for large crowds. The section shows how the breaking of the bread, which at first was for Jewish men *(andres)* only (6:34-44) came to include Gentiles as well. Along with Gentiles, the breaking of the bread would include women as well as men (8:1-9). The section also shows what was needed, on the Jewish side and on the Gentile side, for those developments to be possible.

TABLE II

A Comparison of the Stories of the Breaking of the Bread in
Mark 6:34-44 and Mark 8:1-9

Mark 6:34-44	*Mark 8:1-9*
(34) When he disembarked and saw the vast crowd,	In those days (1) when there again was a great crowd without anything to eat, he summoned the disciples and said,
his heart was moved with pity for them,	(2) "My heart is moved with pity for the crowd,
for they were like sheep without a shepherd; and he began to teach them many things.	because they have been with me now
(35) By now it was already late and his disciples approached him and said,	for three days
"This is a deserted place and it is already very late.	and have nothing to eat.
(36) Dismiss them so that they can go	(3) If I send them away hungry

to the surrounding farms and villages and buy themselves something to eat."

(37) He said to them in reply,
"Give them some food yourselves."
But they said to him,
"Are we to buy two hundred days' wages worth of food
and give it to them to eat?"
(38) He asked them,
"How many loaves do you have? Go and see."
And when they had found out they said,
"Five loaves and two fish."
(39) So he gave orders to have them sit down in groups on the green grass.
(40) The people took their places in rows by hundreds and by fifties.
(41) Then, taking the five loaves
and the two fish
and looking up to heaven,
he said the blessing, broke the loaves,
and gave them to [his] disciples
to set before the people;

he also divided the two fish

among them all.
(42) They all ate and were satisfied.
(43) And they picked up

twelve wicker baskets full of fragments
and what was left over of the fish.
(44) Those who ate [of the loaves]
were five thousand men.

to their homes,

they will collapse on the way, and some of them have come a great distance."

(4) His disciples answered him,
"Where can anyone get enough bread
to satisfy them here
in this deserted place?"
(5) Still he asked them,
"How many loaves do you have?"

"Seven," they replied.
(6) He ordered the crowd
to sit down on the ground.

Then, taking the seven loaves

he gave thanks, broke them,
and gave them to his disciples
to distribute,
and they distributed them to the crowd.
(7) They also had a few fish.
He said the blessing over them
and ordered them distributed also.
(8) They ate and were satisfied.
They picked up the fragments left over —
seven baskets.

(9) There were about
four thousand people.

Mark's presentation of the Church's universal mission revolves around the two stories of the breaking of bread, the first on the Galilean side of the Sea of Galilee (6:34-44), the second in the Decapolis (8:1-10).[9] Together, the two say a great deal about the Church's mission to all peoples, to Gentiles as well as Jews, Greeks, and barbarians, both male and female, whether slave or free (See Gal 3:28; Col 3:11). They show how the Church fulfills its mission, really and symbolically, when taking bread, blessing (6:41) or giving thanks (8:6), breaking the bread, and giving it to the hungry.

The two stories of the breaking of bread highlight the challenge of mission and the resistance it is apt to meet. Crossing the sea from the Jewish to the Gentile shore proved extremely difficult. The *sectio panis* shows how Christians can and must respond to the challenge and deal with the resistance, both internal and external.

The background for this Eucharistic teaching on mission is given earlier in scenes of hospitality where Jesus heals Simon Peter's mother-in-law (1:29-31) and joins tax collectors and sinners at dinner (2:13-17). Occasions when Jesus and others found it impossible to eat (3:20) or when Jesus ordered that someone be given something to eat (5:43) also are part of the background. The heart of Mark's teaching on the Eucharist and mission, however, is in the *sectio panis* and its two stories of the breaking of bread.

In many respects, the two stories are very similar, but they are also very different. Both show how Jesus and the disciples nourished a huge crowd with very little bread and fish. For five thousand men *(andres)*, they had but five loaves and two fish. For four thousand people, they had seven loaves and a few fish. In both stories, Jesus took the loaves, blessed or gave thanks, and broke the loaves, but did not personally give them to the crowd. Instead, he gave them to the disciples, and it is they who distributed the loaves to the crowd; it was they, too, who gathered several baskets, twelve and seven respectively, of the bread that was broken *(klasmata)*.

Both accounts, like the four others in the New Testament (Matt 14:13-21; 15:32-39; Luke 9:10-17; John 6:1-14), follow the general line of a story in 2 Kings, telling how Elisha ordered his servant to set twenty barley loaves made from the first-fruits and fresh grain in the ear before a hundred men. When Elisha's servant objected that this was far too little for so many, Elisha persisted, "Thus says the LORD, 'They shall eat and there shall be some left over.'" And so it happened, as the Lord had said (2 Kgs 4:42-44).[10]

Both stories also use key expressions from the Lord's Supper to describe what Jesus did. Not that the event was actually a celebration of the Eucharist. The Eucharist makes sense only in relation to Christ's passion-resurrection of which it is the memorial. Still, there is a way of viewing the event as Eucharistic.

Like Paul, who viewed Israelite stories of the exodus through a Christian lens and spoke of them as baptismal and Eucharistic (1 Cor 10:1-5), Mark viewed events in the life of Jesus and the stories based on them through later Christian experience and presented them as Eucharistic. In this way, as Paul had done for the Old Testament, Mark showed what stories of Jesus meant years later for the early Christians. He could have given an explanation, as we do in exegesis and hermeneutics, but he took a simpler and more effective way. He retold the story in terms of the early Church and the Eucharistic assembly.

The two stories of the breaking of bread are also quite different, not only in particulars such as the size of the crowd, the number of loaves and fish, and the amount that was gathered after people had eaten, but also in their theological emphases.

The first story (6:34-44) places great emphasis on ecclesiology and the mission of Jesus' followers, who misunderstood their role, felt overwhelmed by the demands of their ministry, and asked Jesus to send the crowd away to find food and lodging for themselves. Ignoring their request, Jesus told them to give the crowd something to eat. Deeply moved on behalf of the people because they were like sheep without a shepherd, Jesus asked his disciples to be shepherds with him and assist him in nourishing them.

The second story (8:1-10) places greater emphasis on Christology, highlighting Jesus' initiative. Jesus himself brings up and then dismisses the idea of sending the crowd away. People had come a great distance and would collapse on the way. The disciples then ask a rhetorical question: where could anyone find enough bread in such a deserted place? Jesus responds by taking bread, giving thanks, breaking, and giving the bread for them to distribute.

Regarding the Eucharist, the first story evokes the banquet setting of a symposium, a formal banquet such as communities held in the home of a member on the first day of the week. Jesus asked the disciples to have the people, the five thousand, recline by symposia of fifties and one hundreds. The scene is that of an assembly of assemblies, a symposium of symposia, for one great Eucharistic symposium, as it were, of the universal Church. In the assembly of assemblies, each community was required to share not only with its own members but with all the others.[11]

In its Eucharistic expressions, the first story adheres more closely to the event's preliturgical setting in Jesus' ministry, indicating that Jesus took not only the five loaves but the two fish, blessed [God] and broke the loaves (*tous artous*). The second story separates the fish from the main action and shows Jesus taking the seven loaves, giving thanks, and breaking, this time without mentioning the loaves a second time. In this is reflected a stage of liturgical development that is closer to the formula in Mark 14:22-25, where the Lord's Supper no longer consists of a full meal.

Mark's stories of the breaking of the bread reflect two stages in the development of the Eucharist, one shaped by the community's earlier Jewish setting (6:34-44), the other shaped by a later setting, in which Christians of Gentile origin had been integrated into the community (8:1-9). In the earlier setting, the Eucharist remained a full meal. In the later setting, it had become a symbolic meal.

The clearest indication of this development lies in the various references to the fish. In Mark's first story of the breaking of the bread (6:34-44), the fish were part of the available fare, "five loaves and two fish" (6:38). They were also mentioned in the liturgical formula, "Taking the five loaves and the two fish" (6:41), and they were included among the leftovers, "and they picked up twelve wicker baskets full of fragments and what was left of the fish" (6:43).

In Mark's second story of the breaking of the bread, fish were not part of the available fare, consisting of "seven loaves" (8:5), instead of the "five loaves and two fish" (6:43). Nor were they included in the liturgical formula, "then taking the seven loaves" (8:6). Instead, they were mentioned separately as a postscript: "They also had a few fish. He said the blessing over them (*eulogesas auta*) and ordered them distributed also" (8:7). The mention of the fish recalls the story's earlier stage when the Eucharist was still a full meal. Mentioning them apart from the bread suggests that the story was also adapted to a later stage when the Eucharist no longer was a full meal. Nor were the fish included among the leftovers, "they picked up the fragments left over — seven baskets" (8:8). We understand then why this second story, unlike the first, makes no mention of a symposium or symposia, which would have presupposed a full meal.

The first story, the breaking of bread for the five thousand men (*andres*), comes from a tradition that developed in a community of Jewish origin. In Mark's Gospel it shows Jesus and the disciples breaking bread in a Jewish setting on the eastern side of the Sea of Galilee (see 6:45). Accordingly, the Greek term for baskets, *kophinoi,* refers to baskets commonly found in a Jewish setting.

The second story, the breaking of bread for the four thousand people, comes from a tradition that developed in a community of Gentile origin. In Mark's Gospel it shows Jesus and the disciples breaking bread in a Gentile setting on the western side of the Sea of Galilee (see 7:31). Accordingly, the Greek term for baskets, *spurides,* refers to baskets found in Greek or Gentile settings. The blessing of the fish also indicates a Gentile setting. In a traditional Jewish setting, only persons, including God, were blessed.

The Gospel tells how Jesus made the disciples embark for the Gentile shore and how personal resistance and a strong headwind kept them from reaching the other shore (6:45-56). "They had not understood the incident of the loaves. On the contrary, their hearts were hardened" (6:52).[12] They had not understood that the breaking of the bread, the Eucharist, was intended for Gentiles as well as Jews and for women as well as men.

Jesus had to teach them, first on the Jewish side, about the traditions of the fathers regarding ritual purification and the priority of God's word (7:1-23). On the Gentile side, he had to show them the faith of the Gentiles, represented by a Syro-Phoenician woman (7:24-30), as well as Christ's gift of hearing and speech to the Gentiles (7:31-37). Only then would the disciples be able to cross to the Gentile shore of the sea and be able to join with Gentiles as well as Jews in the breaking of bread (8:1-10).[13]

Even after the breaking of bread with the five thousand and the four thousand, the disciples did not understand (8:14-21). Jesus warned them against the leaven of the Pharisees, whose hearts were hardened (3:5; see 7:52 and 8:17) and who kept looking for signs (8:11-13). He warned them also against the leaven of Herod, who saw in Jesus no more than John the Baptist, risen from the dead and pursuing his Jewish mission of moral reform (6:14-16).

What would it take for the disciples to understand? Mark answers the question in the second major section of the Gospel. Peter confessed that Jesus was the Christ, the Messiah, but this was not enough (8:29). Mark's readers, like Peter and the Twelve, had to see that Jesus, the Christ, was also the Son of Man who had to suffer greatly, be put to death and rise after three days (8:31). In the same way, it was not enough to see the Eucharist as a Messianic banquet. Mark's readers, like Peter and the Twelve, had to see the Eucharist as a sharing in the Messiah's passion, death and resurrection.

Drinking the Cup

Mark's story of Eucharist reaches its second climax in the passion-resurrection (14:1–16:8) at Jesus' Last Supper with the Twelve (14:17-26). The first part of the Gospel emphasized the symbol and theme of bread, the breaking of bread and eating. The second part emphasizes the symbol and theme of the cup and drinking the cup.

The cup and drinking the cup are introduced at the height of a section on the following of Christ to his passion, death and resurrection (8:22–10:52; see 10:38-39). The cup is also highlighted at the Last Supper (14:22-25), where one verse refers to the bread (14:22) and three verses refer to the cup (14:23-25).[14] Finally, Mark refers to the cup in Jesus' prayer at Gethsemane: "Abba, Father, all things are possible to you. Take this cup away from me, but not what I will but what you will" (14:36).

With the symbol of bread and the theme of eating, the first section of the Gospel focused on the *breadth* of the Church and the universality of its mission. With the symbol of the cup and the theme of drinking, the second focuses on the *depth* of commitment needed to fulfill the Church's universal mission.

Mark first refers to the cup (10:38-39) in a unit outlined by two stories in which Jesus opens the eyes of the blind (8:22-26; 10:46-52). Disciples have to see with Christ-given sight to follow him on the way to Jerusalem (10:32, 52), where the Son of Man will be handed over and be put to death but will rise after three days (10:33-34). Three times Jesus announces the passion-resurrection of the Son of Man (8:31; 9:31-32; 10:32-34). Three times the disciples refuse to deal with Jesus' announcement (8:32; 9:32-34; 10:35-37). And three times Jesus addresses them directly in the matter (8:33; 9:35-37; 10:38-40).

The first time, Peter took Jesus aside and rebuked him, and Jesus rebuked him in return, ordering him back into his following. The second time, the disciples did not understand and argued who among them was the greatest. That is when Jesus told them, "If anyone wishes to be first, he shall be the last of all and the servant of all" (9:35). The third time, James and John asked that in his glory they sit one at his right and one at his left. That is when Jesus introduced the cup and asked if they were willing and able to drink it: "Can you drink the cup that I drink or be baptized with the baptism that I am baptized?" (10:38). They said they could, and Jesus responded: "The cup that I drink, you will drink, and with the baptism with which I am baptized, you will be baptized . . ." (10:39).

The cup in Jesus' response to the sons of Zebedee is a symbolic event. Like baptism, it refers not to an object but an event. The cup-event is, first, Jesus' drinking of the cup, and, second, the disciples' drinking the same cup, that is, the cup that Jesus drinks. As a symbol, the cup, like baptism, refers to Jesus' passion and resurrection.

Mark's view of baptism corresponds to that of Paul as presented in Romans 6: "Or are you unaware that we who were baptized into Christ Jesus were baptized into his death? We were indeed buried with him through baptism into death, so that, just as Christ was raised from the dead by the glory of the Father, we too might live in newness of life" (Rom 6:3-4). The same view of baptism underlies the creed in 1 Corinthians 15:3-5: "Christ died for our sins. . . ." In baptism, Christians die with Christ for the sake of all. They also participate in Christ's burial and resurrection.

Like baptism, the cup-symbol is liturgical and sacramental. It is drawn from the liturgy of the Lord's Supper, the Eucharist, which Mark wants to evoke. Mark's readers needed to see the full implications of the Eucharist as a sharing in the passion-resurrection of Christ. Jesus developed those implications further in addressing the other Ten, who had heard the exchange with James and John: "For the Son of Man did not come to be served but to serve and to give his life as a ransom for many" (10:45). In drinking the Eucharistic cup of Christ, the Christian community offers its life for the redemption of many.[15]

For the Last Supper, Mark drew on a very ancient liturgical formula (14:22-25), one whose Greek wording stands close to the Hebrew or Aramaic original.[16] For this reason, the formula is considered to be of Palestinian origin.[17]

From a linguistic point of view, the liturgical formula in Mark is the oldest in the New Testament. But from a structural point of view, the formula reflects a later stage of development, when the Eucharist no longer included a full meal. The formula in Mark 14:22-25 presupposes the meal has been eliminated.[18] At one time, the bread formula was spoken at the beginning of the meal and the cup formula after the meal, as can be seen in 1 Corinthians 11:25 and Luke 22:20. When Christians celebrated the Eucharist without a full meal, the two formulas were brought together and their wording was made parallel to one another. Here is Mark's double formula, including his editorial additions to the formula:

"While they were eating
he took bread, said the blessing, broke it
and gave it to them, and said,
    'Take it; this is my body.'
Then he took a cup, gave thanks,
and gave it to them,
and they all drank from it.
He said to them,
    'This is my blood of the covenant,
    which will be shed for many'" (Mark 14:22-24).

Compare Jesus' words in Mark's formula with those of Paul in 1 Corinthians 11:24-25:

"This is my body that is for you," and
"This cup is the new covenant in my blood."

In Mark, the words "this is my body" and "this is my blood" are perfectly parallel. In Paul, the corresponding words, are far from parallel. When the formulas were separated by a full meal, there was no need to make them parallel (see also Luke 22:19-22).

Mark's editorial additions reveal much about his view of the Eucharist and how it contributed to the story of the passion-resurrection.

The first addition, "while they were eating" (14:22) comes at the very beginning. Its function is to situate the Lord's Supper (14:22-26) in the Last Supper (14:17-21) and provide a smooth narrative link from one to the other.

As told in 14:17-21, the Last Supper could be considered complete. That evening, after everything was prepared for the Passover, Jesus came with the Twelve, and while they were reclining at table eating, he announced that one of those eating with him would betray him. One by one they began to protest, "Surely it is not I?" Jesus answered it was one of the Twelve, "the one who dips with me into the dish." It was written that the Son of Man would go this way. Still, woe to the one by whom he was betrayed. It would be better for him if he had not been born.

This Last Supper account (14:17-21) continues the narrative line begun in 14:1-2 and 10-11, with the conspiracy of the chief priests and the scribes and Judas' offer to betray Jesus. That line was twice interrupted, first by the story of the anointing at Bethany (14:3-9), and again by the preparations for the Passover (14:12-16).

It is here in Mark, that, for the first time, the Last Supper is presented as a Passover meal, first in the narrative setting (14:1-2, 10-11) and then in the preparations for the supper (14:12-16). In this Mark would be followed by both Matthew and Luke.

The main narrative line presents the conspiracy against Jesus, the offer of betrayal and a Passover meal at which Jesus and the betrayer are together. Following this line, the passion is a tragedy, as in a Greek drama, and Jesus is the knowing and accepting, but passive and helpless, victim of a plot to destroy him. The Twelve, present at the Supper at which the plot is revealed, are helpless against that which was written, of which one of them is fulfilling.

The stories interrupting the narrative line are essential to the story of the passion, transforming what would be a tragic loss of life into a heroic gift of life and turning the passion into an action. Like Jesus' Gethsemane prayer (14:32-42) after the announcement of Peter's denial (14:27-31), they present Jesus as active, not passive, and the passion as the fulfillment of Jesus' mission, not as its demise.

The liturgical formula for the Lord's Supper was introduced to transform the Last Supper from a betrayal meal into a self-sacrificing meal. The passion was not to be told as a story in which Jesus' life was taken away but as one in which he personally gave his life that all might live.

Mark's second addition, "and they all drank from it," recalls Jesus' exchange with James and John, whether they could drink the cup that he drank (10:38-39). At the Last Supper, they did drink the cup, symbolically participating in Jesus' self-offering and expressing their solidarity with him in the passion. By drinking the cup that Jesus drank (see 10:38-39) the disciples were among the "many" ransomed by Jesus' gift (see 10:45). They also joined in Jesus' sacrifice, offering their own lives with him "as a ransom for many." Like Jesus, the disciples were not tragic victims of a plot to destroy them but participants in a heroic life-giving act.

Since the clause, "and they all drank from it," interrupted the flow of the liturgical formula, separating the first part, "Then he took a cup, gave thanks, and gave it to them," from Jesus' words, "This is my blood of the covenant, which will be shed for many," Mark needed to reestablish the connection, hence his third and final addition, "He [said] to them."

The final reference to the symbolic cup, this time a direct reference to the passion, is in Jesus' prayer at Gethsemane. Jesus had gone ahead to pray. Earlier, when James and John requested a favor, to sit with him in glory, one at his right and the other at his left, they did not know what they were asking. "Can you drink the cup that I drink," Jesus asked, "or be baptized with the baptism with which I am baptized?" They answered boldly and without hesitation, "We can," again not knowing what they were saying.

In his Gethsemane prayer, Jesus models what is expected of his followers. Like him, they must pray that the cup be taken away from them. They should not seek what might overwhelm them. "The spirit is willing, but the flesh is weak" (14:38). Like Jesus, their prayer should be addressed to God as *Abba,* Father, that his will, not theirs, be done. In other words, drinking the cup meant denying themselves, allowing the Father to claim them for the kingdom of God, taking up their cross and following Christ on a way defined by his passion-resurrection. Like its parallel in Matthew and Luke, Mark's account of Jesus' prayer in Gethsemane echoes the Lord's Prayer.

NOTES

1. In the second century, when the four Gospels were gathered into a collection, the name, *kata Markon,* was indicated at the end of the scroll containing Mark's Gospel, to distinguish it from the other scrolls in the collection.

For good commentaries in English on Mark's Gospel, see Vincent Taylor, *The Gospel According to St. Mark* (New York: St. Martin's Press, 1963); Josef Schmid, *The Gospel According to Mark,* ed. and trans. Kevin Condon, The Regensburg New Testament (New York: Alba House, 1968); Augustine Stock, O.S.B., *The Method and Message of Mark* (Wilmington: Michael Glazier, Inc., 1989).

2. In Mark, the term *ophthe* appears in the story of Jesus' transfiguration: "Then Elijah appeared *(ophthe)* to them along with Moses" (Mark 9:4).

3. The term *anamnesis* does not occur in Mark's Gospel. The verb from which it was derived, however, *anamimnesko,* meaning "to cause to remember," appears twice (Mark 11:21; 14:72), both times in relation to Peter. Seeing that the fig tree Jesus had cursed was withered to its roots, Peter was made to remember *(anamnestheis)* (Mark 11:21). When the cock crowed a second time, Peter was made to remember *(anemnesthe)* the word Jesus had spoken to him (Mark 14:72). The noun *anamnesis* shares in the causative sense of the verb from which it is derived.

A related but quite different word is used in the anointing story (Mark 14:3-9) when Jesus announces: "Amen, I say to you, wherever the gospel is proclaimed to the whole world, what she has done will be told in memory *(mnemosyne)* of her" (Mark 14:9). The noun *mnemosyne* is derived from the verb *mnemoneuo,* meaning "to think about again." Telling what she did would enable people to remember what she did and see it as part of the gospel.

4. *Paradosis* appears several times in Mark 7:1-13 in Jesus' controversy with the Pharisees over "the tradition of the elders."

5. Nero's persecution lasted from the summer of A.D. 64 until his death on June 9 of the year A.D. 68.

6. While those who wrote the gospels addressed communities and situations at a particular time and place, they did not limit their readership to those they knew or those living at a particular time and place. Everyone was a potential reader. No one was excluded.

7. As traditional stories, apart from Mark's Gospel, the story of Jesus eating with Levi and tax collectors (2:13-17) and the dispute over feasting and fasting (2:18-22) may not have been Eucharistic. Their context in Mark's Gospel, however, makes them part of Mark's story of the Eucharist. Related to Jesus' passion (see Mark 3:6), they should also be read in relation to Jesus' Last Supper (Mark 14:17-26).

8. Associating the Eucharist with the exodus and God nourishing the people in the desert had been traditional for many years, as we see from 1 Corinthians 10:1-13. Told in Exodus 16, the story was integrated into Jewish wisdom (see Wis 16:20-21) and was celebrated in Israelite and Jewish worship (see Pss 78:17-32; 81:10; 104:27-28; 105:40-41).

9. Over the years, these stories have been given various titles, reflecting what was considered either their most salient or a fairly neutral feature. Highlighting the activity of Jesus and the size of the crowd, the New American Bible gave them the titles, "Jesus Feeds Five Thousand" and "Jesus Feeds Four Thousand." The Revised New Testament of the New American Bible entitled them more simply, "The Feeding of the Five Thousand" and "The Feeding of the Four Thousand," without mentioning Jesus.

Focusing on the stories' miraculous nature, the Jerusalem Bible and the New Jerusalem Bible described them as "the first miracle of the loaves" and "the second miracle of the loaves."

Bypassing the gospel stories, popular imagination refers directly to the event and focuses on the nature of the miracle, calling it "the multiplication of the loaves."

10. The Elisha story from 2 Kings 4:42-44 underlies all six of the New Testament stories in which Jesus breaks bread for a large crowd (see also Matt 14:13-21; 15:32-39; Luke 9:10-17; John 6:1-14). Early Christian storytellers must have had the Elisha story in mind when they first told the story of Jesus and the crowd, before the development of the various traditions reflected in the six New Testament accounts.

11. The story provides a gospel parallel for the Pauline collections on behalf of the poor. According to 1 Corinthians 16:2, the collection was to be made "on the first day of the week," that is at the community assembly for the Lord's Supper.

12. What the disciples did not understand was related to the twelve baskets of the bread broken that was left over. The twelve baskets correspond to the Twelve, the community of the Twelve, whose mission was to all human beings, Gentiles as well as Jews.

13. The situation in Mark is similar to the one referred to by Paul in Galatians 2:11-14, where Christians of Jewish background who once ate with those of Gentile background, symbolically sharing in one loaf (see Mark 8:14), began to eat separately when those who clung to traditional Jewish observance came from Jerusalem.

In his letter, Paul argued for one common meal, using the rhetoric of direct address. In his gospel, Mark did the same, but with the narrative power of a story.

14. In Greek, the bread-verse (14:22) has eighteen words, and the cup-verses (14:23-25) have fifty-one words.

15. The term, "many," a semitism for "all," is drawn from Isaiah 53:12, "And he shall take away the sins of many, and win pardon for their offenses."

16. See Joachim Jeremias, *The Eucharistic Words of Jesus* (Philadelphia: Fortress Press, 1966) 160–201.

17. See P. Benoit, O.P., "The Accounts of the Institution and What They Imply," in J. Delorme, et al., *The Eucharist in the New Testament, A Symposium* (Baltimore: Helicon Press, 1964): "The Aramaic tone of his account is a sign of a very ancient Palestinian origin, while Paul seems to be handing on the tradition of a 'hellenistic' Church, such as Antioch," 72.

18. The same formula at the stage of development reflected in 14:22-25 is referred to in the story of the breaking of bread with the four thousand (8:6). The formula in the breaking of bread with the five thousand may reflect the earlier stage of the same formula in a Greek wording that is closer to its Palestinian origins and the preliturgical telling of the story.

5

For the Forgiveness of Sins:
The Eucharist in Matthew's Gospel

Matthew's Gospel was written around
the year A.D. 85, some fifteen years after Mark
wrote "The beginning of the gospel of
Jesus Christ [the Son of God]."
Heir to Mark's Eucharistic tradition,
Matthew followed Mark in many
ways, but he also showed great
independence, retelling the story for a
community rich in Jewish background
and tradition, but now cut off from
the synagogue and newly committed to
the Gentile mission.

The forgiveness of sins is something one rarely hears anyone talk
about anymore. Instead, people talk of reconciliation. When they do
talk of forgiveness, it often has nothing to do with sins.

Today's silence regarding forgiveness and the forgiveness of sins
contrasts with the New Testament, where "the forgiveness of sins" is
associated with the preaching of John the Baptist, the mission and
ministry of Jesus, the preaching of the apostles, conversion *(metanoia)*,
baptism, and even the Eucharist.

Before Vatican II, the forgiveness of sins was the reason for "going to
confession," and good Catholics "received" the sacrament of penance
at least once a month. Since Vatican II, confession and the forgiveness
of sins have been renewed liturgically as part of the celebration of
penance in various rites of reconciliation. Rarely, however, is the forgiveness of sins related to the celebration of Eucharist.[1]

For Matthew,[2] "the forgiveness of sins" was a primary purpose of the Eucharist. In Jesus' Last Supper and the Church's Lord's Supper, Matthew followed Mark (see Matt 26:26-29; Mark 14:22-25) quite closely except for one major addition: "for the forgiveness of sins."

In Mark, Jesus' words regarding the cup were shorter and simpler:

"This is my blood of the covenant,
which will be shed *for* many" (Mark 14:24).

In Matthew, these words became:

"For this is my blood of the covenant,
which will be shed on behalf of many
for the forgiveness of sins" (Matt 26:28).

Every addition or change is significant, but the most striking come in the conclusion, giving the purpose for the shedding of Jesus' blood: *"on behalf of* many *for the forgiveness of sins."*

Christ's death was "on behalf of many for the forgiveness of sins." So was the sacramental offering of his blood in the Eucharist. In taking and drinking the Eucharistic cup, the disciples participated in his "blood of the covenant." As they joined him in forgiving others, their own sins were forgiven, and the purpose of the Eucharist was fulfilled.[3]

Matthew's Gospel had already made the forgiveness of sins a central concern, beginning with Jesus' basic catechesis on prayer (6:5-15) in the Sermon on the Mount (5:1–7:29).

The Lord's Prayer, which is at the heart of that catechesis (6:9-13), contains many of Matthew's most basic themes, and Matthew could have chosen any of them for additional development. He chose the petition for forgiveness: "and forgive us our debts, as we forgive our debtors" (6:12), commenting, "If you forgive others their transgressions, your heavenly Father will forgive you. But if you do not forgive others, neither will your Father forgive your transgressions" (6:14-15).[4]

Matthew added a more extensive development on the forgiveness of sins in Jesus' discourse on relations among members of the Church (18:1-35). Jesus had just given a short instruction on reconciliation (18:15-20), and Peter asked how often he should forgive a brother or sister who sinned against him, suggesting that seven times would be very generous (18:21). Jesus multiplied Peter's suggestion to "seventy-seven times" (18:22) and continued with a parable about an unforgiving servant (18:23-34). Applying the parable to the disciples, Jesus concluded: "So will my heavenly Father do to you, unless each of you forgives his brother from the heart" (18:35).

The Eucharist in Matthew and Mark

Like Mark, Matthew included the theme of Eucharist at various
points in his Gospel, giving us a story of Eucharist. As I have indicated,
the forgiveness of sins is especially important in the story's climax in
the Last Supper and the Eucharistic words of Jesus from the Lord's
Supper (Matt 26:28). But the forgiveness of sins was introduced earlier in Matthew's story of Eucharist, at least implicitly, in the closely
related theme of healing (Matt 14:14; 15:30-31).

To appreciate Matthew's contribution to the New Testament theology of the Eucharist, we must consequently look at his entire story of
Eucharist, as we did for Mark.

Table III
An Outline of Matthew's Gospel

Introduction-Prologue:	
Origins, birth, and manifestation of Jesus	1:1–2:23
Book I. Proclaiming the Kingdom of God	3:1–7:29
1. Narrative: the beginnings of Jesus' Ministry	3:1–4:25
2. Discourse: the Law of Christ	5:1–7:29
Book II. Mission in Galilee	8:1–9:38
1. Narrative: the miracles of Jesus	8:1–9:38
2. Discourse: the mission	10:1–11:1
Book III. Opposition from Israel	11:2–13:53
1. Narrative: conflict with Israel	11:2–12:50
2. Discourse: the parables	13:1-53
Book IV. The Church	13:54–18:35
1. Narrative: forming the disciples	13:54–17:27
Breaking the Bread for five thousand men,	
not counting women and children (14:13-21)	
Breaking the Bread for four thousand men,	
not counting women and children (15:32-39)	
2. Discourse: the Church	18:1-35
Book V. Mission in Judea and Jerusalem	19:1–25:46
1. Narrative: the authority of Jesus	19:1–22:46
2. Discourse: judgment and eschaton	23:1–25:46
Conclusion: Passion, resurrection and commission	26:1–28:20
The Last Supper (26:20-30)	
"Let this cup pass from me" (26:36-46)	

On the surface, the Eucharist in Matthew's Gospel is very much like that in Mark.

- We recognize the same two stories of *the breaking of bread*, one for the five thousand (Matt 14:13-21; Mark 6:34-44) and one for the four thousand (Matt 15:32-38; Mark 8:1-10).
- We also recognize the exchange between Jesus and the sons of Zebedee, whether they could *drink the cup* Jesus would drink (Matt 20:20-23; Mark 10:35-40).
- The stories of the *Last Supper* are also very similar (Matt 26:20-30; Mark 14:17-26, including, as we saw earlier, the same basic *liturgical formula* (Matt 26:26-29; Mark 14:22-25).
- So are the stories of Jesus' prayer at Gethsemane that *the cup* be taken away from him (Matt 26:36-46; Mark 14:32-42).

In all of these stories, Matthew followed Mark's story line fairly closely. But he also made many changes, dropping, adding, and altering words and phrases at various points in the story. Some of the changes seem to be of no theological consequence. Others are obviously significant. But in fact, all the changes, even the smallest, contribute to a reorienting of the Eucharistic stories, giving not only particular elements, but the stories as a whole, a new and quite different meaning in accord with Matthew's theological, pastoral, and literary purpose.

Matthew and the Matthean Community

The changes Matthew made in relation to Mark's Gospel are related to the nature of the Matthean community as well as to the community's early history and current situation.

Briefly put, the majority in the Matthean community were Christians of Jewish family background, who for years remained close to the synagogue and adhered to Jewish traditions. By the 70s and 80s, however, they were attracting a growing number of Gentiles.

For many years, having members of Gentile background was not a problem for the Matthean community. Nor for several decades had those who were of Gentile origin in the Matthean community been a problem for the synagogue. Judaism was quite pluriform before the destruction of Jerusalem. In welcoming Gentiles, the Christians resembled the Pharisees, who accepted and actively sought proselytes (Matt 23:15).

With the destruction of Jerusalem, however, came a need for greater Jewish uniformity. In the subsequent consolidation of Judaism, the

Christian community's openness to Gentiles was no longer acceptable. Nor was the community's distinctive faith in Jesus Christ, the crucified who had been raised.

Matthew's community had to choose between the synagogue and being Christian. Not all opted for Christ and the Christian community, leaving families divided and friends alienated. Matthew's Gospel addressed those who remained faithful to Christ and for that saw themselves cut off from the synagogue and thrust into the Gentile world, "like sheep without a shepherd" (Matt 9:36).

Matthew addressed the community at this stressful time of transition (*circa* A.D. 85),[5] showing how the community was entering a new period in its history. Instead of retrenching, it had to forge ahead, fully embracing the Gentile mission, which Matthew presented as the risen Lord's mandate to the Eleven (Matt 28:16-20).[6]

During Jesus' lifetime, their mission had been only "to the lost sheep of the house of Israel" (10:6), as was that of Jesus (15:24). After Jesus' passion and resurrection, they continued their mission among the Jews, even as they began to welcome Gentile members. But from now on, the mission to the Gentiles would be their major endeavor.

Jesus had prepared them for life and ministry in the Gentile mission by his teaching, adapting, and reformulating the synagogue's interpretation of Scripture and tradition for their new situation. Jesus had also prepared them by his ministry through occasional contacts with Gentiles, notably in a brief foray in Gadarene territory (8:28-34) and in the healing of a Canaanite woman's daughter (15:21-28).

The new situation demanded that they expect persecution (5:11-12), even at the hands of family members (10:16-36), and understand it as meaningful. Jesus had prepared them for these as well. Everyone was a sinner, including themselves. If they wanted their trespasses to be forgiven, they had to forgive the trespasses of others (6:14-15). It is in this spirit they should celebrate Eucharist "for the forgiveness of sins" (26:28).

The Breaking of Bread (14:13-21; 15:32-38)

Like Mark, Matthew has two stories of Jesus breaking bread for a large crowd, the first with five thousand (Matt 14:13-21; Mark 6:34-44), the second with four thousand (Matt 15:32-38; Mark 8:1-10), but the context for Matthew's stories is quite different.

In Mark, the stories were in a part of the Gospel devoted to the mission of the Twelve (6:6b–8:21), the *sectio panis* or "bread section," in which bread and meals are a major motif (see Mark 6:8, 31, 34-44, 52; 7:1-23, 27-28; 8:1-10, 14-21). The "bread section" was itself the third and climactic section of the whole first part of the Gospel (Mark 1:14–8:21).

In Matthew, the stories are not presented in relation to the mission of the Twelve (see Matt 10:1-42) but, in a different part of the Gospel, in relation to the Church as a community of Jesus' disciples (Matt 13:54–18:35), and apart from the two stories, the theme of bread, so prominent in Mark 6:6b–8:21, is much attenuated. In Matthew, Jesus does not ask the Twelve not to bring any bread on their missionary journey (Mark 6:8; see Matt 10:9-10), nor is there reference to the disciples having no opportunity to eat (Mark 6:31; see Matt 14:13), or of their lack of understanding about the loaves (Mark 6:52; see Matt 14:32-33). Matthew also reinterpreted the discussion on the leaven of the Pharisees and the leaven of Herod (Mark 8:14-21) — in Matthew the leaven of the Pharisees and Sadducees — giving it a different and non-Eucharistic sense (see Matt 16:5-12).

In Mark, the stories reflected the development of the Church's mission from the exclusive Jewish world to the inclusive Gentile world. The first story of the breaking of bread was among communities of Jewish origin — in Galilee on the western side of the sea. The second was among people of Gentile origin — in the Decapolis on the eastern side of the sea.

In Matthew, the two stories are situated in Jesus' ministry on the same Galilean side of the sea, among "the lost sheep of the house of Israel." In Matthew, both stories also include women and children, besides the five thousand (14:21) and the four thousand (15:38) men.

It may be that the composition of the Matthean community reflected a development like the one underlying Mark's second story with the breaking of bread for four thousand people. In this case, Matthew would have updated Mark's stories to reflect the actual composition of the Matthean assembly.

However, the very opposite also is possible, that the community at Eucharist in fact corresponded more closely to Mark's first story with its assembly of five thousand men. In this case, mention of the women and children would indicate a need to develop beyond exclusive male composition as the community moved out of the Jewish milieu of its origins into the Gentile world of its mission.

In Mark, the story of Jesus and the Canaanite woman, with its dialogue of sayings about bread, provided the basis for extending the breaking of bread to Gentiles. In Matthew, the story did the same, but as a precedent for that time in the future, after Jesus' death and resurrection (see Matt 28:16-20), when the Church would actually take on the Gentile mission.

In Mark, the two stories were set in the context of Jesus' teaching "many things" to vast crowds: "When he disembarked and saw the vast crowd, his heart was moved with pity for them, for they were like sheep without a shepherd; and he began to teach them many things" (Mark 6:34; 8:1).[7] In the stories of the breaking of bread, Jesus continued to teach. For Mark, the breaking of bread was a teaching as well as a nourishing event.

Matthew followed Mark, but only to a point. Instead of Jesus' teaching, he set the two stories in the context of Jesus' healing of the sick: "When he disembarked and saw the vast crowd, his heart was moved with pity for them, and he cured their sick" (Matt 14:14). In the bread stories, Jesus continued to heal. For Matthew, the breaking of bread was a healing as well as a nourishing event, related to a previous meal at Matthew's home (Matt 9:9-13) as well as to the Lord's Supper and the shedding of Christ's blood for the forgiveness of sins (Matt 26:28).

For Matthew, indeed for the entire New Testament, healing the sick was very closely related to the forgiving of sins. When people brought Jesus a paralytic lying on a stretcher, Jesus said to him: "Courage, child, your sins are forgiven." Reading the thoughts of the scribes, Jesus continued: "Which is easier, to say, 'Your sins are forgiven,' or to say, 'Rise and walk?'" (Matt 9:1-5; see Mark 2:1-12; Luke 5:17-26). Healing and forgiving were two aspects of the same reality.

Matthew also made a number of changes in the stories themselves, simplifying them and eliminating anything that might distract from their relation to the Eucharist as celebrated in the Matthean community. The changes were made both in the dialogue portion of the stories as well as in the meals.

In the first story, the disciples come to Jesus and ask him to send the crowd away to provide for themselves (Mark 6:35-36; Matt 14:15). In Mark, we then have the following dialogue:

"He said to them in reply,
  'Give them some food yourselves.'
But they said to him,
  'Are we to buy two hundred days' wages worth of food
  and give it to them to eat?'
He asked them,

'How many loaves do you have?
Go and see.'
And when they had found out they said,
'Five loaves and two fish'" (Mark 6:37-38).

In Matthew, the dialogue has been greatly reduced:

"[Jesus] said to them,
'There is no need for them to go away;
give them some food yourselves.'
But they said to him,
'Five loaves and two fish are all we have here.'
Then he said,
'Bring them here to me'" (Matt 14:16-18).

Matthew's much simpler presentation highlights the role of Jesus and portrays him as quite firm and assertive, issuing declarations and commands. Jesus knows what the crowd needs and will personally provide it. The same decisive attitude appears in the second story, with Jesus declaring, "I do not want to send them away" (Matt 15:32), instead of, "If I send them away" (Mark 8:3). Later, at the Last Supper, Jesus reveals the same attitude with the commands: "Take and eat," and "Drink from it, all of you" (Matt 26:26-27).

As "sheep without a shepherd," the Matthean community needed strong and authoritative leadership. Jesus had provided such leadership for his disciples, showing the way for the difficult time of transition the community would later experience.

For the actual meal, Matthew again simplified the arrangements for the community, eliminating Mark's reference to symposia and groups of one hundreds and fifties, focusing instead on the principal liturgical elements, with no mention of the fish in the meal distribution and in the gathering of fragments (Matt 14:19-20; see Mark 6:39-43). Like Mark, Matthew said that Jesus took "the five loaves and the two fish" (14:19), but he did not mention that "he also divided the two fish among them all" (Mark 6:41).

In the second story (15:32-38; see Mark 8:1-9), Matthew reintegrated the fish into the story, restoring the fish as part of the available fare, "'seven,' they replied, 'and a few fish'" (15:34) and included it in the liturgical formula, "then he took the seven loaves and the fish" (15:36). Having done this, he was able to drop Mark's postscript about the fish, how Jesus blessed them and ordered their distribution (Mark

8:7). In Matthew, only the loaves were distributed (15:36), and once all had eaten, only the fragments left over from the loaves were gathered (15:37).

On the one hand, Matthew stayed closer to early tradition, telling the second story to reflect its original Jewish setting, very likely reflecting the way the Eucharist was celebrated in the Matthean community. On the other hand, Matthew also updated both stories to reflect the community's celebration of Eucharist as a symbolic meal, without a full meal, which would normally have included fish. In the Matthean Eucharist, Jesus was present as the one who took bread, blessed or gave thanks, broke it and gave it to his disciples to give to the crowds. Had he not said: "And behold, I am with you always, until the end of the age"? (Matt 28:20). The Eucharist was their manna in the desert (14:15; 15:33), the gift of Emmanuel — God-with-us — for them to give to the crowds of sick and hungry coming to him for healing and nourishment.

The Cup and the Last Supper (Matt 20:20-23; 26:26-29, 36-46)

Like Mark, Matthew developed the theme of the cup in three stages, beginning with an exchange with the sons of Zebedee (Matt 20:20-23; Mark 10:35-40), then in the story of the Last Supper (Matt 26:26-29; Mark 14:22-25) and finally in relation to Jesus' prayer at Gethsemane (Matt 26:36-46; see Mark 14:32-42).

When the mother of the sons of Zebedee approached Jesus with her two sons, asking that in his kingdom one sit at his right and the other at his left, Jesus asked whether they could drink the cup he was going to drink. When they answered that they could, Jesus assured them they would: "My cup you will indeed drink," but as for sitting at his right and at his left, that was not for him to give (Matt 20:20-23). In the exchange, Matthew focused entirely on Jesus' cup, dropping Mark's reference to his baptism. Jesus would drink the cup with them at the Last Supper and in his passion. They would continue to drink his cup in the Eucharist and in future persecutions.

As in Mark, Jesus sent disciples to prepare the Passover which was to be his Last Supper with them (Matt 26:17-19; see Mark 14:12-16). As in the first story of the breaking of the bread (Matt 14:13-21), however, Matthew simplified the preparations. Gone is the reference to someone carrying a water jar who would meet them. Gone, too, is the reference to the householder, the guest room, and an upper room furnished and ready. Instead of sending two disciples, Jesus sent all of them to prepare the Passover.

TABLE IV

A Comparison of the Last Supper in
Matthew 26:26-29 and Mark 14:22-25

Matthew 26:26-29	*Mark 14:22-25*
(26) While they were eating,	(22) While they were eating,
Jesus took bread	he took bread,
said the blessing,	said the blessing,
broke it,	broke it,
and giving it to his disciples,	and gave it to them,
said,	and said,
"Take and eat;	"Take it;
This is my body."	this is my body."
(27) Then he took a cup,	(23) Then he took a cup,
gave thanks,	gave thanks,
and gave it to them,	and gave it to them,
	and they all drank from it.
	(24) He said to them,
saying,	
"Drink from it,	
all of you,	
(28) for this is my blood	"This is my blood
of the covenant,	of the covenant,
which will be shed	which will be shed
on behalf of many	for many.
for the forgiveness of sins.	
(29) I tell you,	(25) Amen, I say to you,
from now on	
I shall not drink	I shall not drink again
this fruit of the vine	the fruit of the vine
until the day when I drink it	until the day when I drink it
with you	
new in the kingdom of my Father."	new in the kingdom of God."

In Mark, Jesus instructed the two disciples to say: "The Teacher says, 'Where is my guest room where I may eat the Passover with my disciples?'" (Mark 14:14). In Matthew, he instructed the disciples to say, "The teacher says, 'My appointed time draws near; in your house I shall celebrate the Passover with my disciples'" (Matt 26:18). As in the stories of the breaking of bread, Jesus showed himself firm and assertive, not asking questions, but issuing declarations and commands. The same is true in the first part of the meal. Mark leaves the identity of the betrayer unresolved. In Matthew, Judas goes on to ask, "Surely it is not I, Rabbi?" And Jesus answers, "You have said so" (Matt 26:25).

In the Lord's Supper, Matthew also made a number of changes, most of them theologically significant, some merely stylistic, but even these were important for a community living in a Gentile, Hellenistic environment. The dropping of the introductory "and" *(kai)*, for example, a semitism and practically a Markan signature, and the introduction of Jesus' name made for a more graceful Greek introduction: "While they were eating, Jesus took bread" (Matt 26:26; see Mark 14:22).

In the Eucharistic words of Jesus, Matthew either reinforced the command of Jesus or added one. In Mark, Jesus said with regard to the bread, "Take it; this is my body" (Mark 14:22). In Matthew, Jesus said, "Take and *eat*; this is my body."

In Mark, Jesus gave no command regarding the cup. He simply "gave it to them and they all drank from it," recalling Jesus' response to James and John in Mark 10:39: "The cup that I drink, you will drink." Matthew made no mention of the disciples drinking the cup, but he did add the command: "Drink from it, all of you" (Matt 26:27). Jesus' Eucharistic word regarding the cup then gives the reason why they all must drink it:

"for this is my blood of the covenant
which will be shed on behalf of many
for the forgiveness of sins" (Matt 26:28).

The disciples — all of them — were to drink from the cup because this was Jesus' "blood of the covenant on behalf of many for the forgiveness of sins." If they wanted to have their sins forgiven, they had to join Jesus in his sacrifice "on behalf of many." That is what they did when they drank from the cup that he gave them after giving thanks.

In Jesus' words concerning the cup, Matthew referred at several points to the song of the Suffering Servant in Isaiah 52:13–53:12, emphasizing the sacrificial aspect of the Last Supper. The words, "all of you," for example, may have been included as a reference to Isaiah 53:6, with the needed adjustment from the song's first person, "we all" and "us all," to the second person of Jesus' command:

"*We* had *all* gone astray like sheep,
each following his own way;[8]

But the LORD laid upon him
  the guilt[9] of *us all*" (Isa 53:6).

The cup was Jesus' "blood of the covenant." The expression recalls the Mosaic covenant and its sealing in the blood of young bulls (see Exod 24:3-8). Jesus' covenant was in his own blood, shed on behalf of many. The expression, "on behalf of many"[10] (*to peri pollon;* see also Matt 20:28), replacing Mark's "for many" (*hyper pollon;* see also *anti pollon* in Mark 10:45), again reflects Matthew's interest in Isaiah's song of the Suffering Servant, where the Septuagint used *peri* not *hyper* or *anti:*

"He it is who bore our sins *(tas hamartias)*
  and suffered pain on our behalf *(peri hemon)*" (LXX Isa 53:4).[11]

For Matthew, the Eucharist, like the passion, was a sacrificial event, symbolized above all by the cup, but quite different from other sacrifices. Jesus' sacrifice was a personal act of mercy on behalf of many. As Matthew indicated on two occasions, what God desired was mercy, not sacrifice (Matt 9:13; 12:7; see Hos 6:6), that is, a personal response to God, not the mere sacrifice of animal victims.

The expression, "the forgiveness of sins," further specifies why Jesus' blood of the covenant would be shed on behalf of many, applying it to the situation of the Matthean community, where sin and the forgiveness of sin was a major issue. The issue was raised at a meal with Jesus in Matthew's house (Matt 9:9-13), where "many tax collectors and sinners came and sat with Jesus and his disciples." When the Pharisees objected, Jesus responded, "Those who are well do not need a physician, but the sick do." It is on this occasion that Jesus first introduced the words from Hosea: "I desire mercy, not sacrifice." Jesus concluded, "I did not come to call the righteous but sinners." The mercy God desired was to be shown to sinners through the forgiveness of sins.

Jesus' Eucharistic words end with the announcement: "I tell you, from now on I shall not drink this fruit of the vine until the day when I drink it with you new in the kingdom of my Father" (Matt 26:29). With the expression, "this fruit of the vine," Matthew connects the cup of Jesus' Last Supper with the Eucharistic cup he would drink with them in the kingdom of his Father.

Matthew's story of the Eucharist ends with Jesus' prayer at the Garden of Gethsemane (26:36-46). Like Mark, Matthew indicated that Jesus prayed three times, asking each time that he be spared the cup.

Matthew's version of Jesus' prayer is more modest than that of Mark. In Mark, Jesus prayed:

"Abba, Father, all things are possible to you.
Take this cup away from me,
but not what I will but what you will" (Mark 14:36).

In Matthew, Jesus prayed:

"My Father, if it is possible,
let this cup pass from me;
yet, not as I will, but as you will" (Matt 26:39).

Matthew also gives Jesus' prayer the second time, attenuating it still further, and aligning it with the Lord's Prayer as found in Matthew 6:9-13:

"My Father, if it is *not* possible
that this cup pass without my drinking it,
your will be done" (Matt 26:42).

As in Mark, Jesus was modeling a prayer for the disciples, who like Jesus did not seek the cup but accepted it if that were the Father's will. For Matthew it was much clearer that, as it was for Jesus, drinking the cup was indeed the Father's will. The modesty of Jesus' tone is in keeping with the tone pervading the entire Gospel, refraining, for example, from referring to "the kingdom of God," substituting instead, "the kingdom of heaven."

The Matthean community's response was already in the Lord's Prayer: "Our Father in heaven . . . , your will be done" (Matt 6:9-10). In the Eucharist, they drank the cup of Jesus' "blood of the covenant." They drank it new with him and he with them in the kingdom of his Father, "on earth as in heaven," sacramentally shedding his blood "which is poured out for many for the forgiveness of sins" (Matt 26:27-29 [NRSV]).

NOTES

1. At the popular level, many Catholics view the celebration of Eucharist as a celebration of reconciliation, at least in practice. This development calls for theological reflection and catechesis, relating repentance and the forgiveness of sins to the celebration of penance and to the Eucharist.

2. For full-length commentaries in English on Matthew's Gospel, see W. D. Davies and Dale C. Allison, *A Critical and Exegetical Commentary on the Gospel According to Saint Matthew,* Vols. I and II, The International Critical Commentary

(Edinburgh: T. & T. Clark Limited, 1988, 1991); John P. Meier, *Matthew,* New Testament Message 3 (Wilmington: Michael Glazier, 1980); Daniel J. Harrington, S.J., *The Gospel of Matthew,* Sacra Pagina 1 (Collegeville: The Liturgical Press, 1991).

3. In the New Testament, the forgiveness of sins is closely related to repentance and reconciliation, and all three, with varying emphases, are important in celebrating Eucharist. Mark emphasized the repentance or conversion aspect of Eucharist, Luke emphasized the reconciliation aspect, and Matthew emphasized the forgiveness of sins.

4. Like Matthew, Luke presented the Lord's Prayer in a short catechesis on prayer (Luke 11:1-13), with a commentary by Jesus on one of its petitions (Luke 11:5-13). In Luke, Jesus' commentary develops various aspects of the petition for "our daily bread."

5. See Eugene A. LaVerdiere, S.S.S., and William G. Thompson, S.J., "New Testament Communities in Transition: A Study of Matthew and Luke," *Why the Church?,* ed. Walter J. Burghardt, S.J., and William G. Thompson, S.J. (New York: Paulist Press, 1977) 23–53. The introduction, the section on Matthew, and the conclusion were written by Thompson.

6. After Judas' defection, the Twelve of Christ became the Eleven, as we find at the end of the Gospel of Luke (Luke 24:9, 33) and of Matthew (Matt 28:16). The same is true of the later alternate ending provided for Mark's Gospel (Mark 16:9-20; see 16:14). For Luke, however, it was important to restore the Twelve, a designation inspired by the Twelve of Jacob (see Acts 7:8). This was done at the beginning of the Acts of the Apostles (see Acts 1:15-26; see 6:2). When Luke continued to refer to the Eleven, it was to distinguish them from Peter (see Acts 2:14). In Matthew 28:16, the reference to the Eleven includes Peter. The event, appropriately referred to as "the great commissioning" (28:16-20) has Jesus sending the Eleven disciples to go and "make disciples of all nations" (28:19), suggesting that the Eleven needed symbolically to be completed, that is, made the Twelve, by the Gentiles.

7. The entire section was introduced by a short summary of Jesus' life and ministry as a teacher: "He went around to the villages in the vicinity teaching" (Mark 6:6b). The term "again" *(palin)* in Mark 8:1, recalls the previous time a great crowd gathered without anything to eat.

8. In this context we should recall, Matthew's insistence on the mission of Jesus and the Twelve as being "only to the lost sheep of the house of Israel" (Matt 10:6; 15:24) and the description of the crowds and perhaps of the Matthean community as "troubled and abandoned, like sheep without a shepherd" (Matt 9:36).

9. Instead of the word "guilt" used in the Hebrew text of Isaiah 53:6 ("But the Lord laid upon him the *guilt* of us all"), the Septuagint has "our sins" ("And the Lord laid on him *our sins — tais hamartiais hemon*). Matthew's evocation of Isaiah 53:6 thus points to Jesus' words, "for the forgiveness of sins."

10. The term "many" is a semitism referring to "all." The alternative to "many" is consequently "one" or "few."

11. The translation of the Hebrew for this passage is quite different:

"Yet it was our *infirmities* that he bore,
    our sufferings that he endured."

6

Dining in the Kingdom of God:
The Eucharist in Luke's Gospel

Like Matthew, Luke wrote around
the year A.D. 85, some fifteen years after Mark
wrote his Gospel. Again like Matthew,
Luke also drew on Mark's story of
the Eucharist, but also on the tradition
Paul quoted in 1 Corinthians 11:23-25.
But, unlike Matthew, Luke wrote for
Christians of Gentile origin.
Luke presents the origins of the Eucharist
in a series of ten meals with Jesus,
showing the relationship of
the Eucharist to every aspect of
Christian life, mission, and ministry.

The Eucharist. The Last Supper. The theological relationship between
the Eucharist and the Last Supper is very close, so close that there is
no understanding one without the other. But they are not the same.

The Last Supper was a formal meal with Jesus. As host, Jesus welcomed those invited and personally attended to them. The disciples
were Jesus' guests. Jesus loved everyone at table and was ready to lay
down his life for them, including the one who betrayed him. As a participant, Jesus also personally nourished the disciples, inviting them
to do the same for one another. The Last Supper was part of Jesus'
mission for the kingdom of God.

The Eucharist also is a formal meal with Jesus, at which Jesus is the
host and we his guests. As host for the Eucharist, Jesus welcomes all

who respond to his invitation. He loves us, even when we betray him, and offers his life for us. At Eucharist, Jesus is present among us as a participant, but also as nourishment, sharing his person with us and inviting us to do the same. In the Eucharist, we dine with Jesus in the kingdom of God, even as he continues his mission: "Your kingdom come. Give us each day our daily bread."

Recognizing the relationship between the Eucharist and the Last Supper, the New Testament invites seeing the Last Supper as the first celebration of Eucharist with Jesus as celebrant. So it is that Paul and the Synoptic Gospels presented the Last Supper, not as distinct from the Lord's Supper but as actually fulfilled in the Lord's Supper.[1] Each account includes a traditional Eucharistic formula. Placing the formula in the historical context of the Last Supper is what makes it an institution narrative and transforms Jesus' Eucharistic words into words of institution.

In the New Testament, no one showed the relationship between the Eucharist and the Last Supper more clearly than St. Paul: "The Lord Jesus, on the night he was handed over, took bread, and after he had given thanks, broke it and said, 'This is my body that is for you. Do this in remembrance of me'" (1 Cor 11:23-24).

In their story of the Last Supper, Mark and Matthew also situated the Eucharist at the Last Supper, which they showed unfolding in two parts, the first dominated by Jesus' announcement that one of the Twelve would betray him (Mark 14:17-21; see Matt 26:20-25), the second by the Eucharist, when Jesus "took bread, said the blessing, broke it, and gave it to them saying, 'Take it; this is my body'" (Mark 14:22-25; see Matt 26:26-29).

Luke's account is very different.[2] As a theologian, Luke included the Eucharist in Jesus' farewell discourse at the Last Supper, inviting further reflection on their relationship. As a historian, Luke also distinguished the Eucharist from the Last Supper, inviting reflection on the difference between the two.

While the Last Supper was a formal Jewish meal with Jesus of Nazareth, the Eucharist is a formal Christian meal with the Lord Jesus. When Jesus took his place at table for the Last Supper, the passion may have been imminent, but still lay in the future. The Last Supper was a prepassion meal. For the Eucharist, the passion lies in the past, as does the resurrection. As the memorial of Christ's passion and resurrection, the Eucharist is a postresurrection event. Without the resurrection and apart from the risen Lord, there would not be any Eucharist.[3]

Luke was both a theologian and a historian. In the New Testament, no one distinguished more clearly between the Last Supper and the Lord's Supper while shedding additional light on their theological unity.[4]

Luke distinguished historically between the Last Supper, a unique and unrepeatable event announcing the passion-resurrection, and the Lord's Supper, a repeatable, liturgical event after the passion-resurrection:

"I have eagerly desired to eat this Passover with you before I suffer" — Last Supper — "for, I tell you, I shall not eat it [again] until there is fulfillment in the kingdom of God" — Lord's Supper (Luke 22:16; see also 22:18).

Luke also joined the Last Supper (22:14-18) and the Lord's Supper (22:19-20) theologically within Jesus' farewell discourse (22:14-38) as one Passover event (22:14-20). In this Luke showed how the Last Supper is fulfilled in the Lord's Supper and how the Lord's Supper gives meaning to Jesus' Last Supper. Without the Lord's Supper, Jesus would have had a last meal, but not what we know as the Last Supper.

The liturgical formula (22:19-20), like the Last Supper (22:14-38), is a theological unit with its roots in history, providing the historian with a window into what Jesus did, taking bread and giving thanks the night he was handed over. The liturgical formula also shows what the Last Supper meant for "those who were eyewitnesses from the beginning" and handed it down to us as "ministers of the word" (see Luke 1:2).[5]

Luke's story of the Last Supper and Lord's Supper are part of a bigger story, that of the passion-resurrection (Luke 22:1–24:53). And the story of the passion-resurrection is part of a bigger story yet, that of "the events that have been fulfilled among us" (Luke 1:1). Like the other gospel writers, Luke made the story of the Last Supper an integral part of his gospel, and that is how we must read it.

The Eucharist in Luke's Gospel[6]

Comparing the Eucharist in Luke's Gospel with the other gospels and 1 Corinthians brings out Luke's unique contribution. Several features are quite distinctive, in particular Luke's great interest in history, in liturgical tradition, in the discourses of Jesus, and in the meaning of meals.

We note first Luke's sense of history, his concern for historical organization, and the way he distinguished various periods in salvation history. Mark included the mission to the Gentiles in Jesus' earthly mission and ministry. That is why Mark's Gospel contains two stories of Jesus breaking bread, one in Galilee with a Jewish crowd of five thousand (Mark 6:34-44), and one in the Decapolis with a mixed, Jewish and Gentile crowd of four thousand (Mark 8:1-10).

TABLE V

An Outline of Luke's Gospel

I.	Preface	1:1-4
II.	Prologue	1:5–2:52
III.	Background and preparation	3:1–4:13
IV.	Jesus, his mission and ministry	4:14-44
V.	Origins of the Church in the ministry of Jesus	5:1–9:50
	1. A people called	5:1–6:11
	Banquet at the home of Levi (5:27-39)	
	2. The community of the Twelve	6:12–8:56
	Dinner at the home of Simon (7:36-50)	
	3. A people sent on mission	9:1-50
	The breaking of the bread in Bethsaida (9:10-17)	
VI.	Destiny of the Church in the journey of Jesus	9:51–24:53
	1. In the villages of Galilee	9:51–13:21
	At the home of Martha (10:38-42)	
	At the home of a Pharisee (11:37-54)	
	2. From Galilee to Jerusalem	13:22–19:48
	At the home of a leading Pharisee (14:1-24)	
	At the home of Zacchaeus (19:1-10)	
	3. In the temple of Jerusalem	20:1–21:38
	4. From Jerusalem to God	22:1–24:53
	The Last Supper (22:14-38)	
	The breaking of the bread at Emmaus (24:13-35)	
	With the entire community in Jerusalem (24:36-53)	

Luke, who did not include the mission to the Gentiles in Jesus' earthly ministry, distinguished the origins of Eucharist in the life of Jesus from its development in the apostolic Church. The first he told in the Gospel, the second in the Acts of the Apostles. That is why Luke retained only one story of Jesus breaking bread, the one with the Galilean crowd of five thousand (Luke 9:10-17). Omitting the second, he returned to the breaking of the bread later in the Last Supper (Luke 22:19) and in the story of Emmaus (24:13-35) as well as in the Acts of the Apostles (2:42-47; 20:7-11; 27:33-38).

Like Matthew, Luke followed Mark in presenting the Last Supper, but only in part. Instead he took up the Antiochene tradition cited by Paul in 1 Corinthians 11:23-25. Turning also to other elements of gospel tradition, Luke created a unique synthesis on the origins of the Eucharist and its implications for the life of the Church.

Luke's development of discourses, especially the farewell discourse at the Last Supper (Luke 22:14-38), brings to mind the Eucharistic discourses in John's Gospel (John 6:22-59; 14:1–17:26). These discourses, which were given after the meal was over, associate the Eucharist with formal banquets known in the Hellenistic world as symposia. At a symposium, wine was served only after the tables had been cleared. Those participating in the symposium then joined in planned dialogue, listened to a discourse, or were treated to poetry, music or some other form of entertainment.

Luke's Gospel tells the story of the origins of the Eucharist in a series of ten meals with Jesus, along with some parables and a few sayings where eating and meals are the basic theme. Through a carefully unified substory of meals, Luke's Gospel shows how the Eucharist gradually unfolded in the course of Jesus' ministry. Each of the ten meals is related to a basic aspect of Christian life and Church ministry.

Luke even related the Eucharist to Jesus' birth. Mary laid the firstborn in a manger, an eating trough, because there was no room for them in the inn, that is, in the hospitality of the city of David (Luke 2:7). The Greek word translated as "inn" is *katalyma*, a general term which can refer to any place of hospitality. At the Last Supper, the *katalyma*, this time translated as "guest room," would consist of a "large upper room" (Luke 22:11-12). Denied hospitality at birth, Jesus offered hospitality at death, in the Last Supper and its fulfillment in the Lord's Supper.[7]

Here is the list of the ten meals with Jesus in Luke's Gospel:
1. a great feast at the home of Levi (5:27-39),
2. a dinner at the home of Simon the Pharisee (7:36-50),
3. the breaking of bread in the city of Bethsaida (9:10-17),
4. hospitality at the home of Martha (10:38-42),
5. a noon meal at the home of a Pharisee (11:37-54),
6. a Sabbath dinner at the home of a leading Pharisee (14:1-24),
7. hospitality at the home of Zacchaeus (19:1-10),
8. a Passover meal, the Last Supper (22:7-13, 14-38),
9. the breaking of the bread at Emmaus (24:13-35),
10. a community meal in Jerusalem (24:36-53).

Some of Luke's meals, like those in Matthew, have Mark as their source. This is true of the great feast at the home of Levi (5:27-39; see Mark 2:13-17, 18-22), the breaking of bread at Bethsaida (9:10-17; see Mark 6:34-44) and part of the Last Supper (22:7-13, 14-38; see Mark 14:12-16, 17-26). Like Matthew, Luke retold these Markan stories and adapted them for his readers according to his pastoral and theological concerns in writing the gospel.

Most of the stories appear uniquely in Luke's Gospel. At times, we note the influence of traditions common to Luke and John (7:36-50 and 10:38-42; see John 11:2; 12:1-11). And there is the old Antiochene tradition for the Lord's Supper, the same to which Paul referred. In every case, Luke transformed his sources and traditions, giving each meal story a peculiarly Lukan literary stamp.

Luke and the Lukan Communities[8]

At the onset, the Markan community was mainly Jewish in origin. But when Mark wrote his gospel (*circa* A.D. 70), most of the members were Gentile. Even so, many wanted the community to return to the Jewish traditions of its origin. This, of course, meant holding back on the mission to Gentiles. With his story of Eucharist, Mark did all he could to counter both of these tendencies. This explains Mark's emphasis on the missionary dimension of the Eucharist and the following of Christ.

The Matthean community was also of Jewish origin, and when Matthew wrote his gospel (*circa* A.D. 85), it remained very Jewish, but with a growing number of Gentile converts.[9] After the destruction of Jerusalem in the First Jewish Revolt (A.D. 66–73), efforts at consolidation in Judaism led to the Matthean community's separation from the synagogue. With his story of the Eucharist, Matthew wanted to help the community situate itself historically, deal with its internal and external conflicts, and move fully into the Gentile world. This is why Matthew emphasized the healing aspect of the Eucharist and the forgiveness of sins.

The Lukan community was very different. For example, it consisted not in one, but in many communities, whose members were mainly of Gentile origin from the very beginning. Luke wrote his Gospel and the Acts of the Apostles for communities that had been established during the great Pauline missions and for those they themselves founded later.

Like the Matthean community, the Lukan communities were in transition. They had already seen the center of Christianity shift away from Jerusalem, home of the first Christian community, to Antioch, a great missionary center to which they owed their Christian faith. For years, Antioch remained the center of their Christian world. Now they were seeing a second shift, with Rome, the capital of the Empire, displacing Antioch, the capital of the province of Syria.

Christianity was spreading "to the ends of the earth" (Acts 1:8) and fulfilling its promise of universality. Luke wrote his Gospel and Acts (*circa* A.D. 85) to help the communities see themselves as part of a universal, that is catholic, Church. The Lukan communities needed to position themselves in relation to the entire world. With Rome as the center, they would transcend provincialism, see themselves in relation to the whole Empire, and from its vantage point address peoples and empires beyond.[10]

Like the Markan and Matthean communities, the Lukan communities were experiencing a lot of difficulty. But unlike the Markan and Matthean communities, their difficulties did not stem from political factors beyond their control but from their own success. The growth of the communities and the increasing number of prominent members served to highlight how different Christians were from other religious groups and movements in the empire. The fact that in public places, at games and in festivals, Christians did not join in worshiping the emperor must have been the cause of resentment and persecution.

The Lukan communities were also experiencing internal difficulties, especially among their leaders, many of whom seemed more interested in serving themselves than the community and its poor. With the growth of the communities, those in ministry tended to be absorbed by secondary tasks, leaving them no time for prayer and the ministry of the Word. They needed to reexamine the ministry and see how best they might fill the expanding demands of growing communities (see Acts 6:1-7).

Inequities between members who were rich and those who were poor had a direct bearing on the Eucharistic assembly. Since the Eucharist was celebrated in the homes of the wealthier members, which alone could accommodate the community, those hosting the assembly tended to favor members of higher social and economic position.

With all these difficulties, external in the form of persecution, internal in the areas of leadership, wealth and poverty, it was difficult to focus on the mission for which the communities existed. Giving less and less thought to the gospel and their mission, the communities were in danger of being absorbed by their social and cultural environment.

Luke addressed this complex situation in two volumes, The Gospel According to Luke and The Acts of the Apostles, often referred to as Luke-Acts. His story of the origins of the Eucharist played a major role in both volumes.

In the Gospel, he told the story of the origins of the Eucharist in the life and ministry of Jesus, "beginning in Galilee after the baptism that John preached" (Acts 10:37) "until the day he was taken up, after giving instructions through the holy Spirit to the apostles whom he had chosen" (Acts 1:2).

In Acts, he told the story of the origins of the Eucharist in the life and ministry of the apostolic Church, "in Jerusalem, throughout Judea and Samaria, and to the ends of the earth" (Acts 1:8), symbolized by Paul's extended stay at Rome, where "he proclaimed the kingdom of God and taught about the Lord Jesus Christ" (Acts 28:30-31).

Meals with Jesus in the Galilean Ministry

There were seven meals with Jesus before the Last Supper, a series of three in Jesus' Galilean ministry (Luke 5:1–9:50) and a series of four on the journey from Galilee to Jerusalem (Luke 9:51–19:48). Each meal reveals a particular aspect of the Eucharist, beginning with what is most fundamental for Christian life, the call to repentance or *metanoia*, and ending with what is most basic for the mission of the Church, extending salvation in Christ to all of Abraham's children.

The first series of meals, those in the Galilean ministry, deals with the Eucharist in relation to the genesis, constitution, and mission of the Church. In the Eucharist, Christians are called to conversion, reconciled in the community of the Twelve and sent on mission.

The great feast at the home of Levi, the tax collector (5:27-39), presents the Church as a people called to repentance and the Eucharist as a sacrament of evangelization. The Eucharist is a gospel event, issuing Jesus' call to conversion — *metanoia* — and welcoming all who respond to his call: "I have not come to call the righteous to repentance but sinners" (Luke 5:32). All are sinners. The call excludes no one. Those called, however, can exclude themselves. In the story, Levi and the tax collectors have accepted Jesus' call. The Pharisees and their scribes have not.

The dinner at the home of Simon the Pharisee (Luke 7:36-50) shows the Church, the community of the Twelve, as a people called to reconciliation and the Eucharist as a sacrament of reconciliation. A woman who was a sinner but became a disciple has repented and been forgiven. This is shown by her presence "at Jesus' feet" and her loving gesture. "So I tell you, her many sins have been forgiven; hence, she has shown great love" (7:47). Shocked by the way Jesus welcomed her, Simon, Jesus' host, questions Jesus' prophetic authenticity. The woman is reconciled. The Pharisee has yet to learn its meaning.

The breaking of bread for the five thousand at Bethsaida (Luke 9:10-17) focuses on the mission of the Church and shows the Eucharist as a sacrament of mission. Jesus teaches the crowds about the kingdom of God, preparing people to dine in the kingdom. But come evening and dinner time, the disciples want him to send the crowd away. Jesus shows the disciples what their mission is: "Give them some food yourselves" (Luke 9:13). Their mission is to nourish the crowds, not just in word but in deed, with the bread Jesus gave them when he took the loaves, spoke a blessing and broke the loaves for the disciples to set before the crowd. As the Church of the Twelve, their mission was to serve at the banquet of the kingdom of God.

Meals with Jesus on the Journey to Jerusalem[11]

The second series of meals, those on the journey from Galilee to Jerusalem, deals with the major Eucharistic issues in the life and ministry of the Church. Those issues include the quality of service and the primacy of discipleship (Luke 10:38-42), the need for interior purification and commitment versus merely external performance (11:37-54), attitudes in the community towards other participants (14:1-24) and the significance of Eucharistic hospitality for salvation (19:1-10).

The hospitality Jesus received at the home of Martha (Luke 10:38-42) contrasts the attitude of Martha, who was busy and anxious about many things, with that of her sister, Mary, who was attentive to the one thing necessary. Mary's position at the Lord's feet (see 7:38; 8:35) listening to the word of the Lord presents her as a true disciple: "There is need of only one thing" (10:42). Like Mary, those who minister at the table of the Lord must be true disciples, attentive to the person of the Lord and listening to his message. The one thing necessary gives meaning to everything else in their ministry.

The noon meal at the home of a Pharisee (Luke 11:37-54) contrasts the insistence of Pharisees and scholars of the law on external observance and purification with Jesus' teaching on the priority of interior attitudes and purification. In the Eucharist, external observance must flow from what is within a person: "But as to what is within, give alms, and behold, everything will be clean for you" (11:41). Giving alms assures the right attitude and makes everything clean for those at table with Jesus.

The Sabbath meal at the home of a leading Pharisee (Luke 14:1-24) deals with the attitudes of the participants toward one another. In a brief discourse, Jesus focuses first on the attitudes and behavior of the guests (14:7-11) and then on those of the host (14:12-14). Seeking the last place assures the guest a position of honor. Inviting the poor, the crippled, the lame, and the blind aligns the meal with Jesus' mission:

"The Spirit of the Lord is upon me,
  because he has anointed me
    to bring glad tidings to the poor.
He has sent me to proclaim liberty to captives
  and recovery of sight to the blind,
    to let the oppressed go free,
and to proclaim a year acceptable to the Lord" (Luke 4:18-19).

The story of Zacchaeus (Luke 19:1-10) is the second meal with Jesus at the home of a tax collector (see 5:27-39), this time a chief tax collector. It shows Zacchaeus going to extraordinary lengths to see Jesus and Jesus announcing the necessity *(dei)*[12] that he stay at his home that day. Responding to the grumbling of the crowd, Zacchaeus announces he will give alms to the poor, even as much as half his possessions (see Luke 11:41): "Today salvation has come to this house, because this man too is a descendant of Abraham" (Luke 19:9). Jesus declares Zacchaeus a son of Abraham, one who, like the prodigal son (15:11-32), was lost but now is saved. As a sacrament of salvation, the Eucharist is intended for all.

The Last Supper

For years there has been much discussion whether the Last Supper was a Jewish Passover meal. In John's Gospel, the Last Supper took place before Passover and Jesus died on the day the Passover lambs were sacrificed (see John 19:14). John's purpose in this is theological, showing Jesus as the Lamb of God (John 1:29). Whether or not the Last Supper was in fact a Jewish Passover meal, Luke clearly presented it as a Passover, a Christian Passover. In this his purpose was mainly theological.

TABLE VI

A Synoptic Comparison of the Liturgical Formula in
Luke 22:19-20, Mark 14:22-24, and 1 Corinthians 11:23-25,
translated by the author

Luke 22:19-20	*Mark 14:22-24*	*1 Corinthians 11:23-25*
		(23) The Lord Jesus, on the night in which he was handed over,
(19) AND	(22) AND while they were eating	
TAKING BREAD *HAVING GIVEN THANKS* HE BROKE AND GAVE TO THEM saying:	TAKING BREAD having blessed HE BROKE AND GAVE TO THEM and said: "Take;	took bread (24) and *HAVING GIVEN THANKS* broke and said:
"THIS IS MY BODY (TOUTO ESTIN TO SOMA MOU) which is given *FOR YOU.* *DO THIS IN MY REMEMBRANCE.*"	THIS IS MY BODY (TOUTO ESTIN TO SOMA MOU)"	This is my body (touto mou estin to soma) *FOR YOU.* *DO THIS IN MY REMEMBRANCE.*"
(20) *AND LIKEWISE THE CUP AFTER THEY HAD EATEN,*	(23) then he took a cup,	(25) *AND LIKEWISE THE CUP AFTER THEY HAD EATEN*
	gave thanks, and gave it to them, and they all drank from it.	
SAYING, "*THIS CUP IS THE NEW COVENANT IN MY BLOOD,* WHICH IS POURED OUT for you."	(24) He said to them, "This is my blood of the covenant, WHICH IS POURED OUT for many."	*SAYING* "*THIS CUP IS THE NEW COVENANT IN MY BLOOD.* Do this, as often as you drink it, in my remembrance."

(Table VI continued)

To highlight the similarities and differences, Luke 22:19-20, Mark 14:22-24, and 1 Corinthians 11:23-25 have been translated very literally. The terms and expressions Luke has in common with Mark are given in UPPER CASE, while those in common with 1 Corinthians are in *UPPER CASE ITALICS*. Words found only in Luke or whose grammatical form in Greek is specific to Luke are in lower case.

For Luke, the preparations for the Passover were made on the day of the Feast of Unleavened Bread, when it was necessary *(edei)* to sacrifice the Passover (22:7). Like John, Luke associated Jesus with the Passover sacrifice. John, however, showed how Jesus' death brought the ancient Passover sacrifice to fulfillment. Luke showed how the Passover sacrifice was fulfilled in Jesus' Last Supper. The Eucharist, the memorial of Jesus' passion-resurrection is a Passover sacrament.

In Luke's Gospel, the Last Supper is presented in the form of a farewell discourse.[13] In the ancient world, whether biblical or extra-biblical, throughout the Hellenistic world, a farewell discourse enabled a historical figure such as Jesus of Nazareth to address situations that occurred much later, at the time the discourse was written down. Jesus' farewell discourse at the Last Supper (Luke 22:14-38) enabled Jesus to address the principal issues facing the Lukan communities when Luke wrote his Gospel around A.D. 85.

So it is that Luke had Jesus speak not only to the betrayal that occasioned his passion and death (22:21-23) but also to the ongoing betrayal by leaders of the Christian community who lorded it over the others and sought recognition as big benefactors (22:24-30). In the same way, Luke had Jesus address not only the coming denial of Peter in the courtyard of the high priest (22:31-34), but the denials of the Christian community responding to persecution with violence (22:35-38).

It is here also that Luke distinguished most clearly between the Last Supper and the Lord's Supper or Eucharist. At the Last Supper, Jesus told how he had eagerly desired to eat this Passover with his disciples before he suffered, also to drink of the cup with them. He would not eat it or drink of the fruit of the vine again until the kingdom of God came (Luke 22:15-18). This was clearly the Last Supper.

But there would be a new supper when there would be fulfillment in the kingdom of God. That new supper would first be realized in the Christian community's Lord's Supper but fully realized only in the heavenly banquet. In the Lord's Supper, Christians would participate in the body of Christ and in the cup of the new covenant in his blood (Luke 22:19-20).

The liturgical formula in Luke 22:19-20 represents the same tradition Paul quoted in 1 Corinthians 11:23-25 but with a Markan framework. In this way, Luke connected the liturgical experience of his readers with the traditional gospel story. Situating the Lord's Supper as an integral part of the life and story of Jesus, Luke invited his readers to see it as an integral part of their own lives and stories.

For the beginning of the formula and for the ending, Luke relied mainly on Mark 14:22-25. For the rest, especially for the action and words of Jesus regarding the cup, he relied on the Antiochene formula used at the Lord's Supper in the Lukan communities. The relationship between Luke 22:19-20 and its sources can be seen from the synoptic comparison in Table VI.

From the beginning up to Jesus' words, "This is my body," Luke basically followed Mark, but with a few changes. In Mark, the expression, "while they were eating" (Mark 14:22), links the liturgical formula to the meal begun in Mark 14:17. But since Luke distinguished the Lord's Supper (22:19-20) from the Last Supper (22:15-18), such a connective link was not needed.

Luke also substituted the words, "having given thanks," which were familiar to his readers, for the words, "having blessed," which came to Mark from the formula's original semitic, Palestinian environment. Luke's "having given thanks" (see also 1 Cor 11:23) corresponded to the formula's development in a Gentile, Greek-speaking environment.

Luke also dropped the command that the disciples, "Take." In Mark and Matthew, the command challenged the disciples to take on the challenge of discipleship in the following of Christ. In Luke, the command, "Do this in memory of me," serves much the same purpose.

Jesus' discourse at the Last Supper emphasized the thanksgiving (eucharistia) aspect of Eucharist — "Then he took bread, gave thanks, broke it" — addressing communities who were children of God by grace (charis) not by ancient heritage. Christians of Jewish background spoke rather of being blessed by God and of their blessing God in return, as they had done under the old covenant. Those of Gentile background celebrated the grace granted them in the new covenant. The proper response to grace (charis) is thanksgiving (eucharistia).

The discourse also emphasizes the relationship between the Eucharist and the Eucharistic community. "This is my body, which will be given *for you*" (Luke 22:19; see 1 Cor 11:23). In the same way, Jesus speaks of the cup "which is poured out *for you*" (Luke 22:20), that is, for those present at the supper. In Mark, Jesus speaks of the cup "which will be shed *for many*" (Mark 14:24).

Mark and Matthew stressed the Church's commitment to the mission of Christ. Luke and Paul stressed the need for communities to be integrated in a Church that was missionary. Universal in principle, called to be universal in fact, the Church is of its nature missionary. The same applied to the Eucharist. Universal in principle, called to be universal in fact, the Eucharist is of its nature missionary.

Meals with the Living One

Luke's story of the origins of Eucharist did not end with the Last Supper. It could have done so, in view of Luke's distinction between the Last Supper and the Lord's Supper and the way he united them in one Passover event. But instead the gospel develops aspects of the Eucharist related to Jesus' presence after the passion-resurrection.

There are two meals in Luke's account of Jesus' resurrection: the one with the disciples of Emmaus (24:13-35) and the one with the assembled community in Jerusalem (24:36-53). The meals are introduced by the story of the women who went to the tomb in search of the body of Jesus, only to find the tomb open at which time two men in dazzling garments appear to them: "Why do you seek the living one among the dead?" (Luke 24:5).

The story of Emmaus then shows where the communities were to seek the living one, that is, among the living. The final meal in Jerusalem shows the universal and missionary implications of Jesus' presence to them as the living one. With those two meals, Jesus' personal mission on earth is complete. As he ascends to heaven, he blesses the assembled community. The promise made to Abraham is fulfilled. In his progeny all the families of the earth would be blessed.

Finding and recognizing the living one — the risen Lord — among the living was not easy for the Lukan communities. Nor is it easy today.

The story of Emmaus shows disciples profoundly disheartened by the events of the passion and abandoning Jerusalem, the city of fulfillment. It was the first day of the week, the day of the new creation. There was no reason for their discouragement. Jesus was with them. But they were unable to recognize him.

The disciples were still fixed on images of "Jesus the Nazarene, who was a prophet mighty in deed and word before God and all the people" (Luke 24:19). Despite all of Jesus' power, the chief priests and rulers had sentenced him to death and crucified him. The disciples had lost all hope. That is why they were going away from Jerusalem and the community.

To recognize the living one among them, they first had to understand Jesus' passion. The passion was not the end of Jesus' life, but only the end of his earthly life: "Was it not necessary that the Messiah [Christ] should suffer these things and enter into his glory?" (Luke 24:26). The passion was Jesus' way into a new and glorious life, which did not remove him from them but allowed him to remain with them in a new way. Years later, the Church would refer to that way as sacramental.

Still not recognizing Jesus in their midst, the disciples were nevertheless moved by his message, but it is only after their eyes were opened in recognition that they became conscious of the profound effect his words had on them. "Stay with us," they said, and he did so. Jesus accepted the disciples' hospitality. In their eyes, however, he remained a stranger until they were at table and "he took bread, said the blessing, broke it, and gave it to them." Luke's message was clear. For those who accept the gospel of the passion-resurrection, the living one can be recognized in "the breaking of the bread."

For Luke the Eucharist was "the breaking of the bread," a sharing event in which the participants blessed God and raised their minds in thanksgiving. It is primarily in that event that the living one was present to the assembled community and recognized by its members, only, however, if they were present to him as he was present to them.

The disciples immediately returned to Jerusalem and joined the assembled community. The gospel and the breaking of the bread had to be shared. Jesus was risen and among them, even more powerful in deed (the breaking of the bread) and word (the gospel of the passion-resurrection) before God and all the people.

While they were still speaking, Jesus again appeared in their midst, bringing peace to them and requesting hospitality. "Have you anything here to eat?" he asked (Luke 24:41). The disciples of Emmaus had recognized Jesus in the breaking of the bread. Jesus eating with the community now becomes the springboard for the Christian mission (Luke 24:36-53).

After eating, Jesus addressed them as he had done at earlier meals, but this time about their mission. Eating with Jesus, they became witnesses to Jesus' passion and resurrection and how the Scriptures were fulfilled in them. The message of the passion-resurrection was a call for repentance promising the forgiveness of sins. Those who shared at the table of the Lord were to preach this message "in his name to all nations, beginning from Jerusalem" (Luke 24:47).

The story of the meal at Emmaus, as well as that of the final meal in Jerusalem, announces many of the Eucharistic themes developed in the Acts of the Apostles. For that we need to take a close look at Luke's second volume.

NOTES

1. In this context, recall the opening words of Luke's preface: "Since many have undertaken to compile a narrative of the events that have been fulfilled among us" (Luke 1:1). The Last Supper was one of those events. Like those who came before him, Luke did not present the Last Supper precisely as it happened but "as an event fulfilled among us."

2. For a full commentary on Luke's Gospel in English, see Joseph A. Fitzmyer, *The Gospel According to Luke I–IX, XII–XXIV*, The Anchor Bible 28, 28A (Garden City: Doubleday & Company, Inc., 1981, 1985); see also Luke Timothy Johnson, *The Gospel of Luke*, Sacra Pagina 3 (Collegeville: The Liturgical Press, 1991); Eugene LaVerdiere, S.S.S., *Luke*, New Testament Message 5 (Collegeville: The Liturgical Press, 1980).

3. Without the passion and resurrection, Jesus certainly would have had a last meal, but that is all it would have been, his last meal. It might have been the last meal of "Jesus the Nazarene, who was a prophet mighty in deed and word before God and all the people" (Luke 24:19), but it would not have been Christ's Last Supper.

4. Theologically and literally, the Last Supper and the Lord's Supper form a single symbolic event, introducing and embodying the passion-resurrection.

5. Discussing the oldest attainable form of the tradition and more specifically whether it consisted in a liturgy or a historical account, Joachim Jeremias concluded that *"at the beginning there stands not liturgy, but historical account."* Various elements in the Last Supper liturgical formulas point back "to a very old pre-liturgical narrative tradition" (*The Eucharistic Words of Jesus*, trans. Norman Perrin [Philadelphia: Fortress Press, 1966] 191–193).

6. For a detailed presentation of the Eucharist in Luke's Gospel, see Eugene LaVerdiere, *Dining in the Kingdom of God, The Origins of Eucharist According to Luke* (Chicago: Liturgy Training Publications, 1994).

7. See E. LaVerdiere, "Mary's Son, God's Firstborn," *Church* 10 (Winter 1994) 5–9.

8. For a description of the Lukan communities at the time Luke wrote the Gospel and Acts, see Eugene LaVerdiere, *Luke* (Collegeville: The Liturgical Press, 1980) xiii–xviii. See also Eugene A. LaVerdiere, S.S.S. and William G. Thompson, S.J., "New Testament Communities in Transition: A Study of Matthew and Luke"

in *Why the Church?*, ed. Walter J. Burghardt, S.J., and William G. Thompson, S.J. (New York: Paulist Press, 1977) 23–53. The section on Luke was written by E. A. LaVerdiere.

9. That is why Mark needed to explain ordinary Jewish traditions related to meals: "For the Pharisees and, in fact, all Jews, do not eat without carefully washing their hands, keeping the tradition of the elders. And on coming from the marketplace they do not eat without purifying themselves. And there are many other things that they have traditionally observed, the purification of cups and jugs and kettles [and beds]" (Mark 7:3-4). The story of Jesus had been clear for Christians of Jewish background, but was no longer clear for Christians of Gentile background. While following Mark at this point in his Gospel, Matthew dropped Mark's explanatory parenthesis. His community, largely of Jewish origin and still close to Judaism had no need of such explanations.

10. The story of Pentecost, with "devout Jews from every nation under heaven staying in Jerusalem" reveals Luke's view of the universality of both gospel and Church. Note that the list of those present begins with "Parthians, Medes, and Elamites, inhabitants of Mesopotamia" (Acts 2:9), all of them outside the sphere of the Roman Empire.

11. The journey narrative in Luke's Gospel can be viewed in two different ways. Thematically, the journey is to Jerusalem as the place of the ascension (Luke 9:51; see 9:31). As such the journey includes Jesus' teaching in Jerusalem (20:1–21:38), as well as the passion-resurrection (22:1–24:53). Geographically, however, the journey ends with the cleansing of the temple when Jesus has arrived in Jerusalem (19:38).

12. In Luke and Acts, such "necessity" is associated only with the mission of Jesus and the great events of salvation (see, for example, Luke 22:7, 37; 24:7, 26, 44).

13. See E. LaVerdiere, "A Discourse at the Last Supper," *The Bible Today* (March 1974) 1540–1548.

7

The Breaking of the Bread:
The Eucharist in the Acts of the Apostles

> Luke wrote the Acts of the Apostles
> as the continuation of his Gospel.
> In the Gospel, Luke did not treat
> the development of the Church
> after Jesus' resurrection and
> ascension. He took it up in
> the Acts, relating the Eucharist
> to various phases of the Church's
> growth and showing how the Eucharist
> contributed to its understanding.
> In the process, he also added to
> our understanding of the Eucharist.

Luke was a historian, the first to write a history of the origins and development of the Church.[1] Luke was also a theologian and introduced his work as "a narrative of the events that have been fulfilled among us" (Luke 1:1). His narrative is presented in two volumes, The Gospel According to Luke and the Acts of the Apostles.

For the Christian Middle Ages, building on foundations set centuries earlier by St. Augustine, theology was "faith seeking understanding" (*fides quaerens intellectum*). The view was popularized by St. Anselm. For St. Luke, building on foundations set by "those who were eyewitnesses from the beginning and ministers of the word" (Luke 1:2), theology was faith seeking historical understanding.

Luke presented his narrative in two scrolls or volumes. In the New Testament, the first volume, called the Gospel According to Luke, was placed between the Gospel According to Mark and the Gospel

According to John. The second volume, called the Acts of the Apostles,[2] was separated from the first by the Gospel According to John. The arrangement helps to see the unity of the gospel story, but it distracts from the unity of Luke's two-volume work.

The Gospel According to Luke and the Acts of the Apostles, conceived as one work, were meant to be read sequentially. The gospel presupposes what Luke would present in Acts, and Acts presupposes what he wrote in the Gospel. There is no understanding one without the other. To emphasize that unity, many today refer to Luke's two-volume "narrative of the events that have been fulfilled among us" (Luke 1:1) as "Luke-Acts."

Luke showed himself a historian in the preface he wrote for the Gospel (Acts 1:1-4), a classic of the form used by Greek and Roman writers to introduce a historical work. He also wrote a secondary preface, as ancient historians did, to introduce his second volume, the Acts of the Apostles (Acts 1:1-2).[3]

As a historian, Luke was far more than a chronicler of past events. Schooled in the art of Hellenistic historiography, he wrote of the past to illumine the present and provide direction for the future. As such, he wrote of matters he considered important for the Church in the mid-80s of the first century.

As a biblical historian, Luke was also steeped in the historical writings of the Bible, especially those of prophetic inspiration. He saw deeply into situations and events as the prophets did and wrote so that readers might see what he saw and respond accordingly.

As a Christian historian, Luke was also immersed in Christian tradition, in earlier writings such as Mark's Gospel, in the liturgical life of the Church and in the Church's expanding mission. Luke knew the life of the Church, as it began in Jerusalem on Pentecost (Acts 2:1-41), as it developed in the apostolic age, and continued to develop even as he wrote Luke-Acts.

In Luke-Acts, Luke gave us a two-volume history of the Church. In the Gospel, he told the story of the origins of the Church in the life, mission, and ministry of Jesus. In the Acts, he told the story of the development of the Church in the apostolic community.

An important part of Luke's Gospel story is that of the origins of the Eucharist. Luke showed the *origins* of the Eucharist primarily through a series of ten meals with Jesus, the first in the home of a tax-collector named Levi (Luke 5:27-39), the last after his resurrection with the community of disciples assembled in Jerusalem (Luke 24:36-53).

In his story of origins, Luke also included some of Jesus' teaching that contributed to understanding the Eucharist. He even showed how the Eucharist was related to Jesus' birth and the historical origins of his mission.

An important part of the Acts' story of the apostolic Church is that of the *development* of the Eucharist. The literary presentation in Acts, however, is very different from that in the Gospel. Instead of a whole series of meals, the Acts recounts only three meals, all three of them involving Paul (Acts 16:25-34; 20:7-12; 27:33-38). In the Acts, the development of the Eucharist is shown mainly in other ways, such as through summaries of life in the primitive community, community assemblies, apostolic discourses, missionary experiences, and community decisions affecting the Church as it grew and became more diversified.

The Eucharist in the Acts of the Apostles

As in the Gospel, the story of the Eucharist in Acts begins with the book's introduction, consisting in a secondary preface to the reader and a prologue for the work itself (1:1-14). In the Gospel, Luke related the Eucharist to Jesus' birth, when the city of David denied him hospitality, and Mary, the servant of the Lord — literally the slave *(doulos)* of the Lord — laid him in a manger, thereby offering him as nourishment for the flock (Luke 2:7). The story of Jesus' birth pointed to the end of Jesus' life, when the city of David again rejected Jesus. The one who was denied hospitality at birth offered hospitality at death, giving himself as nourishment in the Last Supper and the Lord's Supper.

TABLE VII

An Outline of the Acts of the Apostles

Preface and prologue		1:1-14
Taking salt during forty days (1:3-4)		
Part I. Growth and development of the Church		1:15–19:20
Section 1. Beginnings in Jerusalem	1:15–5:32	
The breaking of the bread (2:42-47)		
Section 2. From Jerusalem to Antioch	6:1–12:25	
Diakonia *(6:1-7)*		
Discourse to the household of Cornelius (10:34-43)		
Section 3. Missions from Antioch	13:1–19:20	
Dietary laws (15:13-29)		
Deliverance from prison (16:25-34)		

Introducing the Acts, Luke showed how the Eucharist has firm foundations in Jesus' meals with the apostolic community — literally "taking salt with" *(synalizomenos)* them — during forty days between the resurrection and the ascension (1:3-4). As part of the introduction (1:1-14), it helps readers see how events and developments in the Acts are related to the Gospel. More particularly, the reference to Jesus' eating with the disciples brings out the strong relationship between the development of the Eucharist in the apostolic Church and its origins in the life and mission of Jesus.

After the introduction (1:1-14), the Acts of the Apostles can be divided into two parts. The first tells of the growth and development of the Church (1:15-19:20), paralleling the story of the foundations of the Church in Luke 5:1–9:50. The second tells of Paul's great journey to Rome (19:21–28:31), paralleling Jesus' journey to Jerusalem in Luke 9:51–24:53.[4] Each part can be divided into three large sections, with all but one contributing to the story of the development of the Eucharist in the life of the Church. The Eucharist is a pervasive theme in Acts' entire story of the development of the Church.

The first part of Acts (1:15-19:20) starts with the Church's beginnings in Jerusalem (1:15–5:32). In a summary describing the life of the primitive Christian community in the city of its birth (2:42-47), the Eucharist is referred to as "the breaking of the bread" (2:42, 46).

The account continues with the spread of the Church from Jerusalem to Antioch (6:1–12:25). The Eucharist is referred to in the opening episode, spelling out the difficulties the community was experiencing in the matter of service *(diakonia)* at table (6:1-7). It also lies in the background of the story of Peter at Joppa, Caesarea, and Jerusalem (10:1–11:18) and figures prominently in Peter's address to the household of Cornelius (10:34-43).

The third section, devoted to the growth and development of the Church (13:1–19:20), tells of the Church's missions from Antioch, the first leading up to and including the general assembly at Jerusalem (13:1–15:35), the second implementing the assembly's decisions (15:36–

19:20). One of the central questions before the assembly was whether Jewish dietary laws applied to the Gentiles. It consequently had a direct bearing on the celebration of the Eucharist in communities whose members were of Gentile origin (15:1-35). A second reference to the Eucharist may be found in the story of the deliverance of Paul and Silas from prison at Philippi (16:25-34).

The second part of Acts, the story of Paul's great journey to Rome (19:21–28:31), also unfolds in three sections, as outlined in 19:21-22. The first has Paul traveling through Macedonia and Achaia (19:21–20:38). That is when Paul breaks bread with the community at Troas on the first day of the week (20:7-12). The story is very important for its description of an early Christian community assembled and actually celebrating the Eucharist. This is the only passage in the New Testament that tells the story of a celebration of the Eucharist by a Christian community.

The second section of the journey, which has Paul going on to Jerusalem (21:1–23:11), is the only section in the Acts that does not refer to the Eucharist. The third and last section, the journey from Jerusalem to Rome (23:12–28:31), contains a very important story concerning the Eucharist at the height of a great storm at sea (27:33-38). Unlikely as the setting may be, its reference to the Eucharist is unmistakable.

While Eating Salt with Them (Acts 1:1-14)

Acts' story of the development of the Eucharist in the apostolic Church begins with the introduction, which is in the form of a preface and prologue (1:1-14).[5] As part of the introduction, Luke sums up his first volume, focusing especially on Jesus' concluding appearance and the ascension (Luke 24:36-53): "In the first book, Theophilus, I dealt with all that Jesus did and taught until the day he was taken up, after giving instructions through the holy Spirit to the apostles whom he had chosen" (Acts 1:1-2).

At this point, we expect Luke to announce the contents of the second volume. Instead he adds further developments on the period between Jesus' resurrection and the ascension, again in the form of a summary description: "He presented himself alive to them by many proofs after he had suffered, appearing to them during forty days and speaking about the kingdom of God. While meeting with them, he enjoined them not to depart from Jerusalem, but to wait for . . ." (Acts 1:3-4a).

At this point, we expect Luke to report what Jesus said. Instead, the summary passes from indirect discourse to direct discourse, quoting Jesus' words to them during that time: ". . . the promise of the Father about which you have heard me speak; for John baptized with water, but in a few days you will be baptized with the holy Spirit" (Acts 1:4b-5).

This second summary (1:3-5) describes the way Jesus presented himself alive to the disciples after the passion *(to pathein)* for forty days. During this period, Jesus was appearing *(optanomenos)* to them, telling *(legon)* them about the kingdom of God, and while eating with them *(synalizomenos)*, he told them not to leave Jerusalem, but to await the promise of the Father (see Luke 24:49). The present passive participle, *synalizomenos,* like the two other present participles, refers to what Jesus did, not on one particular occasion during the forty days, but over and over again throughout the forty days.[6]

The verb *synalizo,* meaning literally "to eat salt *(alizo)* with *(syn),"* clashes with modern day sensibilities, repeatedly warning us against the unhealthy effects of adding salt to our food. It would never occur to us today to want to eat salt with people we love. Not so in the ancient world, where salt was prized not only as a preservative agent but for its medicinal qualities as well as a condiment.[7] For Job, the calamitous situation that had befallen him was like being reduced to eating bread without salt (Job 6:6). Aristotle quoted a proverb in which "consuming salt together" *(halas synanalosai)* spoke of being bound by close ties of hospitality,[8] and another referring to old friends as having "eaten a bushel of salt together."[9] It takes a lot of meals together for bonds of friendship to become strong and deep.

With an awareness and appreciation for ancient sensibilities, we can understand why the Israelites spoke of their covenant as "a covenant of salt forever before the Lord" (Num 18:19 [NRSV]) and of the "salt of the covenant with your God" (Lev 2:13 [NRSV]). We understand also why "to eat salt together" could become a very powerful metaphor.

By eating bread with his disciples, Jesus shared his life with them and made them one with him. Jesus' eating salt with the disciples spoke of the quality and depth of his sharing with them. Doing so during forty days spoke of the profound and lasting effects of that sharing.

It took a lot of meals with the risen Lord to become strong witnesses to his resurrection. Those meals during forty days between the first day of the week after Jesus suffered and the day he ascended to his Father strengthened the relationship between the disciples and Jesus, their risen Lord, preparing them to be the witnesses they needed to be to the ends of the earth.

The Breaking of the Bread (Acts 1:15–5:42)

The first part of the Acts of the Apostles tells of the development of the Church from its beginnings in Jerusalem's primitive Christian community (1:15–5:42), as it spread from Jerusalem to Antioch (6:1–12:25) and then to the completion of Paul's missions from Antioch (13:1–19:20).[10]

The account of the beginnings in Jerusalem opens with an introductory passage on the community of apostles. Judas, who betrayed Jesus and suffered the fate of a betrayer, had to be replaced. The community of Peter and the Eleven had to be reconstituted. The body of the section consists of a series of events, discourses, reactions to these, and of summaries of the community's life and activities.

Three longer-than-average summaries stand out (Acts 2:42-47; 4:32-35; 5:12-16) as transitions both separating and joining various units in the story and providing insight into the community's life and ideals.

The first of these summaries (Acts 2:42-47) is the most basic, including themes that would be further developed in the other summaries. It also has a special focus of its own on "the breaking of the bread," Luke's expression for the Eucharist (2:42; Luke 24:35). In the section, the summary comes after the Pentecost event, including the descent of the holy Spirit, Peter's discourse and the crowd's favorable reaction to it.

The community described in Acts 2:42-47 was born of the holy Spirit at Pentecost (Acts 2:1-13), of Peter's first great act of witness once "the promise of the Father" was fulfilled (2:14-36; see 1:8) and of the baptism "with the holy Spirit" of which Jesus had spoken (2:37-41; see 1:5). The community described was an ideal community, one which Luke's readers could recall as the Church's golden age.

The summary begins with a summary of its own (Acts 2:42), a summary of the summary, giving the distinctive qualities or characteristics of the Christian community, before giving the summary in fuller detail (2:43-47). The Eucharist, the breaking of the bread, is one of those distinguishing characteristics. It is also referred to in the expanded summary (2:46).

In modern times, we speak of the Church as having four traditional and characteristic marks. These marks describe the Church as one, holy, catholic, and apostolic. Each mark is real. Each mark is also an ideal. Luke also described the Church in its beginnings as having four real and ideal marks: "They devoted themselves to the teaching of the apostles and to the communal life, to the breaking of the bread and to the prayers" (Acts 2:42). Such were the most fundamental realities in the life of the Church community.

Luke presented the four marks of the early Church in two sets of two. The first set consisted in "the teaching of the apostles" *(he didache ton apostolon)* and "the communal life" *(he koinonia)*. These form the general life setting for the second set, "the breaking of the bread" *(he klasis tou artou)* and "the prayers" *(hai proseuchai)*.

The community was engaged, first of all, in apostolic teaching (see Acts 4:2, 18; 5:21, 25, 28, 42). The expression, "the teaching of the apostles," does not refer to a body of apostolic teachings but to the activity of apostolic teaching. Devoting themselves to the teaching of the apostles means they were faithful to their mission of apostolic teaching. The community did have special teachers, such as Peter and John (Acts 4:2, 18), indeed all the apostles (Acts 5:21, 25, 28, 42), but the whole Church identified with their teaching mission and made it their own.

To be effective teachers, the apostles and those with them had to live what they taught. As witnesses to Jesus' resurrection, their life had to reflect and announce the implications of the resurrection. They did this by their "common-union" *(koinonia)*, that is, by the way they were united with one another through their union with Jesus Christ, the risen Lord.

Their common-union was made visible in their attitudes toward one another, in the way they treated one another in daily life and genuinely shared with one another. The community was thus apostolic in word *(didache)* and deed *(koinonia)*.

The first set of distinctive traits, devotedness to the teaching of the apostles and the common-union, found its highest expression in the second, the breaking of the bread and the prayers. These also consisted in activities, more specific than the first pair but not less significant. The apostolic teaching and the common-union penetrated and pervaded the community's daily life (see Acts 5:42), which breaking of the bread and prayers epitomized.

The expression "the breaking of the bread" has its origins in an Old Testament and Jewish ritual gesture associated with family meals. At the beginning of the meal, the head of the family or a special guest took bread, spoke a blessing, broke it and gave it to those at table. In the Old

Testament, the gesture of breaking bread can be traced back at least to the time of Jeremiah (Jer 16:7). From frequent references to it in the New Testament, we must assume that Jesus broke bread with his disciples and others.

For the early Christians, the person of Jesus, the way he communicated with those at table, what he communicated to them, and his relationship to them, gave the breaking of bread new and distinctive meaning. This was not just the breaking and sharing of bread, but Jesus' breaking of bread and Jesus' sharing of it as an expression of his very person. For the Christians, the bread was broken in memory of Jesus. It was "the breaking of *the* bread" by apostles with whom Jesus the risen Lord had eaten salt over forty days and who were closely united with him.

In the New Testament, "the breaking of the bread" and related expressions using the verb "break" continued to evoke the ancient Jewish gesture and especially Jesus' breaking bread in the course of his ministry, but they now referred to the entire Eucharistic meal, one of the distinctive activities of the Christian community and the first expression of their apostolic teaching and their *koinonia*.

In Luke-Acts, as in the other gospels, the act of breaking bread is closely associated with the early Christian experience and ideal of the Eucharist. Literally, the Eucharistic breaking of bread, "the breaking of the bread," transforms all the meals in Jesus' gospel story and relates them to the Eucharist. This is especially true of the breaking of the bread with the five thousand (Luke 9:10-17), of the Last Supper (Luke 22:14-38), and of the recognition of the risen Lord at Emmaus (Luke 24:13-35).[11]

At Jewish meals and the meals in Jesus' ministry, the gesture of breaking bread came after a prayer of blessing, which explains the close relationship between "the breaking of the bread" and "the prayers." For the Christians, these prayers included blessings but also thanksgiving and praise (Acts 2:47).

The prayers referred to included any that were associated directly with the Eucharist, "the breaking of the bread," but also pointed beyond such prayers, even beyond the celebration of the Eucharist. The definite article in the expression, "the prayers," suggests the existence of distinctively Christian prayers. The Lord's Prayer (Luke 11:2-4) comes immediately to mind. It also refers to the community's fidelity to the traditional hours of prayer, for which they assembled in the temple area (Acts 2:46; 3:1) and in their homes (see Acts 12:12).

From Jerusalem to Antioch (Acts 6:1–12:25)

After describing the beginnings of the Church in Jerusalem (Acts 1:15–5:42), Luke tells how it spread from Jerusalem to Antioch (6:1–12:25). The story of the beginnings presented the primitive Church as a distinct community with roots in Judaism, developing in a Jewish milieu.

The story of its spread to Antioch shows how the Church expanded from a Hebrew or Aramaic speaking community to one that included Greek-speaking Jews. It then shows how the Church expanded still further from a linguistically mixed community into one that included Gentiles. In the process, the community also moved beyond the Jewish milieu of its origins to the Gentile milieu of Antioch, from which it would send missionaries to the ends of the earth.

Such developments did not come about without difficulty. As we might expect, the difficulties came up most sharply in relation to community assemblies and Eucharistic meals. Issues that affect the life of the community at large become magnified when the community comes together.

Difficulties first surfaced in Jerusalem (Acts 6:1-7) where the community not only had grown quite dramatically, but had also become ethnically and linguistically diversified. There were those who spoke Hebrew and Aramaic. There were also newer members who spoke Greek. Growth and diversification put a strain on the community's resources, leading to complaints that the widows among the Greek-speaking members were being neglected in the daily distribution of food.

To resolve the difficulty, the Twelve called the community together and said, "It is not right for us to neglect the word of God *(ton logon tou theou)* to serve at table *(diakonein trapezais)*" (Acts 6:2). The response of the Twelve went beyond the matter of equitable distribution and addressed some of the broader issues of the Eucharistic ministry.

The problem in Jerusalem was analogous to the situation at the home of Martha, when Martha complained of being burdened with much serving *(diakonia)* while Mary sat at the feet of the Lord *(pros tous podas tou kyriou)* and listened to his word *(ekouen ton logon autou)*. Martha wanted Mary to help her serve *(diakonein)* but Jesus defended Mary's position as a disciple[12] attending to the word of the Lord (Luke 10:38-42).

At the home of Martha, the gospel's concern was to affirm the priority of discipleship and the word. In the community at Jerusalem, Acts' concern was to resolve the conflict between ministering at the Eucharistic table *(diakonein trapezais)* and the ministry of the word *(he diakonia tou logou),* along with the attendant need for prayer *(he proseuche).*

The Twelve therefore proposed that responsibility for the service at table be shared with others. Such was the origin of the Seven who would supplement the Twelve in assuring adequate Eucharistic service (Acts 6:3-6). With that "The word of God continued to spread, and the number of disciples in Jerusalem increased greatly" (6:7).

The community was thus able to continue devoting itself "to the teaching of the apostles and to the communal life, to the breaking of the bread and the prayers" (Acts 2:42). Essential elements in the community's life and ideals had been threatened, resulting in the need for something to be done.

The second story with implications for the Eucharist is the long account of how Peter evangelized the household of Cornelius (Acts 10:1–11:18). The issue had to do with accepting hospitality from Gentiles, entering their homes and sharing in their life, along with the question of eating foods that were considered ritually unclean. Such matters prevented the Christian community from reaching out to the Gentiles and forming communities with them.

This second issue was far more serious than that of managing an influx of Jews who differed ethnically and linguistically from the earliest Christians. It had to do with Christian identity and its relationship to both Judaism and the Gentile world.

In his discourse to the household of Cornelius (Acts 10:34-43), Peter addressed the matter from a Christological point of view. The identity of Christians and Christian communities depended on the identity of Jesus, whom Peter introduced as "Jesus Christ, who is Lord of all" (Acts 10:36). "God anointed Jesus of Nazareth with the holy Spirit and power," and "he went about doing good and healing all those oppressed by the devil, for God was with him" (Acts 10:38). The disciples of Emmaus had spoken of Jesus in similar terms (Luke 24:19).

Raised from the dead, however, Jesus Christ (the anointed) is Lord of all. That is why those who are his witnesses, "who ate and drank with him after he rose from the dead" (Acts 10:41; see 1:4 and Luke 24:36-53) must be his witnesses before all human beings, both Jew and Gentile. All are invited to share at the table of the one who is Lord of all. From a Christological point of view, the key to the universal mission of the Church and the nature of its Eucharistic assembly is the Lordship of Jesus.

The Missions from Antioch (Acts 13:1–19:20)

The second section of the Acts told how the Church spread from Jerusalem to Antioch (Acts 6:1–12:25). The third section tells of the missions from Antioch (13:1–19:20). The community's expansion from Jerusalem to Antioch came as a result of persecution. The next stage of its expansion, from Antioch to the whole Aegean world, came by missionary initiative.

The difficulties regarding the presence of Gentiles in the community and of developing Gentile communities in the Church had already been faced in the story of Peter and the household of Cornelius, first by Peter in Caesarea (Acts 10:24-49) and then by the community when Peter went to Jerusalem (11:1-18).

In the story of Peter and the household of Cornelius, the Church's opening to the Gentiles was dealt with on the level of understanding and faith. God showed Peter that he "should not call any person profane or unclean" (Acts 10:28). Those who ate and drank with Jesus after he rose from the dead on the third day were his witnesses, commissioned to bring the Gospel of salvation to all peoples (10:40-43). There was no withholding baptism from those who received the Holy Spirit, be they Jews or Gentiles (10:44-49).

In this section on the missions from Antioch, the same issues are dealt with on the level of policy and implementation. It was one thing for the Church to open up to the Gentiles (Acts 10:1–11:18). It was another to integrate the Gentiles into the community's life and history, and to do this without prejudice to compatible aspects of their culture and background.

Finding and establishing a common policy was Paul and Barnabas' purpose in calling a general assembly in Jerusalem at the end of the first mission (Acts 15:1-35).[13] The assembly decided that Gentiles should be asked only "to abstain from meat sacrificed to idols, from blood, from meats of strangled animals, and from unlawful marriage." If they kept free of these, they would be doing what is right (Acts 15:29). They would be integrated into the eucharistic community of the Church, devoting "themselves to the teaching of the apostles and to the communal life, to the breaking of the bread and the prayers" (2:42).

In the second mission, Paul and Silas applied the policy established in their evangelization of Macedonia and Achaia as well as in the province of Asia. At the beginning of the mission, while at Philippi, they shared a meal in the home of the one who had been their jailer

(Acts 16:25-34). While in prison, Paul and Silas were praying and singing hymns when an earthquake released them. But instead of leaving, the prisoners remained to evangelize the jailer and his household. Once these were baptized, the jailer brought Paul and Silas "into his house and provided a meal (*paretheken trapezan*, literally "set out a table") and with his household rejoiced at having come to faith in God" (Acts 16:34). Paul and Silas thus joined at the table of the Lord with a newly-formed Gentile community in the home of a Gentile.[14]

On the Journey to Rome (Acts 19:21–28:31)

The first part of the Acts told of the growth and development of the Church from its beginnings in Jerusalem to its spread throughout the Aegean world. Those called to be Jesus' witnesses had fulfilled their mission, at least in principle.

The biblical expression "to the ends of the earth," a geographical image, refers to all peoples. Through Peter's witness, especially in Jerusalem, Judea and Samaria, and Stephen's witness, which resulted in the Church's going as far as Antioch, and Paul's witness in the missions from Antioch, the gospel had been preached "in Jerusalem, throughout Judea and Samaria, and to the ends of the earth" (Acts 1:8). There were now Christian communities among both Jews and Gentiles. But how would the mission be realized in fact?

In the second part of the Acts, Luke tells of a great journey, in which Paul, after traveling through Macedonia and Achaia and passing through Jerusalem, travels to Rome (Acts 19:21–28:31). Like the journey of Jesus in the gospel, this is no ordinary journey.

Jesus' journey to Jerusalem (Acts 9:51–24:53) was a journey to the ascension and the kingdom of God, inspiring Christians in their own journey to the kingdom of God. Paul's journey to Rome is an epic missionary journey, bringing the gospel to the very heart of the Roman Empire. Paul's epic journey was written to inspire those who came later and benefited from Paul's mission. It was written for Christians whose mission was to bring the gospel even further. As the list of those present at Pentecost showed (Acts 2:9-11), the ends of the earth went well beyond the boundaries of the Roman Empire.[15]

There are two meal stories in the epic of Paul's journey to Rome, the first at the beginning, at Troas, where it became obvious Paul was embarking on a great journey to distant places and that the community at Troas would see him no more (Acts 20:7-12). The second is at the end of the journey on a storm-tossed ship which is about to capsize, and whose passengers were weak due to lack of food (27:33-38).

Like the meal at Emmaus (Luke 24:13-35) and the meal with the assembly in Jerusalem (Luke 24:36-53), the meal with Paul at Troas was held on "the first day of the week" (Acts 20:7; see Luke 24:1). For the early Christians, the day was associated with creation, the resurrection of Jesus, and the beginning of a new creation.

On the first day of the week, the Christians of Troas gathered "to break bread" (Acts 20:7, 11) as did the primitive Christian community in Jerusalem (2:42, 46). Since Paul was to leave the next morning, this was their last supper with him. As Jesus did at the Last Supper, Paul also spoke to them at length, but the story reports nothing of what he said. Paul's farewell discourse would come a bit later at Miletus, where Paul addressed the elders of the Church at Ephesus (20:17-35).

The story is dramatically told, highlighting the fatal fall of a young man from a fourth-story window[16] to the ground (Acts 20:9). But this was truly "the first day of the week," a day for celebrating the resurrection and the new creation. The Eucharistic assembly, Paul's ministry of the Word, and the breaking of the bread are presented as life-giving. Like Elijah in 1 Kings 17:21 and Elisha in 2 Kings 4:34, Paul threw himself on the boy and raised him to life (Acts 20:10).

The second meal story is even more dramatic. After appealing to Caesar, Paul was being taken to Rome. Off the coast of Crete, a great storm arose. The ship was driven off course and was tossed about for many days until it ran aground and began to break up (Acts 27:6-44). Throughout the ordeal, Paul is presented as an epic hero.

At the height of the storm, Paul spoke up, urging everyone to take some food. They had eaten nothing for some fourteen days. They needed to take some food if they wanted to survive (Acts 27:33-34). The Greek term used for "survival" is *soteria*, which in Christian parlance referred to salvation. Eating was, therefore, a matter of salvation. The story's emphasis on salvation recalls the story of Zacchaeus, where Jesus announced it was necessary that he stay at Zacchaeus' house that day, later specifying that salvation had come to Zacchaeus' house (Luke 19:5, 9).

After urging everyone to eat, Paul "took bread, gave thanks to God in front of them all, broke it, and began to eat" (Acts 27:35). Encouraged by Paul's example, the others then took some food themselves.

Paul gave them the example of what everyone needed to do in order to be saved. The reference to the Eucharist is unmistakable. The event, however, should not be interpreted as describing an actual Eucharist, but as a literary analogy. Just as Paul, the sailors, and the other passengers had to eat in order to have the strength they needed to survive, so also the Christians needed to join in the Eucharistic meal if they wished to be saved. Like Paul, they would then be able to pursue their mission to the ends of the earth, proclaiming the kingdom of God and teaching about the Lord Jesus Christ.

NOTES

1. In his letters, Paul included elements of autobiography and sometimes referred to historical events. His interest in these, however, was not so much historical as evangelical and prophetic, calling communities and individuals to consistency with and fidelity to the gospel they had received.

Mark also told of historical events, but again his reason for doing this was not so much historical as liturgical and prophetic. Mark told stories that were familiar to the community from their initiation catechesis to renew his readers in their baptismal commitment.

Matthew, like Luke, was sensitive to historical distinctions, but his primary concern was catechetical. Matthew retold the story of Jesus and his disciples, adapting it for the community now separated from the synagogue and taking on the mission to the Gentiles.

2. For full-length general commentaries available in English on the Acts of the Apostles, see Ernst Haenchen, *The Acts of the Apostles, A Commentary* (Philadelphia: The Westminster Press, 1971); Luke Timothy Johnson, *The Acts of the Apostles*, Sacra Pagina 5 (Collegeville: The Liturgical Press, 1992).

3. The secondary preface in Acts (1:1-2) flows almost imperceptibly into a prologue (1:3-14). The shift comes in reporting Jesus' message (1:4-5). At first Jesus' message is reported indirectly: "he enjoined them not to depart from Jerusalem, but to wait for." But then, in midsentence, it shifts to direct discourse: "the promise of the Father about which you have heard me speak; for John baptized with water, but in a few days you will be baptized with the holy Spirit."

4. There are various ways of dividing the book of Acts. The one here proposed respects the unity of the journey narrative (19:21–28:31) as well as the structural parallel between Luke's two volumes.

5. As a preface, the introduction speaks directly to the reader. As a prologue, it announces the major themes of the book of Acts. The introduction clearly begins as a preface (1:1-2) but moves from the preface to the prologue almost imperceptibly (1:3), making readers aware of the transition only after it has already taken place (1:4-5). Luke takes personal responsibility for the narrative in the gospel (Acts 1:1-2), but introduces the authoritative voice of the risen Lord for the development of the Church in the Acts.

6. All three present participles, *optanomenos, legon, synalizomenos,* characterize the way Jesus presented himself to the apostles during forty days. Part of this message during those forty days was to await the promise of his Father before leaving Jerusalem. The shift from indirect to direct discourse gives the impression that

verses 4 and 5 refer to one of the appearances during the forty days, but the present participle of *synalizomenos* associates these verses with the entire theological period of forty days.

7. See Pliny the Elder, *Natural History,* Book XXXI, xxxix–xlv.

8. *Nicomachean Ethics,* Book VIII, iii, 8.

9. *Eudemian Ethics,* Book VII, ii.

10. With the summary in 19:20, the first part of the Acts comes to a close. The second part begins by referring to the first as complete, "as these things were now fulfilled" *(hos de eplerothe tauta),* before outlining the second part: "Paul made up his mind to travel through Macedonia and Achaia, and then to go on to Jerusalem, saying, 'After I have been there, I must *(dei)* visit Rome also'" (19:21).

11. See Eugene LaVerdiere, *Dining in the Kingdom of God, The Origins of the Eucharist According to Luke* (Chicago: Liturgy Training Publications, 1994).

12. To sit at someone's feet does not refer to someone's physical posture but to being a true disciple. In Acts, this is very clear from Paul's reference to having been educated "at the feet of Gamaliel" (22:3).

13. Acts did not approach the Church as an idea, or ideal form, transcending peoples and cultures, and so able to be realized in various cultures independently of other realizations. From the beginning, the Church was an incarnate reality that needed to make room within itself for new peoples and cultures and relate them to its existing historical reality.

14. See Philippe H. Menoud, "The Acts of the Apostles and the Eucharist," in *Jesus Christ and the Faith,* trans. Eunice M. Paul (Pittsburgh: The Pickwick Press, 1978) 89–90.

15. Among those who heard the apostles in their own tongue were Parthians, Medes and Elamites and inhabitants of Mesopotamia. At the time of Luke's writing, none of these territories belonged to the Roman Empire.

16. The Greek term *tristegos* refers to the "third" *(tris)* "roof" *(tegos),* hence, at least in American usage, the fourth story, not the third, as it is often translated.

8

Bread from Heaven:
The Eucharist in John's Gospel

John's Gospel developed over a period of
about fifty years, beginning in the 50s with a
rich store of traditions and going through
several editions, each new and enlarged
until its completion in the late 90s.
During those years, the situation in the
community changed, over and over again,
and John's Gospel reflects those changes.
One thing, however, remained constant:
the need to take Jesus' incarnation,
the Word made flesh, seriously.
For John, this meant taking the Eucharist,
the sacrament of the Word made flesh,
seriously.

"In the beginning was the Word, and the Word was with God, and
the Word was God" (John 1:1). John's Gospel[1] tells the story of the
Word, from the beginning, before human history began, when the
Word was with God — indeed was God (1:1-5) — until the Word became flesh in the person of Jesus and dwelt among us (1:14).

John's Gospel also tells how Jesus, the Word made flesh, was "the
bread of life" (6:48), "the living bread that came down from heaven"
(6:51a), to give his "flesh for the life of the world" (6:51c).

As the story of the Word made flesh, John's Gospel is unique in its
telling of the gospel. The story of bread which came down from

heaven to be the bread of life is also unique in its reflection on the Eucharist.

In Paul and the Synoptic Gospels, the Eucharist is related primarily to Christ's passion and resurrection, in which the assembly and Christ's followers are invited to join Christ in that event, offering themselves as he did. For Paul and the Synoptics, the Eucharist was above all the sacrament of Jesus' climactic redemptive acts.

In John, the Eucharist is related primarily to Jesus' incarnation, the Word of God made flesh, inviting Jesus' disciples, indeed all who believe, to be one with him as he and the Father are one. For John, the Eucharist was above all the sacrament of Jesus, the incarnate Word of God, dwelling among us as God's personal revelation.

With John's Gospel we enter a world of symbol and sacrament, where the eternal, creative, life-giving Word of God becomes flesh and dwells among us (1:1-5, 14), where water becomes wine (2:1-11) and people are born anew of water and Spirit (3:1-15), where the water Jesus gives becomes a spring welling up to eternal life (4:4-15), and where Jesus, as heavenly bread, comes down from heaven and gives his flesh for the life of the world (6:52-59).

At the heart of John's world of symbol and sacrament, there is the person of Jesus, the Word made flesh. There are also Jesus' signs,[2] revelatory acts of the Word made flesh, some of which are Eucharistic, as well as Jesus' teaching, the spoken word of the Word made flesh, some of which bears on the Eucharist.

So many things can be said about the Eucharist in John's Gospel. Like Paul and the Synoptic Gospels, John presents the Eucharist as a liturgical, salvific event, integral to the life of the Church and celebrated in memory of Christ's death and resurrection. John, however, viewed the event primarily as life-giving for those who actually believe and partake.

Like Paul and the Synoptic Gospels, John also presents the Eucharist as a symbolic event, a unique Christian synthesis of symbol, gesture, deed, and word,[3] and as a sacramental event, in which Christ acts in and through a Christian assembly, proclaiming the death of the Lord.[4] For John, however, the event is viewed primarily from the point of view of Christ's personal presence, sustaining, challenging, nourishing, and uniting the Church on its journey to the Father.

As presented in John's Gospel, the Eucharist can be summed up as *the Word of God made flesh made sacramental nourishment* for all who believe.

The Eucharist in John's Gospel

As a symbolic and sacramental event in the life of the Church, the Eucharist is very much at home in John's world of symbol and sacrament. We sense its presence just about everywhere, if not at the center of attention, at least on the periphery and as a pervasive atmosphere.

John's tendency is to presuppose the Eucharist, rather than speak of it directly, and to focus on its significance and implications for the life of Christians. There is more than one way for a story, discourse, or symbol to be Eucharistic.

Table VIII
An Outline of John's Gospel

I.	Prologue	1:1-18
II.	The book of signs	1:19–12:50
	A. The beginnings of Jesus' ministry	1:19–4:54
	The wedding feast at Cana (2:1-11)	
	B. Public ministry in Galilee, Judea and Jerusalem	5:1–12:50
	The bread from heaven (6:1-71)	
III.	The book of glory	13:1–20:31
	The Last Supper (13:1–17:26)	
IV.	Epilogue	21:1-25
	The breakfast by the sea (21:1-14)	

The gospel prologue (1:1-18), for example, may not be directly and explicitly Eucharistic, but it does invite reflection on the Eucharist. Like every gospel prologue, John's prologue contains the entire Gospel in miniature, announcing the various themes that would be developed in the body of the gospel. The prologue's reference to the Word made flesh (1:14) is therefore not an isolated statement. As an expression of John's theology of the incarnation in miniature, it already contains the Gospel's further development of that theology, including its sacramental realization in the Eucharist.

The prologue's declaration that "the Word became flesh" (1:14) is related to Jesus' declaration concerning the bread he distributed to the five thousand (6:1-15): "and the bread that I will give is my flesh for the life of the world" (6:51c). It is also related to Jesus' subsequent challenge to the crowd: "Amen, amen, I say to you, unless you eat the flesh of the Son of Man and drink his blood, you do not have life within you" (6:53). As such, welcoming Jesus as the Word made flesh implies welcoming him as the true bread from heaven and the life-giving sacrament of the Word made flesh.[5]

The reference at the end of the passion to the flow of blood and water, when a soldier thrust his lance into Jesus' side, also invites reflection on the Eucharist as it does on the closely related sacrament of baptism (19:34).

The flow of blood refers, first of all, to the reality of Jesus' passion and death, but it also calls to mind Jesus' challenging declaration that his blood was true drink (6:55) and a source of eternal life (6:54). In so doing, the flow of blood associates the Eucharist with the passion of the Word made flesh.

Like the blood, the water flowing from Jesus' side refers to his passion and death, but it also calls to mind Jesus' teaching to Nicodemus about being born again of water and Spirit (3:3-5) and to the Samaritan woman about "living water," indeed "a spring of water welling up to eternal life" (4:14). As the symbol of blood did for the Eucharist, the flow of water associates baptism with the passion of the Word made flesh.

The Eucharist is closer to the center of attention, but still secondary, in the story of the wedding feast at Cana (2:1-11), where the primary focus is on the new era or covenant brought by Jesus. A number of elements, however, beginning with the setting, a wedding feast, and the symbol of wine, but especially the proximity to the Jewish feast of Passover (2:13)[6] and the reference to Jesus' hour (2:4),[7] evoke the Eucharist as a symbol of the new era.

Besides these indirect or secondary references to the Eucharist, John contains three passages in which the reference to the Eucharist is primary. The first is the story popularly known as "the multiplication of loaves" (John 6:1-15) together with Jesus' discourse to the crowd (6:22-59) and the ensuing dialogue with the disciples (6:60-71). The second is the story of the Last Supper (13:1-38) and the farewell discourses that follow it, climaxing in a great synthesis of Jesus' mission in the form of a prayer (14:1–17:26). The third is in the Gospel's epilogue, a story of a breakfast with Jesus on the seashore (21:1-14) followed by a special message to Simon Peter (21:15-23).

The story of Jesus giving bread to eat to a crowd of some five thousand is the most directly and explicitly Eucharistic in the whole gospel. Like the story of Jesus breaking bread in the Synoptic Gospels, it includes expressions taken and adapted from a liturgical formula used in the early Christian Eucharist: "Then Jesus *took* the loaves, gave thanks, and distributed them to those who were reclining" (6:11). Later the discourse speaks of the bread as Jesus' very person come down from heaven (6:35-51b) and then as the bread Jesus would *give*, his flesh for the life of the world (6:52c-58).

John's account of the Last Supper is very different from those in the Synoptic Gospels. In John, the meal is mentioned but mainly as the setting for a symbolic action, Jesus' washing the feet of his disciples (13:1-20), his announcement of Judas' betrayal (13:21-35) and of Peter's denial of him (13:36-38),[8] and a series of farewell discourses (14:1-31; 15:1-17; 15:18–16:4a; 16:4b-33) followed by a concluding prayer (17:1-26). The discourses spell out the implications of the Last Supper for successive historical situations in the life of the community.

John does refer to the supper, to being at supper (13:2), rising from supper (13:4), reclining at table (13:12, 23, 28) and dipping and giving a morsel to Judas, probably a bitter herb dipped in salt (13:26-27). John does not, however, include a liturgical formula such as we find in 1 Corinthians 11:23-25 and in the Synoptic Gospels (Mark 14:22-25; Matt 26:26-29; Luke 22:19-20).

John's account is more like a homiletic reflection on the Last Supper and the Eucharist, showing and drawing out their implications for the life of the community. This is especially true of the discourses Jesus gives during the supper (John 13:12-20, 31-35) and after the supper, as well as in the prayer. But even the washing of feet, a symbolic act, and the announcements of betrayal and denial may be seen as commenting homiletically on Jesus' Last Supper and the Eucharist.

The story of the breakfast by the seashore (John 21:1-19) tells of a bread-and-fish meal with Jesus and so comes closest to the story of Jesus' giving bread to the five thousand (6:1-15). In the story of Jesus' giving bread and its discourse (6:22-59) and dialogue (6:60-71) commentary, John shows how the Eucharist is a real sharing in Christ's life-giving flesh and blood. The breakfast by the seashore relates the Eucharist to the mission of the apostolic Church (21:1-14) and to Simon Peter's special role in the life of the Church (21:15-19).

John and the Johannine Community

Like Paul, the Synoptic Gospels and the book of Acts, John emphasized the aspects of the Eucharist that responded to concrete situations in the Johannine community. Unlike other works in the New Testament, however, each of which was written in a short period of time, John's Gospel was written over a span of some fifty years, drawing on traditions from the early 50s and going through several editions until its completion in the mid or late 90s of the first century.[9] During that time, the situation changed quite dramatically, as can be seen from the succession of farewell discourses after Jesus' Last Supper.[10]

In the first farewell discourse, Jesus addressed a number of general issues related to continuity and perseverance in the community after Jesus' departure (John 14:1-31). The second discourse, based on the image of the vine and the branches, emphasizes the need for unity (15:1-17). The third provides a pastoral theology of persecution (15:18–16:4a). The fourth deals with the coming of the Advocate, the Spirit of truth, the community's need for further revelation, the Spirit's role in the community, and the Spirit's relation to what Jesus taught his disciples (16:4b-33).

The various discourses witness to the changing situation in the community, with new and urgent needs continually displacing the old. Some needs, however, were constant. Through much of its history, the community needed to counter emerging docetic and proto-gnostic tendencies that were at least downplaying, if not denying, the incarnation.

Responding to these tendencies, John emphasized the full reality of the incarnation and the humanity of Jesus. In reading John's Gospel, it is both striking and moving to see Jesus, the Son of God (John 1:18), emotionally overcome (11:33) and weeping at the death of his friend Lazarus: "See how he loved *(ephilei)* him," observed some Jews who were present (11:35). In John's Gospel, the Son of God has friends: "No one has greater love *(agapen)* than this, to lay down one's life for one's friends *(hyper ton philon)*. You are my friends *(philoi)* if you do what I command you" (15:13-14). The alternative was to be Jesus' slave: "I no longer call you slaves *(doulous)*, because a slave *(ho doulos)* does not know what his master *(ho kyrios)* is doing; I have called you friends *(philous)*, because I have told you everything I have heard from my Father" (15:15).[11]

John's most important and very distinctive response to those who saw little or no value in Jesus' humanity came in his theology of the Word made flesh: "And the Word became flesh and made his dwelling among us, and we saw his glory, the glory as of the Father's only Son, full of grace and truth" (John 1:14).

John's pastoral theology of the Word made flesh was at the heart of his Eucharistic theology, emphasizing the need to partake of the Word made flesh: "Amen, amen, I say to you, unless you eat the flesh of the Son of Man and drink his blood, you do not have life within you" (John 6:53).

It is as the Word made flesh that Jesus is glorified, that the Father is present in him and that he reveals the Father. It is as the Word made flesh that Jesus died, rose again, is exalted, and is now present to us in sacrament.

At stake was not only the reality of the incarnation but that of the Church as the sacrament of the incarnate Word and the whole sacramental life of the Church. Hence the pervasive role of the incarnation and of the Eucharist, the primary sacrament of the incarnate Word, in John's Gospel.

For John, there could be no neglecting the earthly concerns of fleshly existence. As a living sacrament of the incarnate Word, the Church had to take seriously the hunger, thirst, and suffering of human beings. Important in themselves, hunger, and thirst were also signs of a much greater hunger and thirst. Like Jesus, the Church had to respond to people's personal hunger and thirst, both physical and spiritual.

By becoming flesh in Jesus, the Word of God came into the world and lived a mortal human life. As the sacrament of the Word of God made flesh, the Eucharist puts those who believe in touch with God's personal Word and introduces them to eternal life.

The Johannine community included members of Jewish, Samaritan, and Gentile background,[12] living in a cultural milieu pervaded by a variety of religious movements and mystery cults, with their initiation rites, emphasis on rebirth, small communities, and ritual meals.[13] Members of the community were bound to be influenced by some of these movements and cults. It was not easy for them to maintain the proper balance between the Spirit and the flesh. Competing values quickly became divisive.

Throughout its history, the Johannine community needed to be reminded that in Jesus the Word of God really became flesh and that partaking of the Word-made-flesh-made-sacrament was a condition for eternal life.

Given this background, we can appreciate the achievement of John and others in the community who first developed and successively refined the Gospel's sacramental synthesis of Word and flesh, while maintaining Spirit and flesh in delicate balance. We can also appreciate the gospel's emphasis on Christian unity and the Eucharist's role in realizing and maintaining that unity while pursuing Christ's mission: "I pray not only for them, but also for those who will believe in me through their word" (17:20).

Bread for the Five Thousand (John 6:1-71)

The most important passage on the Eucharist in John's Gospel is 6:1-71. It is here in chapter 6 that John sets out his basic theology of the Eucharist, providing a synthesis and point of reference for all further reflection on the Eucharist in his gospel.

John's chapter 6 also represents the highest point in the Eucharistic theology of the New Testament. Paul and the Synoptic Gospels presented the Eucharist as an event in which the Church does what Jesus Christ did in memory of him. From various points of view, each focused on the action of Christ giving himself as nourishment. John largely presupposes the action of Christ and focuses on the person and personal presence of Christ giving himself as nourishment and its effect on those who receive him in faith.

The chapter can be divided into four sections, beginning with a story in which Jesus gives bread to a crowd of five thousand (John 6:1-15), continuing with a second story in which Jesus comes to the disciples on the sea as "It is I" (*ego eimi*, literally, "I am") (6:16-21), and concluding first with a discourse and then with dialogue in which Jesus interprets the event for the crowd (6:22-59) and for the disciples (6:60-71).

The two stories present two of Jesus' revelatory signs, the fourth and the fifth in a series of seven whose story is told in the first part of the gospel (John 1:19–12:50).[14] Together the two signs reveal the Eucharist as a personal gift of Jesus. In the first sign, the Gospel focuses on Jesus' gift of five barley loaves to a crowd numbering about five thousand. In the second, it focuses on Jesus' revelation to the disciples of his personal identity as "It is I *(ego eimi)*." The two signs are very closely related. There is no separating the gift from the giver. Who Jesus is makes all the difference for the nature of the gift.

In the discourse, Jesus interprets the event for the crowd (John 6:22-59). In the dialogue, he then interprets the discourse for the disciples (6:60-71). His discourse on the bread of life, the bread come down from heaven, and the bread that he will give, speaks "the words of eternal life." Just as there is no separating the gift from the one who gives it, there is no separating the words from the one who speaks them. Again, who Jesus is makes all the difference.

Jesus, the Crowd, and Five Barley Loaves (John 6:1-15)

John's story of Jesus giving bread to a crowd of about five thousand has its closest parallel in Mark's account of Jesus breaking bread for a similar crowd of five thousand (Mark 6:34-44). Like all the other New Testament stories in which Jesus breaks bread for a large crowd, John's telling of the story was influenced by that of Elisha in 2 Kings 4:42-44, in which twenty barley loaves were enough to feed one hundred men and there was some left over. John actually stayed closer to the story's Old Testament prototype, specifying that the loaves were made of barley (6:9).

John's telling of the story is distinctive in many other ways, most of which are related to the discourse and the dialogue that follow it. From this we conclude that the story was written with the discourse and the dialogue in mind, and vice versa.

The uniqueness of John's version of the story appears even in the evocation of the Eucharist where there is a notable omission. Jesus took *(elaben)* the loaves, and having given thanks *(eucharistesas)*, distributed *(diedoken)* them, but he did not break *(eklasen)* the loaves as we find in every other New Testament account of the event (John 6:11). Indeed, for the Synoptic Gospels, the gesture of breaking was one of the most significant, serving as the basis for Luke's designation of the Eucharist as "the breaking of the bread" (Luke 24:35; Acts 2:42).

Omitting all mention of Jesus' breaking, John highlights Jesus' act of giving to each, that is of distributing, an emphasis which corresponds perfectly to his interpretive announcement at the beginning of the second part of the discourse: "and the bread that I will give *(doso)* is my flesh for the life of the world" (6:51). The discourse's specifically Eucharistic section (9:51-59) is thus integral to the theology of chapter 6. The Eucharistic teaching in John 6:51-59 may have been added at a later stage in the composition of the discourse, but there is no question of its being spurious or even secondary in John's thinking. What it does is spell out explicitly something that was already implicit in the telling of the event.

In both John 6:1-15 and Mark 6:34-44, the crowd numbers about five thousand men *(andres)*. At least in John, however, the term "men" *(andres)* is equivalent to "people" *(anthropoi;* see 6:10). Both also mention that there was grass in the place, in John "a great deal of grass" (6:10), in Mark "green grass" (Mark 6:39).

Again both also specify that there were five loaves and two fish, and that twelve baskets *(kophinoi)* of broken fragments *(klasmata)* were gathered. In Mark 6:34-44, as in all its parallels, there is no indication that Jesus multiplied the loaves, as the popular description would have it. In John, not only is there no indication that Jesus multiplied the loaves, but such an explanation is positively excluded: What the disciples collected were "fragments from the five barley loaves, that had been more than they could eat" (John 6:13).

What the stories actually do is confront the listener with the mystery and the extraordinary nourishing quality of the bread that Jesus gives. To call the event "a multiplication of loaves" provides a rational, albeit miraculous, explanation for it and draws attention away from its intended Eucharistic significance.

The similarities between John 6:1-15 and Mark 6:34-44 point to their drawing from the same basic tradition. The differences between the stories, however, are equally striking, indicating independent developments of that tradition along with the creativity of their authors.

John alone stresses why the crowd was following Jesus, namely, "because they saw the signs he was performing on the sick" (6:2).[15] Later, after Jesus gave them bread, they continued to seek him. This time, John has Jesus confront them with the reason: "Amen, amen, I say to you, you are looking for me, not because you saw signs, but because you ate the loaves and were filled" (6:26).

John also situates the event on the mountain (6:3) instead of a "desert place" (Mark 6:32-35) and relates it to the approaching feast of Passover (John 6:4). He also introduces a special role for Philip (6:5-7), Andrew, "the brother of Simon Peter" (6:8) and an unnamed boy (6:9). Throughout the story, however, Jesus is the one who takes the initiative (see 6:5-6, 10, 11, 12, 15), to the point of personally distributing the bread to the entire crowd (6:11). There is no mistaking that this is the bread that Jesus gives (see 6:51-52).

Jesus Reveals Himself as "It Is I" (John 6:16-21)

After the story of Jesus and the five barley loaves (John 6:1-15), John tells the story of Jesus walking on the sea and revealing himself to the disciples as "It is I" (6:16-21). In this, John follows the pattern found in Mark 6:34-52, where after breaking bread for the five thousand (6:34-44) Jesus came to the disciples across the troubled sea (6:45-52). Finding the same relationship between the two stories in both John and Mark points to a common underlying tradition in which the stories were handed down together.

The relationship between the stories is clearest in Mark. After the breaking of the bread for the five thousand, Jesus made the disciples get into the boat to precede him to the other side, toward Bethsaida on the Gentile side of the sea, where he would join them later. The breaking of the bread was meant for the Gentiles as well as for Jews. For this, the disciples had to cross the sea. At the time, however, the disciples did not understand this about the breaking of the bread and resisted crossing to the other side (Mark 6:52).

In John, the relationship between the stories is less clear. After Jesus gave bread to the five thousand on a mountainside across the sea from Capernaum (6:1-3, 16-17), the disciples had no compelling reason to cross the sea. In Mark, crossing was necessary to include the Gentiles in the breaking of the bread (see Mark 8:1-9). At stake was the universality of the Christian mission. In John, the disciples were simply returning to Capernaum.

Because the crossing itself has no special significance in John, the story of Jesus' walking on the sea (6:16-21) seems out of place, separating the meal event (6:1-15) from the discourse and the dialogue that interpret it (6:22-71). Normally, a discourse or dialogue comes right after the meal, especially when it bears on issues related to it. Such is the case, for example, at the Last Supper (13:1-38) which is followed immediately by Jesus' farewell discourse (14:1–17:26), and at Jesus' breakfast on the seashore (21:1-14), which is followed by Jesus' dialogue with Simon Peter (21:15-23).

In some ways, the story's presence between the bread sign (6:1-15) and the discourse (6:22-59) does break the gospel's narrative flow. Even so, the sign of Jesus coming to the disciples on the sea is critical for understanding John's teaching on the Eucharist, but in a way very different from Mark. For Mark, the crossing itself was at the center of attention and everything else was related to it. For John, the crossing was insignificant, leaving Jesus' walking on the sea and revealing himself to the disciples as "It is I," at the center of attention.

When people saw what Jesus had done with the five barley loaves, they concluded, "This is truly the Prophet, the one who is to come into the world" (6:14), a prophet-like Moses as announced in Deuteronomy 18:15. Jesus realized, "they were going to come and carry him off to make him king" (6:15). In the circumstances, it was extremely important for Jesus to make plain his identity.

Such was John's purpose in telling the story of Jesus' walking on the sea, dominating chaos, and revealing himself as "It is I." Everything in the story's tradition that could have obscured this purpose has been stripped away. Jesus was far more than a prophet like Moses. He was "It is I,"[16] the presence of God in the world, to his disciples and to the

Johannine community. "I AM" *(ego eimi)* as God revealed to Moses (see Exod 3:14), means "I AM (with you)," making you what you are, accompanying you, revealing myself to you, supporting you, guiding you, in divine solidarity with you.

It is as *ego eimi* that Jesus distributed the five barley loaves to the crowd of five thousand. The five loaves that he gave, which were more than the crowd could eat, were the gift of *ego eimi*.

In the discourse that follows, Jesus pursues these same themes, contrasting his identity with that of Moses and specifying how he was *ego eimi* to them, namely as "the bread of life" (John 6:35, 48), indeed "the living bread that came down from heaven" (John 6:51).[17]

Discourse to the Crowd: Jesus, the Bread of Life (John 6:22-59)

The discourse begins with a narrative introduction (John 6:22-24). The place where the crowd "had eaten the bread when the Lord gave thanks" (John 6:23) was across the Sea of Galilee from Capernaum (6:1). Since the disciples had to return across the sea to Capernaum (6:16-18) and Jesus had gone out to be with them (6:19-21), it was necessary once again to gather the crowd, this time at Capernaum (6:24) for the discourse (6:25-58), which Jesus delivered in the synagogue there (6:59).

The discourse then continues with a dialogue introduction (John 6:25-31), in which Jesus challenges the crowd to work for the food that endures for eternal life, the food the Son of Man would give (6:27). This would mean doing the work of God, believing in the one he sent (6:28-29). The crowd, which was looking for Jesus not because they saw signs but because they had eaten their fill (6:25-26) challenged Jesus in return. What sign could he do that they might see and believe? Their ancestors ate manna in the desert, as it is written: "He gave them bread from heaven to eat" (6:30-31; see Ps 78:24). Could Jesus do as much?

The discourse itself is divided into two parts (John 6:25-50, 51-58). The first concerns the bread Jesus is, the true bread from heaven. The second concerns the bread Jesus gives, his flesh for the life of the world. Jesus' teaching on the bread that he gives, his flesh and blood in the Eucharist, must not be separated from the bread of life that he is.

Underlying and unifying both parts is the Old Testament theme of the banquet of wisdom (see Prov 9:2-5; Sir 24:19-21; Isa 55:1-3). Jesus, the Wisdom of God incarnate, nourishes us through his personal presence (John 6:25-50) and personally sets out a banquet for us (John 6:51-58).

The discourse then closes with a very simple conclusion, indicating that Jesus said these things "while teaching in the synagogue in Capernaum" (John 6:59).

In the first part of the discourse proper (John 6:25-31, 32-50), Jesus gives the true meaning of Psalm 78:24, "He gave them bread from heaven to eat" (John 6:31), by contrasting the bread Moses gave with the bread his Father gave, that is, Jesus' very person, the bread of God which comes down from heaven and gives life to the world. "I am *(ego eimi)* the bread of life," Jesus declares, "whoever comes to me will never hunger, and whoever believes in me will never thirst" (6:32-35). Jesus then addresses the matter of belief and unbelief in relation to the will of his Father (6:36-47). Repeating, "I am *(ego eimi)* the bread of life," he concludes the first part of the discourse, by returning to the contrast between the bread their ancestors ate and his person as the bread come down from heaven (John 6:48-50).

Jesus' interpretation of the verse provides an excellent example of midrash, a popular literary form in ancient Judaism, whose purpose was to interpret or reinterpret a passage from Scripture. John 6:32-50 illustrates how the early Christians appropriated the form and how well it served them.

After a quick summary of the first part (6:51ab), the discourse introduces the second: "and the bread that I will give is my flesh for the life of the world" (6:51c). The first part of the discourse was about the bread Jesus' Father gave, Jesus' very person coming down from heaven and giving life to the world (6:32-50). The second part is about the bread Jesus gave, his Eucharistic flesh for the life of the world (6:51-58). Jesus, the Word made flesh, given as nourishment for the life of the world (6:32-33), gives his flesh as Eucharistic nourishment for the life of the world (6:51).

Jesus' announcement about the bread that he would give is based on a very primitive Eucharistic formula: "the bread that I will give is my flesh for the life of the world" (6:51c), a formula not unlike the one found in 1 Corinthians 11:24: "this [the bread that I will give] is my body [is my flesh] that is for you [for the life of the world]."[18]

After presenting the formula, Jesus provides an authentic interpretation of it (John 6:52-58), as he did for Psalm 78:24. His interpretation is an excellent example of homiletic reflection on the bread that Jesus gives (see John 6:1-15), his Eucharistic flesh for the life of the world (6:51c).

Jesus begins the reflection with a challenge. Eating flesh and drinking his blood is a condition for having life. There is no escaping the demands of the Word made flesh. Sharing in the Eucharist, like sharing in the mystery of Christ's passion and resurrection, is part of the basic message of the gospel. Moreover, Jesus' flesh, the flesh of the Word made flesh, is true food, and his blood true drink. Whoever eats his flesh and drinks his blood has eternal life and Jesus will raise him up on the last day. Sent by the Father, Jesus has life, a life he shares with all who eat his flesh and drink his blood (John 6:52-57).

At the end of the discourse, Jesus returns once again to the contrast between the bread their ancestors ate and the bread that he provided: "Unlike your ancestors who ate and still died, whoever eats this bread will live forever" (6:58; see 6:32-33, 49-50).

Dialogue with the Disciples: The Words of Eternal Life (John 6:60-71)

After the discourse comes a dialogue with the disciples (John 6:60-71), who found Jesus' message very hard. Some of the disciples did not believe. They left him and returned to their former way of life (John 6:66). Judas Iscariot, one of the Twelve, would betray him (John 6:64, 70-71). To the others, however, including Simon Peter, it had been granted by his Father to stay with him (6:67-69; see 6:44).

It is here we best appreciate the extraordinary balance John maintained between spirit and flesh. Yes, the Word was made flesh, and Jesus gave his flesh for the life of the world, and we must eat his flesh to have eternal life. But to understand and accept Jesus' message about the Word made flesh and his Eucharistic flesh, the flesh itself was of no avail. For this they had to be open to the Spirit. Since the words Jesus spoke were Spirit and life, the disciples needed the Spirit which gives life to receive them (John 6:63).

As the dialogue ends, and with it the entire chapter, John returns to the theme of Jesus' identity. It is because Jesus, the Word made flesh, is *ego eimi* (John 6:16-21) that he was able to take five barley loaves, give thanks, and with them provide five thousand people with more than they could eat (John 6:1-15). It is because he is "the bread of life" that those who believe in him have eternal life (6:22-50). It is because Jesus is "the living bread that came down from heaven" that those who eat his flesh and drink his blood have eternal life, indeed the very life of the Father in them (6:51-59). Finally, it is because the disciples, with Simon Peter, confess that Jesus is "the Holy One of God" that they can accept his Eucharistic message as "the words of eternal life" (6:68-69).

NOTES

1. For full-length commentaries available in English on John's Gospel, see Raymond Brown, *The Gospel According to John I–XII, XIII–XXI*, The Anchor Bible 29, 29A (Garden City, New York: Doubleday & Company, Inc., 1966, 1970); Rudolf Schnackenburg, *The Gospel According to St. John*, 3 vols. (New York: The Seabury Press, 1980, 1990). For a short commentary, see George W. MacRae, *Invitation to John*, Image Book (Garden City, New York: Doubleday & Company, Inc., 1978).

2. Rudolf Schnackenburg, *Op. Cit.*, Excursus IV, "The Johannine 'Signs'" I:515–528.

3. See Stephen Happel, "Symbol," *The New Dictionary of Theology*, ed. Joseph A. Komonchak, Mary Collins, and Dermot Lane (Collegeville: The Liturgical Press, 1988) 997–1002: "A symbol is a complex of gestures, sounds, images and/or words that evoke, invite, and persuade participation in that to which they refer" (997); also Karl Rahner, "The Theology of the Symbol," in *Theological Investigations* IV (Baltimore: Helicon Press, 1966) 221–252.

4. See Edward Schillebeeckx, O.P., *Christ the Sacrament of the Encounter with God* (New York: Sheed and Ward, 1963). After showing how Christ is *the* sacrament of God (7–45), and the Church the sacrament of the risen Christ (47–89), Schillebeekx shows how "the Sacraments are the personal saving act of the risen Christ through his visible Church" (91; see 91–32).

5. By its very nature, a symbol, unlike a sign, has more than one referent and can have many layers of meaning, one or some of which are primary while others are secondary.

6. The two most important Johannine passages on the Eucharist, "the multiplication of loaves" (6:1-15) and the Last Supper (13:1-38), together with the discourses following them, are both related to the Jewish feast of Passover. The first took place as "the Jewish feast of Passover was near" (6:4) and the second "before the feast of Passover" (13:1).

7. The hour of Jesus when he would "pass from this world to the Father" begins with the Last Supper, "before the feast of Passover" (13:1).

8. The washing of feet (13:1-20) is told in two parts, the actual washing (13:1-11) and a brief discourse in which Jesus explains what he has done (13:12-20). The announcement of Judas' betrayal (13:21-35) is also told in two parts, the actual announcement in which Judas is identified as the betrayer (13:21-30) and a brief discourse after Judas' departure. The discourse spells out the implications of Judas' betrayal regarding both the glorification of the Son of Man and life in the community after Jesus has gone (13:31-35).

9. Raymond E. Brown, *The Gospel According to John I–XII* (New York: Doubleday, 1966) lxxx–lxxxvi.

10. A farewell discourse in the ancient world was a literary form or device allowing a historical figure like Jesus to address a community long after his death. The content of the discourse arose from the historical figure's life and message but applied these to a new situation in the community. As the situation changed, so did the content of the discourse. See E. LaVerdiere, "A Discourse at the Last Supper," *The Bible Today* (March 1974) 1540–1548.

11. In the Old Testament, Abraham is the only one who was a "friend of God"

(see Isa 41:8, *hon egapesa;* 2 Chr 20:7, *ho egapemenos*). In the New Testament, James 2:23 refers to Abraham as *philos theou.*

12. For Jews in the community, see 2:23; for Samaritans, see 4:39-42; for Gentiles, see 12:20-21 (R. Brown, *Op. Cit.,* I, LXXVII–LXXIX).

13. See Moses Hadas, *Hellenistic Culture* (New York: W. W. Norton & Company, 1959) 182–197; Marvin W. Meyer, "Mystery Religions," *The Anchor Bible Dictionary* (New York: Doubleday, 1992) 4: 941–945.

14. The complete list of signs includes
    1) Jesus making water into wine at the wedding feast of Cana (2:1-11),
    2) his cure of a royal official's son, again at Cana (4:46-54),
    3) his cure of a paralytic at Jerusalem's pool of Bethesda (5:1-9),
    4) the giving of bread to some five thousand on a mountain by the Sea of Galilee (6:1-15),
    5) his walking on the sea as "I AM" (6:16-21),
    6) his cure of a man who was born blind (9:1-7),
    7) and his raising of Lazarus from the dead at Bethany (11:1-44).

15. Throughout the story, John is attentive to the motive for which people acted and the reason for which something happened (6:2, 6, 12, 15).

16. Besides 6:20, the simple, absolute use of "I AM" is attributed to Jesus in 4:26, 8:24, 28, 58; 13:19; 18:5, 6, 8. For a good synthesis concerning the Johannine "I AM," see Raymond Brown, *The Gospel According to John I–XII* (The Anchor Bible 29), Appendix IV: EGO EIMI — "I AM," (New York: Doubleday, 1966) 533–538.

17. Besides 6:35, 48, 51, the use of "I AM" with a predicate is attributed to Jesus in 8:12; 9:5; 10:11, 14; 11:25; 14:6; 15:1, 5; and possibly 8:18, 23.

18. See Joachim Jeremias, *The Eucharistic Words of Jesus,* trans. Norman Perrin from the German third edition (Philadelphia: Fortress Press, 1977) 106–108; Jeremias concludes that "although he (John) does not mention the institution of the Lord's Supper, he introduces the word of interpretation to the bread in the context of a discourse by Jesus, without it thereby (as the history of the research shows) becoming immediately evident as such" (108).

9

On the Lord's Day:
The Eucharist in the *Didache*

> Like John's Gospel, the *Didache*
> represents about half a century
> of writing, editing, adding, and
> transforming an early collection of
> sayings, first into a baptismal instruction
> and then into a community manual.
> We learn from the *Didache* that
> a community can celebrate the Eucharist
> with baptism as a rite of initiation,
> or assemble on the Lord's Day,
> break bread and give thanks,
> and still not have a real Eucharist.

The *Didache* is a remarkable document, a kind of community rule or manual of discipline;[1] it is a treasure trove of early Christian traditions, sayings, instructions, and prayers, each one very striking, even if, as a literary whole, they remain somewhat disjointed.

In its final form, the *Didache*'s sixteen chapters fall into four sections, beginning with a collection of sayings on "the two ways, one of life and one of death" (1–6), continuing with a section on religious practices (7–10), another on leadership roles (11–15), and ending with a collection of eschatological sayings (16).

The Eucharist is treated in the two central sections, first among the religious practices (9–10), and then in relation to leadership roles (14). Among the religious practices, the *Didache* includes a set of extremely beautiful blessings to be said before and after the Eucharistic meal. It also includes what may be the earliest reference to "the Lord's Day."[2]

For years, students of early Christianity knew of a work called the *Teaching of the Twelve Apostles*, the *Didache ton dodeka Apostolon*, also referred to simply as the *Didache*, the "teaching" or "instruction," or in the plural the *Didachai*.[3] That is, they knew the work existed. Clement of Alexandria referred to it, as did Eusebius of Caesarea and Saint Athanasius. They also knew its title, but that was the extent of their familiarity with it. Like so many other ancient writings, the work itself was lost.

Then in 1875, Philotheos Bryennios, the future Metropolitan of Nicomedia in Asia Minor, found a complete Greek text of the *Didache* in a codex, dated 1056, which also included the Letters of Clement of Rome, the Epistle of Barnabas, the Letters of Ignatius of Antioch, and other works. Bryennios followed his announcement with the *Didache*'s publication at Constantinople in 1883.[4]

Since that time, interest in the *Didache* has continued unabated. For students of the origins of Christianity, the *Didache* provides precious data on early Christian tradition and religious practices that are contemporary with the New Testament, especially with the development of Matthew's Gospel. Yet, at the same time, the *Didache* is not part of the New Testament Scriptures, and thereby contributes to our knowledge of the Eucharist in the early Church as it emerged from Judaism.

Most of our knowledge of early Christian tradition, including the Eucharist, comes from analyzing the various works in the New Testament in relation to one another and to their social and cultural milieu. The *Didache* provides an independent witness, one which was not incorporated into the New Testament.

Tradition and Community: A Symbiotic Relationship

But if the *Didache* is so remarkable, why was it not included in the New Testament? There is no knowing the *Didache* or learning something of value from it without answering that question. We need to know why the *Didache* itself was left aside and why its Eucharistic traditions, including the blessing prayers, were not integrated into the New Testament while so many other traditions were. The exclusion has to do not only with the traditions but with the community to which they belonged.

Traditions, including Eucharistic traditions, do not exist by themselves. They need a community. For their part, communities need traditions to develop and maintain an identity. Traditions make the community what it is. As Henri de Lubac put it, "the church makes the Eucharist, and the Eucharist makes the church."[5] That is why we must examine both the community for which the *Didache* was written and its Eucharistic tradition.

A community is formed by people who relate personally to one another. To know a community such as that of the *Didache* we therefore need to know something about its members. Personal relationships alone, however, cannot sustain a community through periods of profound change. For this, a community, made up of personal relationships, needs tradition.

Tradition maintains a community's identity as it meets new challenges and adapts to changing situations, circumstances, and environments. But what if the traditions are inadequate? What if the community clings to inadequate traditions and refuses to meet new challenges?

A community and its traditions enjoy a symbiotic relationship. The community gives life to the traditions, and the traditions do the same for the community. This is especially true of the Eucharist, which epitomizes the community's entire life and existence. The community must be able to meet new challenges, and the traditions must be able to develop. For that, traditions need to be both resilient and open, which is a delicate balance to maintain.

Such a balance can be seen in the development of the Matthean community, whose origins and challenges were quite similar to the community addressed by the *Didache*. It is possible the two may have known one another, especially in the early stages of their development.

The Matthean challenge is well stated at the end of Jesus' parable discourse. "Do you understand all these things?" Jesus asked. The disciples answered, "Yes." "Then every scribe who has been instructed in the kingdom of heaven is like the head of a household who brings from his storeroom both the new and the old" (Matt 13:51-52).

Matthew dealt with the challenge of "the new and the old" at just about every point in his gospel, respecting the old while open to the new, ensuring the viability of the traditions and the vitality of the community. With that, the Matthean community became part of the body of the Church, and its traditions were incorporated into the New Testament as the Gospel According to Matthew.

The *Didache*'s community saw the challenge differently. At every point, we see the community turning away from the new, refusing to take on its challenge, clinging very closely to the old. We see the community rigidly defending its tradition, protecting it and preventing it from absorbing new elements that would have transformed it and kept it viable.[6]

Reading the *Didache*, we see traditions that flowed from Jesus' life and ministry, traditions that had great potential for development. These traditions, however, needed to be enriched Christologically. Of themselves, they had very little biblical and theological depth. The *Didache*'s Eucharistic tradition lacked basic elements needed for a Eucharistic community to survive.

The *Didache*'s tradition was able to maintain the community's life, but only for a time, and resulted in its increased isolation. Tradition was thus the community's riches, which assured growth to a point; it was also its poverty, which ensured its demise. The story of the *Didache*'s community is that of a community fighting to stay alive but slowly dying of inanition for lack of adequate traditions.

There is much to learn from a healthy Christian community like that of Matthew — which remained in communion with other Christian communities and eventually was integrated with them into the Church — and from its Eucharistic tradition, which was welcomed into the New Testament together with many others.

There is also much to learn from a community like that of the *Didache*, which never joined the mainstream of the Church, from its community manual, which was excluded from the New Testament, and from its Eucharistic traditions, which were left aside. Indeed, there may be even more to learn, as with a student of business who very often learns more from a business that failed than from one that succeeded.

The *Didache*

The *Didache* was written over a period of time, perhaps as many as fifty years, from around the year A.D. 50 to A.D. 100. Some parts of the document are very old, whereas some parts were written more recently. Although evidence for the place of origin is not conclusive, some argue for Egypt, while others argue for Antioch. Antioch, the capital of Syria, appears more likely, given the connection between the *Didache* and early strata of the Matthean tradition.[7]

The history of the development of the *Didache* to its final form in sixteen chapters provides an extraordinary view of a Christian community very close to the beginnings of Christianity. Each part, taken independently, puts us in touch with the beginnings of Christian moral instruction, religious practices, including the Eucharist, structures of leadership, the gospel, Christology, and eschatology. We shall examine these in relation to the history of the community. But first, we need to take a look at the *Didache* as a whole, situating the instructions for the Eucharist in relation to the community manual's final form.

Part One

The first part of the *Didache* (1–6) is a presentation of "two ways" *(duo hodoi)*, a traditional form of moral instruction, often referred to in Latin as the *Duae Viae*. One has two options: to follow "the way of life" *(he hodos tes zoes)* or to follow "the way of death" *(he hodos tou thanatou)*. The image is that of two roads, paths, or highways, a common biblical metaphor, especially in Wisdom Literature for a person's basic moral orientation or chosen way of life.

In the Old Testament, the two ways are often presented as the way of the just and the way of the wicked or sinners (Ps 1:1, 6). Those who walk in the way of the just are on the way of wisdom (Prov 4:11), whose path is "like shining light, that grows in brilliance till perfect day" (Prov 4:18). Those who walk in the way of sinners "leave the straight path to walk in the way of darkness . . . whose ways are crooked, and devious their paths" (Prov 2:13, 15).

In the New Testament, Jesus invites his disciples to follow him on the way to his passion-resurrection. Jesus is in the lead (Mark 10:32), preceding his disciples (Mark 16:7) who come after him (Mark 8:34; 10:52). In Acts "the Way" describes the Christian movement, mistakenly thought of as a Jewish sect, but quite distinct from Judaism (Acts 24:1-16). In John's Gospel, Jesus himself is "the way, and the truth, and the life" (John 14:5).

Like the New Testament, the *Didache*'s main focus is on "the way of life" (1:2–4:14), not on "the way of death," whose treatment is much briefer (5:1-2). Based on the twofold commandment of love and the golden rule (1:2; see Matt 22:34-40; Mark 12:28-34; Luke 10:25-28), "the way of life" includes some of Jesus' most distinctive teaching — loving one's enemies and giving without seeking anything in return (*Did* 1:3-6). Developed in terms of the commandments, "the way of life" is grounded in the Torah (2:2-7). As an instruction to "my son" (3:1–4:14; see also 5:1-2), it also stands in Israel's wisdom tradition.

The entire development on the two ways stays very close to the teaching of Jesus, as is true in the Gospels, but unlike the Gospels, the *Didache* does not so much as mention Jesus' name. Amazingly, the *Didache*'s instruction on the two ways has no Christology.

In the greater context of the *Didache*, the instruction on the two ways (cc. 1–6) provides the general setting for the next three parts, on religious practices, structures of leadership, and eschatology. The religious practices (cc. 7–10) and the leadership roles (cc. 11–15) are for a community that rejects the way of death (5:1-2) and opts for the way of life (1:2–4:14) that leads to eschatological fulfillment (c. 16).

Part Two

The instruction on the two ways introduces the second part of the *Didache* (cc. 7:1 –11:2), a set of instructions on baptism and the religious practices of those who accept the way of life and turn away from the way of death. As such the instruction is a summary of baptismal catechesis to be given to a catechumen ("my son") by a leader of the community just prior to the baptism.

Baptism is done "in the name of the Father and of the Son and of the Holy Spirit" (c. 7), the formula given in Matthew 28:19. Besides baptism, the practices include fasting on Wednesday and Friday (8:1) and praying the Lord's Prayer three times daily (8:2-3). The wording of the Lord's Prayer is extremely close to that in Matthew 6:9-13. What comes next are two chapters (cc. 9–10) under the heading, "Regarding the Eucharist" *(peri de tes eucharistias).*

Unlike the first part, this second part does have a certain Christology. Baptism is "in the name . . . of the Son . . ." (7:3). The community is to pray "as the Lord *(ho kurios)* commanded in his gospel *(euaggelion)"* (8:2). In the Eucharistic prayers, Jesus is referred to by name and designated like David, "the servant *(ho pais)* of our Father" (9:2, 3; 10:2, 3).

Surprisingly, however, there is no mention of Jesus' passion, death, and resurrection, nor of Jesus as the Christ, in contrast with the creed Paul cited in Romans 1:3-4, which also associates Jesus to David. The creed tells about God's Son "who descended from David according to the flesh, but was made Son of God in power according to the Spirit of holiness, by his resurrection from the dead: Jesus Christ our Lord."

The contrast is even sharper with the Antiochene baptismal creed in 1 Corinthians 15:3-5, with Paul's theology of baptism in Romans 6:3-11, and with the Antiochene Eucharistic narrative in 1 Corinthians 11:23-25. In the *Didache*, Jesus is Lord *(kyrios)* in relation to the Lord God *(kyrios theos)*, not in relation to Jesus' resurrection.

Part Three

The instruction on the two ways (1–6) concludes with a warning not to be turned away by anyone "from the way of this instruction" *(apo tautes tes hodou tes didaches).* Such a one would be teaching *(didaskei)* as a stranger to God (6:1). The chapter then takes up some religious practices, some regarding the community meal, and provides a transition (6:2-3) to the next part of the instruction, concerning religious practices.

The instruction on religious practices (7:1–11:2) concludes with a similar warning: "If someone comes teaching you all the things just mentioned, welcome him. But if the teacher himself has strayed and teaches other teachings *(didachas),* undermining these things, do not listen to him; but if his teaching promotes justice and the knowledge of the Lord, welcome him as you would the Lord" (11:1-2a). Like 6:1-3, 11:1-2 thus provides a transition to the next part, an instruction concerning community leaders (11:3–15:4).

This third instruction deals first with itinerant apostles and prophets and how to discern between those who are genuine from those who are false (11:3–13:7). While the title Christ is again absent in this third part, a member of the community is referred to as a Christian *(christianos,* 12:4), a descriptive term applied to the disciples for the first time in Antioch (Acts 11:26). The community is warned against a Christian who refuses to work (see 2 Thess 3:6-12). Such a one is "living off Christ" *(christemporos),* taking financial advantage of being a Christian at the expense of other Christians (12:5).

The instruction concerning itinerant apostles and prophets introduces the second passage on the Eucharist (see 10:7), this time as celebrated at the assembly for the breaking of the bread on the Lord's Day (14). For this assembly the community needs to have bishops and deacons worthy of the Lord. Their office is as important as that of prophets and teachers *(didaskaloi,* 15:1-2).

The instruction then concludes with directives on fraternal correction (15:3; see 4:3). Regarding the prayers (see 4:14; 8:2-3) and giving alms (see 1:4-6; 5:2), they should follow the indications given "in the gospel of our Lord" (15:4).

Part Four

In the final section (c. 16), the *Didache* exhorts the community to be watchful: "watch over your life" *(hyper tes zoes hymon,* 16:1), recalling the instructions on "the way of life" (1:2–4:14). In its final form, the *Didache* is oriented to the hour when the Lord will come (see 10:6).

The community is to assemble frequently (16:2; see 4:14). This final reference to the Eucharistic assembly (see 4:14; 9–10) recalls especially the assembly for the breaking of the bread (14). Every aspect of the community's life, including the Eucharist, should contribute to their preparation for the Lord's coming at the final moment.

As the final day approaches, there will be a proliferation of false prophets and internal conflicts will multiply. All will be plunged into a fiery crucible, testing everyone, until great signs appear of the Lord's coming accompanied by all the saints on the clouds of heaven (16:3-8).

The *Didache* and the Community

A second look at the *Didache* shows that it was formed in stages over several decades, as much as half a century (*circa* A.D. 50–100), paralleling much of the writing included in the New Testament. The writing of the *Didache* took place in three general stages, corresponding to stages in the history of the community. With each stage, major additions were made, changing the very form and nature of the document.

In general terms, stage one includes the collection of sayings in the moral instruction on the two ways, the *Duae Viae* (1–6), and the eschatological exhortation (16). Stage two added the instructions on religious practices (7–10), and stage three the directions regarding community leaders (11–15). At each of these stages, however, the writer drew on old traditions and sources and adapted these in making them part of the *Didache*.

Stage One (1–6)

As a whole, the instruction on the two ways (1–6) is the oldest part of the *Didache*. Some have maintained that the core of the teaching (1:1-2; 2:2–5:2) was originally a Jewish instruction, taken over by a Christian community identifying very closely with Judaism. At some point, a distinct collection of Christian sayings (1:3–2:1) was inserted into this older Jewish collection.[8]

Jefford, however, has shown quite convincingly that both collections originated in a Christian community whose members were of Jewish origin and which defined themselves in Jewish terms.[9]

First, there was a collection of sayings (1:1-2; 2:2–5:2), formed in relation to the Old Testament as interpreted by Jesus. This collection provided a synthesis of the community's way of life and moral identity. Like other Jewish communities, that of the *Didache* stressed not so much orthodoxy as orthopraxy. A Christian was one who fulfilled the dual commandment of love (see Matt 22:34-40) as well as the golden rule (Matt 7:12; Luke 6:31). These provided the context for interpreting and the motivation for observing the other commandments.

At this point in its history, possibly as early as A.D. 50, the community saw itself as part of Judaism and patterned itself very closely on other Jewish communities in the diaspora. The purpose of the instruction on the two ways was to help the community maintain itself faithfully in relation to the Law — in the tradition of Jewish wisdom, as good disciples of Jesus — while living in a Gentile environment, the values of which were incompatible with those of the community.

Later, a second collection of sayings based on Jesus' most distinctive teaching was inserted between the golden rule (1:2) and the rest of the commandments (2:2-7). The commandment to love one's neighbor included one's enemies and persecutors (1:3-4). It also required that one give generously to others without requiring anything in return (2:5-6). The eschatological exhortation to be watchful (16) is closely related to this second collection.

It is unclear as to when the second collection was added. Its sayings have parallels with those of source (Q) which Matthew and Luke integrated into their gospel narratives. The underlying tradition is consequently very old. Reference to those persecuting the community (1:3; see Matt 5:11-12, 44-47), however, points to a later stage when the community was separated from other Jewish communities. Remaining very Jewish in spirit, the community had to rely more closely on the tradition of Jesus' prophetic teaching, while awaiting his return as Lord at the final moment.

At the first stage, then, the community was very Jewish in its self-understanding and way of life. Like other Jewish communities in the diaspora, it had to protect itself from the corruptive influence of the greater Gentile world in which they were immersed.

Stage Two (7–10)

At stage two in the *Didache*'s development, the instruction on religious practices (7–10) was added to that on the two ways (1–6), transforming the instruction on the two ways into a pre-baptismal instruction. In the process, chapter 6 was reedited to provide a suitable transition. The community now has distinctive religious practices, beginning with baptism (7), along with a moral code (1–6). Closely related to baptism are the practice of fasting (7:4–8:1), praying the Lord's Prayer (8:2) and the Eucharist (9–10).

These practices and traditions were not new. They were actually very old. What was new was bringing them together into a synthesis of the community's basic religious practices.

At this second stage, the community still clung to its Jewish heritage and identity but it had separated from other Jewish communities. References to other Jews as "hypocrites" indicate the separation was not a friendly one (8:1-2).

Even the community's religious practices had to be different from those of other Jews. Whereas "the hypocrites" fasted on Monday and Thursday, Christians would fast on Wednesday and Friday (8:1). Nor were they to pray like "the hypocrites," but as the Lord demanded in his gospel. Like other Jews they would pray three times a day. Their prayer, however, would be the Lord's prayer (8:2).

Similar references to "the hypocrites" appear in Matthew 6:2, 5, 15 in relation to traditional teaching on giving alms (Matt 6:2-4), prayer (Matt 6:5-6), and fasting (Matt 6:16-18). It seems likely the two communities were excluded from Judaism at about the same time. With regard to other Jews, they reacted similarly. Unlike Matthew's community, however, the *Didache*'s community did not take on the mission to the Gentiles.

Living in a Gentile environment, the community still needed to ward off pagan influences (1:1-6; 16), in particular idolatrous cults. Members had to abstain from meat offered to idols (6:3; see 1 Cor 8–10; Acts 15:20, 29; 21:25). The community seems to have been quite small. On their own, its members found it difficult to fulfill the entire "yoke of the Lord," but should do all they could to do so (6:2).

At this second stage, then, the community continued to be very Jewish in its self-understanding, but as separated from other Jewish communities. It consequently had to distinguish itself and its religious practices from those of other Jews.

Stage Three (11–15)

At the third stage, instructions regarding community leaders were added (11–15). At this point, the community saw its identity threatened not only by Gentile influences (see 1–6) and other Jewish communities (see 7–10) but by other Christian communities and their missionaries.

Other Christian communities, whose members were of Gentile origin, as in the Lukan communities, or who recently took on the Gentile mission and opened their community to Gentiles, as did the Matthean community, were viewed as unfaithful to their Jewish origins and tradition. Still clinging to their Jewish identity, the *Didache*'s community had to protect itself from false apostles, prophets and teachers coming from these communities. It had to select bishops and deacons "worthy of the Lord" (c. 15:1-2) to celebrate the breaking of the bread and give thanks at the community assembly on the Lord's Day (c. 14).

The addition of the instructions — which was in regard to the leaders, both missionary and local — again transformed the *Didache*, this time from a prebaptismal catechesis and a religious practice manual, to a community manual addressed to its elders or presbyters. As in other Jewish communities, it is they who were responsible for passing on the tradition, protecting the community from corruptive influences, discerning the quality of teachers and choosing good leaders of their own. The most likely purpose for such a manual was the formation of presbyters.[10]

To the very end, the *Didache*'s community was unable to let go of its Jewish identity. As Jewish, it maintained itself separate from the Gentile world. As Christian, it eventually separated itself from other Jewish communities. Clinging to its Jewishness, it eventually separated itself from other Christian communities.

Increasingly isolated, it survived on its own for a time but eventually died. A few members may have been absorbed by other communities. They must also have brought their *Didache* with them, assuring its preservation.

There is a great deal of irony in the community's history. Fidelity to what they saw as basic in their identity led to their demise. The greatest irony of all, however, is that at some point in history, their community manual, so strong in maintaining Jewish identity, was renamed "The Lord's Teaching to the Gentiles."

Regarding the Eucharist

Food and meals were very important in the life of the community, as they were for Jews in general and for other Christian communities. So was fasting (1:3; 7:4; 8:1).

Members of the community were to avoid eating meat that had been offered to idols (6:3; see 1 Cor 8–10; Acts 15:19-20, 28-29; 21:25). That would be taking part in the cult of dead gods, joining in idolatry, a practice connected with "the way of death" (5:1). As the Lord taught in his gospel, they were to pray to our Father, "Give us today our daily bread" (*ton arton hemon ton epiousion*, 8:2).

They were also to provide an itinerant apostle the bread needed to reach the next destination, but no more (11:6). A prophet under inspiration who asked the community to set the table for dinner and then partook of it was a false prophet (11:9). Everyone should work for his food (see 2 Thess 3:8-12). The one who refuses to work for his food is "someone who lives off Christ" *(Christemporos)*. An authentic prophet, however, deserves his food, as does an authentic teacher (12:3–13:2; see Matt 10:10).

The first fruits of the wine press, of the threshing floor, of the cattle and the sheep should be offered to the prophets. In the absence of a prophet, the first fruits should be given to the poor. They should do the same when they baked bread or opened a fresh jar of wine or of oil (12:3-6).

The Eucharist is the most important meal in the life of the community.[11] It receives special consideration in Part Two and Part Three of the *Didache*. In Part Two, the Eucharist takes up all of chapters 9 and 10, giving various instructions regarding the meal but including three quite extraordinary prayers.[12] In Part Three, the Eucharist takes up all of chapter 14, concerning the Sunday assembly, as well as 15:1-2, on the need for bishops and deacons who are worthy of the Lord.[13]

As with other parts of the *Didache*, the Eucharistic passages include older traditions. This is especially true of the prayers, which, like the original core of the *Duae Viae*, reach back to the very beginnings of the community. These prayers were provided with a framework of instructions and became part of the *Didache* when chapters 7 to 10 were added to the *Duae Viae* (1–6). It may be at this same time that Jesus' distinctive moral teaching (1:3–2:1) was inserted and the eschatological chapter 16 was added. The section on the Sunday assembly (14:1–15:2) was added still later along with the rest of chapters 11–15.

Given the relationship between the formation of the *Didache* and the history of the community, we can see three major stages in the development of the Eucharist, corresponding to the three major stages in the development of the community.

Stage One

The first stage in the development of the Eucharist corresponds to the community's early years when it was still closely associated with Judaism. From this stage come the prayers in chapters 9 and 10, which were closely patterned on Jewish prayers for religious meals. To this same stage belongs the original instruction on the two ways (1:1-2; 2:5-2).

The Jewish prayers that inspired those of the *Didache* were blessing prayers: for chapter 9, the *Kiddush* and the *Amidah*, for chapter 10, the *Birkath Ha-Mazon*.[14]

The *Kiddush* opens with "Blessed are you, O Lord our God, King of the universe." For the cup, it then continues with "who creates the fruit of the vine"; for the bread, it continues with, "who brings forth bread from the earth."

In the *Didache*, the corresponding prayers were thanksgiving (Eucharistic) prayers addressed to "our Father," as the Lord asked in his gospel (8:2). At this first stage, the prayers were very simple both for the cup, "We give you thanks *(eucharistoumen)*, our Father, for the holy vine of David your servant; to you be glory forever" (9:2), and for the bread broken, "We give you thanks *(eucharistoumen)*, our Father, for life and knowledge; to you be glory forever" (9:3). Reference to "the holy vine of David" introduces a messianic, eschatological note. Reference to "the life and knowledge" connects the bread broken with the banquet of wisdom.

The meal prayers in *Didache* 9 were also inspired by the *Amidah*, announcing the future gathering of Israel's scattered people, and ending with "Blessed are you, O Lord, who gathers together your banished people Israel." Jews prayed the *Amidah* three times daily (see *Berakoth* 14, I) as the early Christians did the Lord's Prayer (8:3).

In the *Didache*, the corresponding prayer referred to the broken bread *(klasma)*, which was scattered on the mountains and then gathered together and became one: "So may your church be gathered together from the ends of the earth into your kingdom" (9:4). Both the prayers of thanksgiving (9:2-3) and this final prayer concluded with a doxology: "For yours is the glory and the power forever" (9:4).

At this point in the community's history, the meals were inspired by and held in direct continuity with those Jesus shared with his disciples in the course of his ministry. The meal prayers, therefore, must have reflected the table prayers Jesus himself used. Just as Jesus' prayers did not contain a Christology, neither did those used by the community.

At this first stage, the expression, "which you have made known to us through Jesus your servant" (9:3), was consequently not part of the prayer. It represents a later addition. The same can be said for the Christological expressions in 10:2, 3.

The *Birkath Ha-Mazon* is in three parts. So is the thanksgiving prayer in the *Didache* 10.

The first part of the *Birkath Ha-Mazon* begins with a blessing, "Blessed are you, O Lord, Our God, King of the Universe, who feeds the whole world with goodness, with grace and with mercy." To this corresponds the second part of the *Didache*'s prayer of thanksgiving, "You, almighty Master *(despota pantokrator)* created all things for your name's sake; food and drink you gave to the children of men *(tois huiois ton anthropon)* to enjoy that they might give you thanks *(eucharistesomen)*; above all we give thanks *(eucharistoumen)* because you are mighty" (10:3-4).

The second part of the *Birkath Ha-Mazon* begins with a prayer of thanksgiving, "We thank you, O Lord our God, for making us inherit a good and pleasant land, the covenant, the Torah, life and food. For all these things we thank you and praise your name forever and ever." To this corresponds the *Didache*'s opening prayer of thanksgiving, "We give thanks *(eucharistoumen)* to you holy Father, for your holy name, which you made dwell in our hearts" (10:2).

The third part of the *Birkath Ha-Mazon* begins with a petition for mercy, "Have mercy, O Lord our God, on your people Israel, and on your city Jerusalem, and on your temple and on your dwelling-place, and on Zion your resting-place, and on the great and holy sanctuary over which your name was called." To this corresponds the *Didache*'s third prayer, evoking the final petition of the Lord's Prayer (8:2; see Matt 6:13b) and asking God to remember, "Remember, O Lord, your church to deliver her from all evil, and to perfect her in your love, and to gather her, the hallowed one, from the four winds into your kingdom" (10:5).

Each part of the *Birkath Ha-Mazon* also concludes with a blessing known as a *chatimah*, "Blessed are you, O Lord, who feeds all"; "Blessed are you, O Lord, for the land and for the food"; "Blessed are you, O Lord, who builds Jerusalem." A *chatimah* is a short *berakah* (blessing) used either to conclude an extended *berakah* or to link distinct parts of a long *berakah*. For each *chatimah*, the *Didache* substituted a simple doxology, for part one and two, "To you be the glory forever," and for part three, "For yours is the power and the glory forever."

Stage Two

At the second stage, the community was separated from other Jewish communities and needed to distinguish itself as a Christian community, albeit still clinging to its Jewish identity. It is at this time that the

Eucharistic prayers became part of an instruction (cc. 7–10) and were related specifically to the role of Jesus. It is through Jesus his servant *(pais)* that Our Father made known to us the vine of his servant David, for which we give thanks (9:2). It is through Jesus his servant that Our Father made known to us the life and the knowledge, for which we give thanks (9:3). We give thanks also "for the knowledge and faith and immortality which you have made known to us through Jesus our servant" (10:2). It is through his servant that God has "graciously given spiritual food and drink and eternal life" (10:3).

The thanksgiving prayers in chapter 10 are supplemented with a final eschatological prayer: "May grace [the Lord] come, and may this world pass away. Hosanna to the God of David; *Maranatha!* Amen." (10:6; see 1 Cor 16:22; Rev 22:20). The addition attunes the prayer to the *Didache's* eschatological conclusion in chapter 16.

The Christology introduced at this second stage relates the Eucharistic prayers to the mission of Jesus but very minimally. Jesus, like David, is our Father's servant, and the one who reveals our Father's gifts. Jesus is not the one who brings our Father's gifts, nor the one through whom our Father fulfills his promise to give them. Nor is Jesus the one through whom we thank our Father for "the holy vine of David" (9:2), "the life and knowledge" (9:3), "the knowledge and faith and eternal life" (10:2), and "the spiritual food and drink" (10:3).

The prayers, however, are related to a formal structure: "Now concerning the Eucharist, or thanksgiving *(peri de tes eucharistias)*, give thanks as follows *(houtos eucharistesate)*. First with regard to the cup *(proton peri tou poteriou,* 9:1-2). . . . Likewise with regard to the broken bread *(peri de tou klasmatos,* 9:3)."[15] The introduction to chapter 10 presupposes that a meal has taken place: "Once you have eaten, give thanks as follows" (10:1).

A special instruction is added, excluding those who are not baptized in the name of the Lord from eating or drinking of their Eucharist. Their exclusion is supported by Jesus' command, "Do not give what is holy to dogs" (9:5; see Matt 7:6). The instruction towards the end of chapter 10 stipulates that "If anyone is holy, let him come; if anyone is not, let him repent" (10:6). Finally, prophets should be permitted to give thanks as they wish (10:7).

Stage Three

It is possible that at stage two the special instructions were simpler; these instructions excluded Jews who were not baptized, and did so without mentioning Jesus' command not to give what is holy to dogs, that is to Gentiles (see Matt 15:26; Mark 7:27). This last might have been added at stage three, when the community needed to protect itself from false apostles, prophets, and teachers and so separate itself from Christian communities who were open to Gentiles. These would have included the Matthean community after its exclusion from the synagogue sometime before the writing of Matthew's Gospel.

The *Didache*'s community was separatist from the beginning. At the first stage, it separated itself along with other Jews from the Gentiles. At the second, it was forced to separate itself from other Jewish communities and to distinguish itself from them. At the third, it separated itself from Christian communities who welcomed Gentiles and celebrated Eucharist with them. Maintaining itself holy, separating itself from the profane and keeping itself from becoming profane was a concern at all three stages.

Here at stage three, with a set of instructions for discerning false from true apostles and prophets and choosing good leaders, bishops *(episkopoi)* and deacons *(diakonoi)* worthy of the Lord (15:1-2), the *Didache* introduces a second major passage on the Eucharist, this time for the community assembly on "the Lord's Day" (14).[16]

The instruction refers to the Lord's Day when the community assembles to break bread and give thanks after confessing their sins, which takes place in the assembly. The purpose for confessing their sins is so that their sacrifice *(thysia hymon)* will not be profaned (14:1). After this come special instructions regarding reconciliation (see 1:2), which must take place prior to the assembly (see Matt 5:23-24). Like the confession of sins, the reconciliation is so that their sacrifice might not be profaned *(me koinothe,* 14:2). To ensure the same, they must choose bishops and deacons who are worthy of the Lord (15:1-2).

If there was any doubt that the *Didache* was actually referring to the Eucharist as celebrated by the Church today, chapter 14:1–15:2, with its reference to the Lord's Day and to the sacrifice, seems to dispel it. Both, however, require close examination.

The expression for "on the Lord's Day" is actually "on the Lord's Day of the Lord" *(kata kyriaken de kyriou),* a very strange expression, so strange that J. P. Audet amended it to "on the Day of the Lord" *(kath' hemeran de kyriou).*[17]

"The Lord's Day," however, which refers to the Lord with an adjective *(kyriakos, e, on)* is not the same as "the day of the Lord," which refers to the Lord with a noun *(kyrios).* With the noun, "the day of the

Lord" refers to the day of the Lord's visitation and judgment. With the adjective, "the Lord's day" refers to Sunday, a day whose meaning comes from the Lord.

In Revelation 1:10, "the Lord's Day" receives its meaning from the person of the risen Lord. But this is not the case in the *Didache*. Nowhere does the *Didache* refer to Jesus' resurrection, nor does it refer to his passion and death, not even in relation to baptism. It does not even use the Christological title "Christ." When it refers to Jesus as Lord, it refers to him not as risen Lord but in relation to the Lord God. As Lord *(Yahweh)*, God is present in a special way to his people Israel, forming them as a people, guiding and protecting them so long as they remained faithful.

By itself, the expression, *kata kyriaken* — the word *hemeran* (day) is understood — would normally associate the Lord's Day with the risen Lord, as it does in Revelation 1:10, making a community's meal assembly a true Eucharist. Adding *tou kyriou* (of the Lord), however, redefines the Lord's Day in terms of the relationship of the Lord Jesus to the Lord *(Yahweh)* God.

In the *Didache*, assembling, breaking bread, and giving thanks celebrates the "Lord's Day of the Lord," and the special relationship of the Lord *(Yahweh)* Jesus to his special people, forming them, guiding them, and protecting them, so long as they opt for "the way of life" and not for "the way of death." For the *Didache*, this special people of the Lord Jesus is faithfully represented by the community of the *Didache*.

The reference to keeping their sacrifice from being profaned refers to their own sacrifice, not to "the sacrifice of Christ." As the sacrifice of Christ, their sacrifice would be a sacrament of Jesus' death and resurrection. Terms to convey that sacrament would be the body or flesh and the blood of Christ, terms that nowhere appear in the *Didache*.

Instead "their sacrifice" is the one referred to by the Lord: "In every place and time, offer me a pure sacrifice, for I am a great king, says the Lord, and my name is marvelous among the nations" (14:3). The reference is a loose quotation of Malachi 1:11-14, calling for a right moral attitude. In *Didache* 14:3, the term sacrifice is consequently a metaphor for their relationship to the Lord Jesus. It does not refer to the Eucharist as we know it in the Church.

We are thus left with a question: Was the Eucharist referred to in the *Didache*, including the Eucharist at its Sunday assembly, a real Eucharist? Did the *Didache*'s community consider it as such?

The answer to the second question is simple. Everything indicates that the *Didache*'s community thought that from the very beginning, it was celebrating a real Eucharistic meal. They may not have used the term "Eucharist" during the first stage, but at the second stage, they applied it to the oldest thanksgiving prayers they had developed for their community meals. They may also have thought of their ordinary community and family meals as participating in those they shared as Sunday Eucharist with the full assembly.

But was what they celebrated really the Eucharist? Everything indicates that it was not. From a Christological point of view, their Eucharistic tradition was too poor. A real Eucharist would have referred to the passion and death of Christ, to the risen Lord and to his body and blood.

Such a Eucharist, however, would have opened the community to all God's people, including the Gentiles. Having died with Christ to live with Christ and gathered at the table of the risen Lord, their Lord and the Lord of all, they would have opened their Christian meal, their Eucharist, to all, especially on the Lord's Day.[18] With that they would have become a community among others in a Church that was catholic in principle and missionary in reality. Instead, they remained a community turned in on itself until it disappeared.

As the sacrament of unity, the Eucharist is not compatible with separatism.

NOTES

1. In some ways, the *Didache* is comparable to the *Manual of Discipline* discovered at Qumran among the Dead Sea Scrolls, setting forth the way of life, exercises, and leadership structures for an Essene community. The *Manual of Discipline*, however, is more highly developed than the *Didache* (see A.R.C. Leaney, *The Rule of Qumran and Its Meaning* (Philadelphia: The Westminster Press, 1966).

For a basic introduction, presentation and commentary on the *Didache*, along with its text in Greek and in French, see Jean-Paul Audet, *La Didache: Instruction des Apotres* (Paris: J. Gabalda, 1958), text on pp. 226–243. For an introduction and translation in English, see James A. Kleist, "The Didache or Teaching of the Twelve Apostles," *Ancient Christian Writers* 6 (Westminster, Maryland: The Newman Press, 1948) 3–25. For another English translation, see J. B. Lightfoot and J. R. Harmer, *The Apostolic Fathers*, 2nd ed., ed. and rev. Michael W. Holmes (Grand Rapids: Baker Book House, 1989) 149–158. For a more recent introduction, and detailed analysis of chapters 1–6 and a fine study of the remainder of the work, see Clayton N. Jefford, *The Sayings of Jesus in the Teaching of the Twelve Apostles* (New York: E. J. Brill, 1989). See also Enrico Mazza, *The Origins of the Eucharistic Prayer* (Collegeville: The Liturgical Press—A Pueblo Book, 1995) 12–41.

2. For other early references, see Revelation 1:10 and Ignatius of Antioch in his letter to the Magnesians 9,1.

3. Jean-Paul Audet showed that the *Didache*'s original title was *Didachai ton apostolon (Teachings of the Apostles)*, a title parallel to that of Luke's second volume, *Praxeis ton apostolon (Acts of the Apostles)* in *Codex Sinaiticus, Vaticanus and Bezae cantabrigiensis*. The title was later expanded to the "Teaching of the Twelve Apostles" to give the document greater authority (see *La Didache: Instruction des Apotres*, 91–103, 247–252).

4. See Philip Schaff, *The Oldest Church Manual Called the Teaching of the Twelve Apostles* (New York: Funk & Wagnalls, 1885).

5. The key passage is in de Lubac's *Meditation sur L'Eglise*, Troisieme edition revue (Paris: Editions Montaigne, 1954): *"Tout nous invite donc a considerer les rapports de l'Eglise et de l'Eucharistie. De l'une a l'autre, on peut dire que la causalite est reciproque. Chacune a pour ainsi dire ete confiee a l'autre par le Sauveur. C'est l'Eglise qui fait l'Eucharistie, mais c'est aussi l'Eucharistie qui fait l'Eglise,"* 113.

6. The New Testament includes several instances in which a tradition was unable to sustain a community faced with new and unexpected realities. This was the case, for example, with the disciples of Emmaus, whose view of Jesus as a prophet like Moses, "mighty in deed and word," "the one to redeem Israel," did not include Jesus' passion and death. As the new Moses, Jesus was not expected to suffer and die (Luke 24:19-24). To be viable, the Emmaus tradition, with its Mosaic Christology, had to be complemented with one based on the Suffering Servant of the Lord. This is what Jesus provided (Luke 24:25-27), enabling the disciples to integrate the passion into their view of Jesus as prophet. In the process, the tradition was not set aside or destroyed but transformed.

7. Early research on the *Didache* concentrated on its place of origin and date of writing. For a good review of that research, see Jefford, *Op. Cit.*, 1–21.

8. See Audet, *Op. Cit.*, 245–357.

9. See Jefford, *Op. Cit.*, 22–92.

10. See Jefford, *Op. Cit.*, 123–129.

11. For general studies of the Eucharist in the *Didache*, see H. J. Gibbins, "The Problem of the Liturgical Section of the Didache," *The Journal of Theological Studies*, XXXVI (1935) 373–386; Maurice Goguel, "La Didache," *L'Eucharistie des origines a Justin Martyr* (Paris: Librairie Fischbacher, 1910) 229–245; Clayton N. Jefford, *Op. Cit.*, 138–140; Willy Rordorf, "The Didache," *The Eucharist of the Early Christians*, trans. Matthew J. O'Connell (New York: Pueblo Publishing Company, 1978) 1–23.

12. For special studies of chapters 9 and 10 and the prayers they contain, see Audet, *Op. Cit.*, 372–433; R. D. Middleton, "The Eucharistic Prayers of the Didache," *The Journal of Theological Studies*, XXXVI (1935) 259–267; John W. Riggs, "From Gracious Table to Sacramental Elements: The Tradition-History of 9–10," *The Second Century* 4:2 (1984) 83–101.

13. For a commentary on chapter 14:1–15:2, see Audet, *Op. Cit.*, 458–467.

14. See Middleton, who showed how the prayers in the *Didache* are related to the Jewish prayers, *Op. Cit.*, 261–265. Riggs went further and showed how *Didache* 10 is older and set the pattern for *Didache* 9, *Op. Cit.*, 93–96.

15. The order, "first with regard to the cup" and then "with regard to the broken bread," is the reverse of 1 Corinthians 11:23-25, but it does correspond to 1 Corinthians 10:16, "The cup of blessing that we bless, is it not a participation in the blood of Christ? The bread that we break, is it not a participation in the body of Christ?"

16. See Audet, *Op. Cit.*, 458–467.

17. Audet, *Op. Cit.*, 460.

18. The community of the *Didache* is comparable to that of the disciples in Mark, when they resisted crossing over to the Gentile side of the Sea of Galilee for the breaking of the bread with Gentiles as well as Jews (Mark 6:45-52). At that point, "They had not understood the incident of the loaves. On the contrary, their hearts were hardened" (6:52).

10

One Flesh, One Cup, One Altar:
The Eucharist in the Letters of Ignatius of Antioch

> Through the *Didache* we are in touch
> with the beginnings of the Eucharist
> in an early Christian Jewish setting,
> striving to celebrate the Eucharist
> authentically, however not quite making it.
> Through the letters of Ignatius of Antioch
> we are in touch with the Eucharist
> in an early Christian Gentile setting,
> an authentic Eucharistic theology
> for the universal Church.

We know very little about the life and personal background of Ignatius of Antioch, the kind of information that would help us situate him in the social and political history of his time.

Eusebius reports that he was the bishop of Antioch, the second to succeed Peter,[1] during the reign of Trajan (A.D. 98–117) and that he was sent to Rome to be devoured by beasts on account of his Christian witness (*Ecclesiastical History*, III, 36).

Fortunately, Ignatius left us seven letters, written on his way to martyrdom. From these, we learn quite a lot about the journey itself, the people who accompanied him, those who came to meet him, and the Churches to which he wrote. All seven of the letters, however, were written over a very short period of time, a few weeks at the very most.[2] Regarding the rest of his life, we are detectives, poring over Ignatius' letters, noting every clue, hoping to uncover additional bits of information, however meager.

Ignatius was quite clearly of Gentile background, but we would like to know more about him, especially how he came to be a Christian. Is it that his parents were Christians? Was he converted personally, independently of his family? If so, at what age and in what circumstances? We would also like to know about his education, his life as a bishop and how the Eucharist was celebrated in the Church he oversaw.

Ignatius seems to have been martyred in Trajan's later years, sometime between 110 and 115. But we would like to know what led to his arrest, in which of those years he was martyred, and how long he had been the bishop of Antioch.[3]

Concerning such factual things, the letters say very little. Concerning Ignatius as a person, however, his personal attitudes and his dedication as a Christian, the letters say a whole lot, more than making up for their silence about his life.

Written within a few weeks, perhaps a few days, of one another, the letters provide a very clear window into Ignatius' mind and spirit as he was being led to martyrdom. They show his attachment to Christ as human and divine, and to the Church as the sacrament of Christ, its catholicity, its mission and its tradition.

The letters also show Ignatius' attachment to the Eucharist as the presence of Christ, human and divine, as central to the being and unity of the Church and as the source and the goal for Christian life. Formed by the Eucharist, Ignatius saw the Eucharist as a great formative force in the Church. Steeped in the New Testament's apostolic tradition, his teaching on the Eucharist provides a bridge from the apostolic to the postapostolic age.[4]

The Letters of Ignatius[5]

Ignatius wrote seven letters between his arrest at Antioch and his martyrdom at Rome. Four of the letters were written from Smyrna where, after the long overland journey from Antioch, the little convoy that was taking him stayed for a few days, perhaps as much as a week. While at Smyrna, Ignatius enjoyed the support of the Church in that city and its young bishop, Polycarp, who, some forty years later, would also suffer martyrdom. He also met with delegations who came from the Churches of Ephesus, Magnesia, and Tralles. Three of the letters were addressed to these Churches. A fourth was entrusted to the Ephesian delegation for the Church in Rome.

Three of the seven letters were written from Troas, where, as at Smyrna, the local Church reached out to him. This time, however, his expected stay was cut short.[6] One of the letters was sent to the Church at Smyrna, and a second to its bishop, Polycarp. The third was sent to the Church in Philadelphia, a city Ignatius passed on the way to Smyrna.

Ignatius' journey took him through Philippi and on to Thessalonica, a route familiar to us from the journeys of St. Paul. According to a letter of Polycarp to the Church of Philippi, written soon after Ignatius passed through that city, members of the Church accompanied Ignatius on part of the journey (Phil I, 1).

The Church of Philippi learned of Ignatius' letters and requested a copy from Polycarp. A copy of Ignatius' letters to Smyrna and to Polycarp and of the other letters, which Polycarp had collected — all except the letter to the Romans — was sent to them.[7] The very existence of such a collection and its circulation, within weeks after the letters were written,[8] show how greatly Ignatius' message was valued by the young bishop and the early Church (Phil XIII, 1–2).

From internal evidence, the letters from Smyrna seem to have been written in the following order: first the letters to the Magnesians and the Trallians, then the letter to the Romans, and then the letter to the Ephesians. Of the letters from Troas, the one to the Philadelphians seems to have been written first, then the letter to the Smyrnians and the letter to Polycarp.[9]

Like the letters of Paul, the spirit and message of Ignatius' letters are profoundly Christian and apostolic. Their form, however, Ignatius follows the conventions of letter writing in the Hellenistic world, unlike Paul, whose letters represent a synthesis of Jewish and Greek elements in a uniquely Christian and apostolic form.[10]

Responding to kindred situations in the various Churches of Asia Minor, the letters have a similar outline.

Each letter opens with a formal greeting, giving the sender's full name, "Ignatius also called (*ho kai*) Theophorus," naming the Church being addressed along with some of its distinctive qualities, and explicitly greeting the Church, "abundant greetings" (*pleista chairein*).

Each letter then continues with a message of praise, recognizing the Church's special blessings and noteworthy qualities. This second section is comparable to the thanksgiving passage in the letters of Paul (e.g., 1 Cor 1:4-9; Phil 1:3-11). In the letter to Polycarp, the praise is integrated into the body of the letter.

The third section comprises the body of the letter, which except for the letters to the Church at Smyrna and to Polycarp, is developed in three parts.

In the letters to the Ephesians, the Magnesians, the Trallians, and the Philadelphians, the body focuses first on the importance of internal unity, Ignatius' most basic concern in all the letters. In the second part, the body deals with a heresy threatening the unity of the Church, either that of docetists (Ephesians, Trallians) or that of Judaizers (Magnesians, Philadelphians). The body then concludes with exhortations to unity. The theme of unity thus frames the central message in which Ignatius warns against heresy.

The body of the letter to the Romans, also in three parts, corresponds to the unique purpose of the letter. First, Ignatius pleads with the Church at Rome not to intercede on his behalf (II–III). He then develops his view of martyrdom (IV–VII) and concludes with a request that the Church pray for him as he approaches martyrdom (VIII).

The fourth section of the letters is a closing greeting along with special regards, particular requests and expressions of gratitude.

Because of his recent visit with the Smyrnians, Ignatius did not need to spell everything out for them. The praise section of the letter stresses the Church's strong faith in the humanity of Jesus (I–III). The body then focuses entirely on the heresy threatening the Church at Smyrna, namely docetism, as was the case at Ephesus and Tralles (IV–IX, 1). The final section is very long, expressing special gratitude to the Church that had been so hospitable and made his stay apostolically fruitful (IX, 2–XIII).

The letter to Polycarp also reflects Ignatius' visit at Smyrna and the close relationship that developed between them. As an older bishop, Ignatius praises, advises, and encourages young Bishop Polycarp (I–V). Through Polycarp, he also addresses the Church of Smyrna (VI–VIII).

Ignatius' letters put us in touch with a Christian consumed by love for Christ and the Church at a point in his life when the goal was in reach. They show a man steeped in the letters of Paul, in particular 1 Corinthians, and in the living tradition of the Church, especially that underlying John's Gospel.[11] As the bishop of Antioch, he also surely knew Matthew's Gospel, most likely from memory.[12]

Making no distinction between the written and the oral gospel, Ignatius drew creatively from the abundant well of tradition, without distinguishing any written texts he may have used from the living faith that produced them. For Ignatius, the gospel was primarily a living reality.

The letters also put us in touch with Ignatius as a preacher, one who had much to say and so little time to say it. Reading the letters, we sense his voice trying to break through the written word. His style is vigorous and direct, driven by faith, love, and boundless hope. His speech is rich in images, gospel allusions, and spiced with aphorisms.

In Ignatius we meet an original mind, immersed in tradition, profoundly apostolic, guided by faith, inspired by love, and drawn by hope. Like the letters of Paul, those of Ignatius reveal extraordinary religious creativity in the service of Christ, the gospel and the Church.

We are not surprised to find Ignatius' letters extremely rich in their Eucharistic theology and spirituality.

Ignatius and the Eucharist

Although not in the same way, Ignatius refers to the Eucharist in every one of his letters except the letter to Polycarp.

He uses Eucharistic vocabulary, including the term "Eucharist" (*eucharistia,* Eph XIII, 1; Philad IV; Smyrn VII, 1; VIII, 1).

He speaks of "the altar of Eucharistic sacrifice" *(thysiasterion)* as a sign and guarantor of Church unity (Eph V, 2; Magn VII, 2; Trall VII, 2; Philad IV) and as a symbol for his own personal sacrifice as Christ's martyr (Rom II, 2).

Using a Pauline expression (1 Cor 11:20), he refers to the Church's "coming together in one place" *(epi to auto)* for the Eucharist (Eph V, 3; XIII, 1; Magn VII, 1; Philad VI, 2; 10, 1; see 1 Cor 11:20).

Ignatius also makes creative use of Eucharistic traditions, in particular the Pauline tradition and the Johannine, but others as well, in developing his theology. For Ignatius, the Eucharist had implications for the unity and universality of the Church, for the humanity and divinity of Christ, for Christian spirituality and the meaning of his martyrdom. He also made extensive use of Eucharistic imagery for his approaching martyrdom, especially in his letter to the Romans.

Ignatius' message concerning the Eucharist is best appreciated in the particular contexts in which he presented it. For that, we now turn to each of the letters, observing the likely order of their writing. After situating the various references to the Eucharist in each letter's context, we shall comment on what Ignatius said about the Eucharist and show how it contributed to his purpose in writing each of the letters.

The Letters from Smyrna

The first time Ignatius dealt directly with the Eucharist was in the letter to the Ephesians, the fourth of his letters from Smyrna. Before that, in the letter to the Magnesians, to the Trallians, and to the Romans, he did so indirectly, referring to the Eucharist's setting in the assembly and by using a lot of Eucharistic imagery. His principal teaching on the Eucharist is in the letter to the Ephesians. What he says in the previous letters, however, is important as background, and as an introduction for his Eucharistic message in the letter to the Ephesians.

To the Church at Magnesia

While Ignatius was at Smyrna, a small delegation visited him from the Church at Magnesia, a city on the river Meander, a few miles east of Ephesus. The delegation included the Church's bishop, Damas, two presbyters, Bassus and Apollonius, and Zotion, a deacon, whom Ignatius describes as his *syndoulos,* his fellow-slave (II, 2). The letter entrusted to them for the Church included greetings from the Church at Ephesus and "from the other Churches," a reference to the Church at Smyrna and very likely to the Church at Tralles (XV).

In his letter to the Magnesians, Ignatius praises the Church at Magnesia (I–II) but expresses concern about its unity (III–VII, XII–XIII), all the more since its bishop, Damas, was still very young (III).

It is in this connection that Ignatius referred to the Eucharistic assembly for the first time: "It is important not only to be spoken of as Christians *(kaleisthai Christianous)* but to be Christians *(alla kai einai).* There are those who speak of the bishop *(episkopon men kalousin)* but in fact do everything apart from him. Those people seem to me not to have a good conscience, for their assemblies *(synathroizesthai)* are worth nothing *(me bebaios)* in relation to the Lord's command *(kat' entolen)"* (IV).

Later, in his letter to the Church at Smyrna, Ignatius took up the same theme, this time referring explicitly to the Eucharist (VIII, 2). His warning echoed Paul's prophetic message regarding factions in the Church at Corinth: "When you meet in one place, then, it is not to eat the Lord's supper" (1 Cor 11:17-22). It also recalls the Lord's command to do what he did in memory of him (1 Cor 11:23-25).

The same opening exhortation on unity (III–VII) concludes with a reference to assembling at the one altar *(epi hen thysiasterion):* "Let all hasten to assemble at the one temple *(naos)* of God, at the one altar, at the one Jesus Christ" (VII, 2). The altar *(thysiasterion)*, that is, the place of sacrifice *(thysia)* or sacrificial area, refers to Jesus Christ's personal sacrifice made present in the Church's assembly. In a sense, Jesus Christ himself is the altar.

The letter's central focus, concerning Judaizing efforts and tendencies (VIII–XI),[13] introduces the Lord's Day as the Christian substitution for the Jewish Sabbath. Rather than "observe the Sabbath *(sabbatizontes),"* Christians "live according to the Lord's Day *(kata kyriaken zontes).*"

Related to Jesus' resurrection and their own baptism, the Lord's Day celebrates the ultimate origins and initial source of their Christian life (IX, 1). Related to the Eucharist, the Lord's Day expresses or implies their entire Christian way of life (IX, 2-X).[14]

To the Church at Tralles

While at Smyrna, Ignatius also received the visit of Polybius, the bishop of the Church at Tralles (I, 1), a city a few miles east of Magnesia. The letter entrusted to him for the Church included greetings from the Smyrnians and the Ephesians. Since no other Churches are mentioned, it must be that the delegation from Magnesia had already departed, bearing Ignatius' letter to their Church (XIII, 1).

The letter to the Trallians is very closely patterned on the letter to the Magnesians, suggesting it must have been written or dictated while the memory of the letter to the Magnesians was still fresh.

Again Ignatius praises the Church (I) but once again is concerned for its unity around the bishop (II–V, XII). He had warned the Church at Magnesia against Judaizing tendencies. He now warns the Church at Tralles against docetism (VI–XI).

Exhorting the Church to take only Christian nourishment *(mone te christiane trophe chresthe),*[15] he warns them against the alien plant of heresy *(allotrias de botanes apechesthe, hetis estin hairesis).* Those who teach heresy are like those who serve honeyed wine laced with deadly poison. Unsuspecting, those enjoying the drink do so to their death (VI, 1–2; see XI, 1; also Philad III, 1).[16]

Christian nourishment refers to the life-giving truth of Christian faith; the poisoned drink refers to the death-dealing error of heresy. In the letter to the Ephesians, Ignatius would develop the same set of images still further. Jesus is the only doctor *(heis iatros,* VII, 2) and the Eucharistic bread is the medicine of immortality, an antidote against death for life in Jesus Christ forever (XX, 2).

Using a Eucharistic image, Ignatius then distinguishes between one who is "inside the altar" or place of sacrifice *(ho entos thysiasteriou)* and one who is "outside the altar" or place of sacrifice *(ho ektos thysiasteriou)* and one who is outside. The first is pure *(katharos estin)*; the second, that is, the one who acts apart from the bishop, the presbyterate *(presbyterion)* and the deacons, is not pure *(ou hatharos estin)* in conscience *(te syneidesei;* VII, 2; see Magn IV and VII, 2).

Ignatius is referring to the heresy of docetism. Jesus Christ, who is of the race of David, the son of Mary, was truly born. He truly ate and drank. He was truly persecuted by Pontius Pilate, was truly crucified, died in full gaze of heaven, earth and hell, and was truly raised from the dead (IX). Such was the true life-giving faith. The atheists, on the other hand, that is the unbelievers *(apistoi)*, say Jesus Christ only appeared *(dokein)* to suffer (X).

The English terms, "docetist" and "docetism" and "docetic," come from the Greek verb *dokein*, meaning "to appear." For the docetists, Jesus was truly divine but merely appeared to be human. If Jesus was not truly human, he did not, indeed could not, truly die on the cross, offering his life that we might live. If Jesus Christ, did not truly die, he did not truly rise, and the Eucharist, the memorial of his passion and resurrection, is meaningless.

To the Church at Rome

While at Smyrna, Ignatius also gave the delegation from Ephesus a letter for the Church at Rome. His greeting to the Church at Rome is by far the most respectful and elaborate, recognizing the Roman Church's preeminence over the "catholic" Church, that is, over the whole Church.

Ignatius' main purpose in writing the letter was to beg the members of the Church, some of whom seem to have been quite influential, not to intercede with the officials on his behalf (I–II). He wishes nothing more than "to be offered as a libation to God *(me paraschesthe tou spondisthenai theo)* while the altar *(thysiasterion)* was still prepared" (II, 2). The altar, an image associated with the Eucharist, is thus introduced to describe Ignatius' own martyrdom. In laying down his life, Ignatius was doing what Christ had done. He was offering his life "for the many" in remembrance of him.

The main part of the letter (III–VIII) contains Ignatius' personal spirituality and theology of martyrdom. Ignatius certainly looked forward to his own martyrdom but not because he wanted to die. Rather, having been condemned to death, he had already accepted martyrdom as the will of God. Martyrdom was the fulfillment of his baptism and of his participation in the Eucharist.

Ignatius' attitude recalls Jesus' response to Simon Peter in the garden of Gethsemane: "Put your sword into its scabbard. Shall I not drink the cup that the Father gave me?" (John 18:11); and later to Pilate: "My kingdom does not belong to this world. If my kingdom did belong to this world, my attendants [would] be fighting to keep me from being handed over to the Jews. But as it is, my kingdom is not here" (John 18:36).

Ignatius wants not only to be called a Christian but to be found (*heuretho*) a Christian (III, 2; see Magn IV). Using Eucharistic images, he describes what he means when he says he wants to be found a Christian: "I am God's wheat (*sitos theou*), and I am ground (*alethomai*) by the teeth of beasts in order to be found (*heuretho*) a pure bread (*katharos artos*) of Christ" (IV, 2). . . . Pray to Christ for me that through these instruments I may be found (*heuretho*) a sacrifice to God (*theo thysia*, IV, 2).

Later he adds: "Allow me to be an imitator (*mimeten einai*) of the passion of my God (*tou pathous tou theou mou*)" (VI, 3). The altar of sacrifice (*thysiasterion*, II, 2) is prepared, and Ignatius himself is to be the sacrifice (*thysia*), just as Christ was the sacrifice in the passion and is now the sacrifice in the Eucharist. Ignatius saw himself doing what Christ did. He was fulfilling Christ's command to do this in remembrance of him.

Later yet, he describes his martyrdom quite explicitly in relation to his baptism and the Eucharist: "The eros in me has been crucified, and the fire of love in me is no more. Within me there is living water (*hydor zon*, see John 4:10; 7:38) murmuring, "Come to the Father (*deuro pros ton patera*, see John 14:12)."

"I no longer take pleasure in perishable food (*trophe phthoras*) or the pleasure of life. I desire the bread of God, which is the flesh (*sarx*) of Jesus Christ, descended from David (see John 7:42; Rom 1:3). As drink I want his blood (*haima*), which is imperishable love (*agape aphthartos*)" (VII, 2–3).

The basis for Ignatius' spiritual reflection is John 4 and 6. He sees himself as the bread of Christ, that is the bread which is Christ offered in sacrifice.

Having received the living water Christ gives, he desires Christ's imperishable food and drink, that is the flesh and blood of Christ, not just in the promise of Eucharistic sacrament and sacrifice, but in the reality they signify.

To the Church at Ephesus

The last and by far the longest of Ignatius' letters from Smyrna was to the Church at Ephesus whose history reached back to the Pauline missions from Antioch. The Ephesian delegation at Smyrna included their bishop, Onesimus, a deacon named Burrhus, and three other members of the community, Crocus, Euplus, and Fronto (I, 3–II, 1).

Representing their Church, the delegation had joined Ignatius in sending greetings to the Churches of Magnesia and Tralles (Magn XV; Trall XIII, 1). They were also entrusted with Ignatius' letter to the Romans (Rom X, 1). In leaving, the delegation from Ephesus also bore a letter to their own Church, which Ignatius recognized as having a special standing among the Churches of Asia Minor.[17] Burrhus, however, who was one of their members, was to stay behind to accompany Ignatius on the journey to Troas (Eph II, 1).

The letter to the Church at Ephesus, most likely the last of the four written from Smyrna, is also the most highly developed. Its structure and content resembles the letters to the Church at Magnesia and to the Church at Tralles, but is more complex. As in those letters, unity is the central theme (III–VI, XI–XIV) and heresy, that of docetism, is a major concern (VII–X). But like one who recognizes this as a final opportunity to address a leading Church, Ignatius returns a second time to the danger of docetism (XV–XX).

The letter to the Ephesians thus continues Ignatius' basic message from Smyrna and develops it even further. A good part of this development bears on the Eucharist.

The letter's first passage on the Eucharist includes an important expression, being "in the altar" or "place of sacrifice," which Ignatius had introduced in the letters to the Church at Magnesia, to the Church at Tralles and to the Church at Rome, and develops the expression still further: "Let no one go astray. One who is not in the place of sacrifice *(entos tou thysiasteriou)*[18] is deprived of the bread of God *(tou artou tou theou)*" (V, 2). The expression, "the bread of God," was taken from John 6:33, "the bread of God is that which comes down from heaven and gives life to the world." The Eucharist is thus a heavenly gift of God as well as the Church's offering to God.

"For if," Ignatius continues, "the prayer of one or two has such power [see Matt 18:20], how much more that of the bishop and the whole Church *(pases tes ekklesias)"* (V, 2).[19] Ignatius thus distinguishes between the gathering of a few members of the Church for prayer and the assembly of the whole Church. In both cases, the prayer may be Eucharistic in quality, since both were a prayer of thanksgiving. Only the second, however, when the prayer of thanksgiving takes place "in the altar," does it consist in the Eucharist itself.

Ignatius describes those who do not come to "the common assembly *(epi to auto)"* as arrogant. The expression *"epi to auto,"* a Pauline expression (see 1 Cor 11:20), is synonymous with "assembling as a church" (1 Cor 11:18). [20]

While emphasizing unity with the bishop in each local Church, Ignatius recognizes the need for unity in the universal Church, whose bishops are established to the ends of the earth in the mind *(gnome)* of Jesus Christ (III, 2).

Later, while addressing the docetist heresy, Ignatius takes up a Eucharistic image he had previously developed in his letter to the Romans: "I am your expiatory offering and I offer myself in sacrifice for you *(peripsema hymon kai agnizomai hyper hymon)* the Church of the Ephesians, whose renown is forever" (VIII, 1; see Rom IV, 2).

Later still, while developing his central theme of unity, Ignatius uses the term "Eucharist" *(eucharistia)* for the first time: "Hasten to assemble *(synarchesthai)* more frequently to give thanks *(eucharistian)* and glory *(doxan)* to God. When you assemble in common *(epi to auto)* frequently, the forces of Satan are put down and his work destroyed by the harmony of your faith" (XIII, 1).

Thanksgiving *(eucharistia)* is broader than the Eucharist *(he eucharistia)*, which is a specific act of thanksgiving, indeed the epitome of Christian thanksgiving, all of which gives glory to God. Ignatius uses the general term, "thanksgiving," in the specific sense of "the Eucharist" in his letters from Troas. In this first instance, the Eucharist is included along with other acts of thanksgiving in the more general term.

Ignatius' best-known passage on the Eucharist is at the conclusion of the letter's second warning against docetism (XV–XX). Promising to write further about "the dispensation *(oikonomia)* relating to the new man *(eis ton kainon anthropon)* Jesus Christ," he describes the dispensation as a new order founded "on his faith, on his love, on his passion and resurrection" (XX, 1).

In the new order or dispensation, "each and every one of them should assemble in common *(koine synerchesthe)* in the grace of the Lord's name, in one faith and in Jesus Christ, who 'according to the flesh was of the race of David' (Rom 1:3), the Son of Man and the Son of God. They would thus obey the bishop and the presbyterate with an undivided mind" (XX, 2).

Having described the assembly, Ignatius turned his attention to its principal activity. In union with the bishop and the presbyterate, they would "break one bread *(hena arton klontes)*, which is the medicine of immortality *(pharmakon athanasias)*, an antidote against death *(antidotos tou me apothanein)* for life in Jesus Christ forever *(alla zen en Iesou Christo dia pantos)*" (XX, 2).

The purpose for assembling in common was to celebrate the Eucharist, and the purpose of celebrating the Eucharist was to give eternal life to Christians who were smitten by death.

Celebrating the Eucharist meant breaking the one bread, and breaking the one bread required an assembly in common. In the Eucharistic assembly, the Church of Ephesus shared one faith in Jesus Christ, who became flesh in the historical family of David and so was Son of Man as well as Son of God.

The Letters from Troas

Ignatius dealt with the Eucharist in two of his letters from Troas, the one he wrote to the Church at Philadelphia and the one to the Church at Smyrna. The only letter that does not refer to the Eucharist is the letter to Polycarp, the very last letter he wrote before boarding for Macedonia.

In his letter to the Church at Ephesus, he used the term "Eucharist" in the broad, generic sense of Christian thanksgiving, including the Eucharist along with other expressions of thanksgiving. In the letters from Troas he uses the term "Eucharist" for the first time with reference to and in the specific sense "the Eucharist."

To the Church at Philadelphia

On the journey from Antioch to Smyrna, Ignatius had passed through Philadelphia, a city in Asia Minor. Members of the Church there surely came out to greet him, but their meeting must have been very brief, since he mentions no one of them by name, not even the bishop, for whom he spoke high praise (I).

Ignatius, therefore, wrote to the Church at Philadelphia, as he had written to the Churches that had sent delegates to meet him at Smyrna. He entrusted the letter to Burrhus, a deacon, one of the delegates from the Church at Ephesus, who accompanied him to Troas (XI, 2; see Eph II, l). The letter also included greetings from the Church at Troas.

The letter's opening exhortation to unity (II–IV) includes one of Ignatius' finest passages on the Eucharist.

On the one hand, Christians were to avoid anyone who did not accept the passion of Christ (III, 3) and the passion's implications regarding the distinction between Judaism and Christianism (V–VI). On the other hand, Ignatius admonished them to see that they participated "in the one Eucharist," that is, in the Eucharist the Church celebrated when it assembled in common (IV, 1).

There were two ways they could separate themselves from Christ's passion. Like the docetists, they might deny that Christ really suffered. Like the Judaizers, they might deny that Christ's passion, together with his resurrection, brought about a new dispensation, fulfilling and transcending Judaism. Either way, the passion was emptied of its meaning. At Philadelphia, as at Magnesia, the problem did not come from docetists, but from Judaizers and Judaizers' tendencies.

The reason they had to avoid all divisions and factions and take part in the one Eucharist (II–III; V–VI) was that "there is only one flesh (*mia sarx*) of our Lord Jesus Christ and one cup uniting us in his blood (*hen poterion eis henosin tou haimatos autou*) just as there is one bishop (*heis episkopos*) with the presbyterate (*presbyterio*) and deacons (*diakonois*), my fellow slaves (*tois syndoulois mou*)" (IV).

The passage is a fine example of how Ignatius drew on tradition, the life of the Church and personal experience to form a unique theological, pastoral, and spiritual synthesis.

The reference to the Lord's flesh and blood was inspired by John 6:51c-58 or a tradition underlying that passage. The Johannine tradition and John's Gospel may have developed in the Church at or around Ephesus, but by the time of Ignatius, they were equally at home in the Church of Antioch and elsewhere.

The reference to divisions and factions, to the cup and to the altar, and the emphasis on unity owes much to Paul's message in 1 Corinthians 1:10-17; 10:16-18; and 11:17-34. The way Ignatius brought the various elements together shows he not only accepted Paul's letter as authoritative but had made Paul's thought his own and could use it creatively.

The reference to the bishop with the presbyterate and the deacons reflects the development of leadership in the Church, not only in Antioch, Syria, and Asia Minor, but throughout the Eastern Mediterranean. Ignatius did not create the monarchical episcopacy, which arose in response to divisions and divisive tendencies in the Church. Ignatius merely recognized the pastoral importance of the monarchical episcopacy for ensuring unity in the one body of Christ.

Ignatius' reference to the deacons as "my fellow slaves" comes from his personal experience as a prisoner on the way to martyrdom. It shows how he integrated that experience in his understanding of service, the following of Christ (see Mark 10:43-44) and how these found sacramental expression in the Eucharist.

To the Church at Smyrna

While at Troas, Ignatius learned that the persecution of the Church at Antioch was over. Part of his purpose in writing to the Philadelphians was to ask them to send a representative to celebrate with the Church of Antioch as the Churches closer to Antioch were doing (Philad x).

He did the same in his letter to the Church at Smyrna (XI) and his letter to its bishop, Polycarp (VII). In his other letters to the Churches, Ignatius referred to the bishop, usually by name, and asked the Church to recognize their bishop's role in maintaining unity. He did not do this in his letter to the Church at Smyrna. Instead, he wrote a separate letter to Polycarp in which he also exhorted the Church to rally around its bishop (VI). The two letters were therefore conceived together and must have been written one immediately after the other.

Toward the end of his letter to Polycarp, Ignatius refers to his unexpectedly quick departure from Troas, making it impossible to write to the other Churches who greeted him on the way between Antioch and Smyrna. He asked Polycarp to write in his name asking all of them also to send representatives to Antioch.

Knowing that his letters to the Church at Smyrna and to Polycarp would be his last, Ignatius addressed only the most important matters. One of those important matters was the Eucharist.

In his other letters, Ignatius spoke of Christ, the historical figure, as truly human. In his letter to the Church at Smyrna, he spoke of Christ's humanity as risen Lord: "As for me, I know and I believe that even after the resurrection he was in the flesh *(en sarki)*." For Ignatius, the risen Lord was present not just bodily but in the flesh, making it possible for Peter and those who were with him to touch him and be united with him both in his flesh and in his spirit (III, 1–2).

Being in the flesh had implications for the Eucharist in which Christ gives not just his body *(soma)* but his flesh *(sarx)* as nourishment (see

Rom VII, 3 and below VII, 1). Ignatius recalls that "after the resurrection, Jesus ate and drank with them, that is, with Peter and those who were with him, as a person with flesh *(hos sarkikos)* while being spiritually united to the Father *(kaiper pneumatikos henomenos to patri)"* (III, 3).

"Body" *(soma),* the term used by the Synoptic Gospels and 1 Corinthians for the Eucharistic bread — "this is my body" — refers to Christ's person. "Flesh" *(sarx),* the term used by John for the nourishment Jesus gives — "the bread that I will give is my flesh" — is far more concrete. Reference to Christ's body *(soma)* or person does not of itself imply his presence in the flesh. Reference to the flesh *(sarx),* associates the Eucharist with the incarnation and refers to Christ's bodily, personal presence in the flesh.

Ignatius was inspired by appearance accounts in which Jesus ate and drank with the apostolic community. He may also have been influenced by Peter's discourse to the household of Cornelius in which Peter spoke of himself and other apostolic witnesses as those "who ate and drank with him (Jesus Christ, who is Lord of all) after he rose from the dead" (Acts 10:41). Each of these early traditions and stories had a history, responding to pastoral situations in the early Church. Ignatius brought them to bear on new pastoral challenges stemming from docetism.

For Ignatius, Christ was truly human, the Word made flesh, in his historical life, in his risen life, and in the sacramental gift of himself in the Eucharist. There is a difference, of course, between the historical and the risen presence of Christ. There is also a difference between his risen presence and his sacramental presence in the Eucharist. There is more than one way of being bodily present in the flesh.

Later in the letter, describing those who think otherwise, who do not accept the grace of Jesus Christ granted us in the incarnation, he states that "they have no concern for charity with regard to the widow, the orphan, the oppressed, prisoners, emancipated slaves, the hungry, and the thirsty. They abstain from the Eucharist and from prayer *(eucharistias kai proseuches apechontai)* because they do not confess that the Eucharist is the flesh *(ten eucharistian sarka einai)* of our Lord Jesus Christ, the same flesh that suffered for our sins and that in his goodness the Father has raised up *(egeiren).* So it is that those who reject the gift of God die of their disputes" (VI, 2–VII, 1; see Eph XX, 2).

Ignatius associates the docetists' disregard for the poor with their disregard for the Eucharist. As Luke described the primitive community in Jerusalem (Acts 2:42-47; 4:32-35), their charity was intimately linked with the Eucharist.[21] In Pauline communities, the collection for the poor in Jerusalem was connected with the Church's assembly on the first day of the week (1 Cor 16:1-4). Presenting the Lukan ideal and Pauline practice in Johannine terms, Ignatius shows that those who have no concern for Christ's flesh in the Eucharist have no concern for the fleshly concerns of the poor and the hungry.

Once again Ignatius refers to the flesh of the risen Lord, the same that suffered for our sins. He uses the term "Eucharist" in two senses, for the Eucharistic celebration and for the "gift of God" (see John 6:31-35), Christ's self-giving presence in the Eucharist. There are those who stay away from the Church's Eucharistic celebrations because they deny the reality of Christ's Eucharistic flesh. In so doing, they are consistent. Docetists regard the incarnation as a continuation of the Eucharistic sacrament.

Ignatius' last reference to the Eucharist returns to the theme of unity, that of the local Church and that of the universal Church: "Let no one do anything that concerns the Church apart from the bishop. That Eucharist alone which is celebrated under the bishop or one whom he has designated has value. Where the bishop appears, let the community gather, just as where Christ Jesus is present, there also is the catholic Church *(he katholike ekklesia)*. It is not allowed to baptize or to celebrate the *agape* (see Rom VII, 3) apart from the bishop" (VIII).

Celebrated by the local Church with its bishop or with one he has designated, the Eucharist is Christ's gift of life (see III). As Christ's sacramental presence in the flesh (see VII), the Eucharist is a celebration of the universal Church (see Eph III, 2).

Ignatius either referred to the Eucharist, used Eucharistic imagery, or reflected upon the Eucharist in all of his letters to the Churches. Focused on his approaching martyrdom, he emphasized the Eucharist as the Church's celebration of Christ's sacrifice. Ever the pastor, concerned for the Churches he was leaving behind, his letters were written sermons on unity, on avoiding heresy and everything that was not in keeping with "the gift of God" and the Eucharistic flesh of Christ.

NOTES

1. According to ancient chronicles, notably those of Eusebius and Jerome, Peter's immediate successor and Ignatius' predecessor was Evodius. It is not clear, however, when the actual title, "bishop," came into use. Ignatius may have been the first in Antioch to hold that title. But even without the title, Peter and Evodius had the equivalent role of leadership.

2. Ignatius' letter to the Romans was written at Smyrna (X, 1) on the ninth day prior to the kalends of September (X, 3), that is, on August 24. An old Antiochene calendar gave October 17 as the date of his martyrdom at Rome. His letters would thus have been written at the end of August and the beginning of September. See P. Th. Camelot, O.P., *Ignace d'Antioche, Polycarpe de Smyrne, Lettres, Martyre de Polycarpe*, 3rd edition (Paris: Cerf, 1958) 12.

3. For Ignatius' background in the Syrian and Hellenistic world of Antioch, see L. W. Barnard, "The Background of St. Ignatius of Antioch," *Vigiliae Christianae* 17 (1963) 193–206; D. S. Wallace-Hadrill, *Christian Antioch, A Study of Early Christian Thought in the East* (New York: Cambridge University Press, 1982) 1–5, 14–26; Glanville Downey, *A History of Antioch in Syria from Seleucus to the Arab Conquest* (Princeton: Princeton University Press, 1961) 202–219, 288–299.

We do not know precisely what led to the brief persecution in which Ignatius was arrested, condemned to death, and sent to Rome for execution. A number of factors, however, indicate how and why such a persecution might have arisen.

Maintaining good order at Antioch was critical for Trajan's position as emperor and for the well-being of the empire. Antioch was strategically situated as the capital of a frontier province, with respect to Rome's long-standing threat from the Parthian empire. Antioch served as the headquarters for Trajan's campaigns against the Parthians. With several Roman legions stationed there, Antioch could easily challenge Trajan's position as emperor should matters deteriorate.

Ignatius' letters show that the Christian community at Antioch was divided into different factions, making it prone to accusations of public disorder. In such a situation, the bishop of the Church would have been the prime target, even if he did make unity his primary objective.

4. For Ignatius' message concerning the Eucharist, see Virginia Corwin, *St. Ignatius and Christianity in Antioch* (New Haven: Yale University Press, 1960) 207–215; Cyril Charles Richardson, *The Christianity of Ignatius of Antioch* (New York: AMS Press, Inc., 1967) 55–59; Raymond Johanny, "Ignatius of Antioch," in Willy Rordorf, *The Eucharist of the Early Christians*, tran. Matthew J. O'Connell (New York: Pueblo Publishing Company, 1978) 48–70.

5. For a good introduction to Ignatius' letters, their text in Greek and a French translation, see Camelot, *Op. Cit.*; for an introduction and a translation into English, see J. B. Lightfoot, *The Apostolic Fathers* (Grand Rapids: Baker Book House, 1976) 53–88.

6. Towards the end of the letter to Polycarp, Ignatius indicates that he was unable to write to all the Churches because of his precipitous departure for Neapolis (VIII, 1). Troas, a Hellenistic city in the vicinity of ancient Troy, was the normal port in Asia Minor for the sea journey to Neapolis, the port of Philippi in Macedonia. From Neapolis, Ignatius proceeded to Philippi. The journey then continued by land along the *Via Egnatia* to Thessalonica and on to the Adriatic port of Durrhachium. From there he would sail to Brundisium for the land journey to Rome along the *Via Appia*.

7. Polycarp obtained copies of the letters from the Churches to whom Ignatius had written. Not enough time had elapsed to obtain a copy of the letter to the Romans. We assume that Polycarp retained the copies he collected and sent a further copy on to Philippi. The process provides a good example of how the letters

of Paul, the Gospels and other works in the New Testament were collected and disseminated.

8. At the time Polycarp wrote to the Church of Philippi, he had not yet received any news from Rome concerning Ignatius' martyrdom (Phil XIII, 2).

9. The order followed by modern publishers is that of Eusebius (*Ecclesiastical History* III, 36), whose first criterion was geographical, giving the four letters written at Smyrna before those written at Troas. The order within those groupings, like that of St. Paul's letters in the New Testament, seems to have been determined by length, from the letter to the Ephesians, by far the longest, to the letter to Magnesians, the next in length, to those to Trallians, Romans, Philadelphians and Smyrnians, roughly of the same length, and the letter to Polycarp, short and the only one written to an individual.

10. See Joseph A. Fitzmyer, S.J., "Introduction to the New Testament Epistles," *The New Jerome Biblical Commentary* (Englewood Cliffs, New Jersey: Prentice Hall, 1990) 768–771; William G. Doty, *Letters in Primitive Christianity,* Guides to Biblical Scholarship (Philadelphia: Fortress Press, 1973).

11. For an excellent presentation of Ignatius' use of Scripture and tradition and the relationship between these in Ignatius' letters, see Robert M. Grant, "Scripture and Tradition in Ignatius of Antioch," *After the New Testament* (Philadelphia: Fortress Press, 1967) 37–54.

12. We need to recognize the importance of memory and memorization in early Judaism and Christianity, indeed in any culture that is primarily oral. Written texts were necessary for communicating with those living at a distance and for preserving one's biblical heritage, but we must not imagine that each one remained bound to the written text.

13. Since in his humanity Jesus was Jewish, Ignatius' warning against Judaizing could have been understood as support for docetism. Hence his warning in X, 3 and XI. Avoiding Judaizing tendencies does not mean setting aside Jesus' humanity. Speaking of Jesus Christ does not imply Judaizing (X, 3). In Ignatius' time, Judaizing and docetism represented two poles, both of which had to be avoided.

14. It is in this context (XI) that Ignatius introduces a new term "Christianism" *(christianismos),* suggested by the already well-known term "Judaism" *(Ioudaismos).* Just as Judaism referred to the whole Jewish way of life, Christianism refers to the whole Christian way of life as flowing from the life and mission of Christ (see also Philad VI, 1).

15. Acts indicated that "it was at Antioch that the disciples were first called Christians" (11:26). Referring to "Christian nourishment," Ignatius, the bishop of Antioch, attests to the adjectival use of the term Christian *(christianos).* In the letter to the Magnesians, he also used the term Christianism *(christianismos,* XI; see also Philad VI, 1; see previous note). Such terms witness to an emerging Christian vocabulary.

16. Ignatius witnesses to the development of Christian doctrines along with Christian vocabulary, both out of need to distinguish what is authentically Christian from what is alien.

17. From Ignatius' letters, we discern an emerging structure of the Church, with Ephesus having a special standing among the Churches of Asia Minor, Antioch a certain eminence among the Churches of the eastern Mediterranean, and Rome a preeminence among all the Churches.

18. "In the place of sacrifice," literally "within the altar," is a symbolic expression for the community of sacrifice and the sacrificial event, in which the Church associates itself with the sacrifice of Christ.

19. Ignatius distinguishes between "the whole Church *(pasa he ekklesia),*" that is, the entire local Church, and "the catholic Church *(he katholike ekklesia)*" (Smyrn VIII, 2), the universal Church made up of local Churches established with their bishops everywhere, even "to the ends of the earth *(kata ta perata horisthentes)*" (Eph III, 2).

20. See E. LaVerdiere, "The Eucharist, Sacrament of the Transformation of the World," *Emmanuel* 99 (September 1993) 378–385.

21. Luke presented the primitive Christian community in Jerusalem as the ideal for all Christian communities.

11

The Food Called Eucharist:
The Eucharist in the Writings of St. Justin

With Ignatius of Antioch,
early in the second century,
Christians dealt with Eucharistic issues
internal to the Christian communities.
The Eucharist was part of Christianism.
With Justin Martyr,
in the middle of the second century,
Christians dealt with Eucharistic issues
arising from the world at large.
With Justin, the Eucharist became
a part of Christian philosophy.

Until Justin, Christianity was concerned mainly with internal matters. With Justin, Christianity took its place as an active player on the world stage.

For more than a century, Christianity was taken up primarily with preaching, initiating new members, catechizing, assembling as a Church, telling the gospel story, shaping identity, sorting out ambiguities, developing a sense of community, and establishing relationships among the various communities. Christianity also had to deal with heretical tendencies and to protect itself from social, cultural, and religious influences that were incompatible with the gospel.

It is in this world of internal concerns that the Eucharist emerged, took shape, and permeated the life of the Church, exercising a major formative influence. As the meaning and implications of Christ's life, mission, teaching, passion, and resurrection were spelled out, so were the meaning and implications of the Eucharist. The story is told in the New Testament and in early Christian writings such as the *Didache* and the letters of Ignatius of Antioch.

In its second century, Christianity became an active player, challenging as well as challenged, on the world stage. With that, its primary concerns shifted from internal to external matters. Internal concerns did not disappear. Preaching and catechesis, for example, were still important, but within a larger context, defined by Christianity's new stance toward the world. Christianity had entered the world of philosophy and apologetics. Its greatest spokesman was Justin, who was a philosopher, apologist, and martyr.

Christianity no longer needed to distinguish itself from Judaism. Separate histories and Christianity's success among Gentiles had moved them apart. Christianity now confronted Judaism as an equal player, a competitor in the interpretation of biblical prophecy.

Nor could Christianity be content with warding off negative cultural, social, and religious influences from its Gentile environment. It had to compete with philosophical schools and mystery cults, with which it was easily confused. In that greater world, Christianity had to present itself and account for itself. It also had to defend itself.

It is in this new world of philosophy and apologetics that the Eucharist was first described and explained for people who were not Christians. For Paul, the Eucharist was proclaimed as part of the gospel. For the Synoptic Gospels and for John, it was part of the Christian story. For Ignatius of Antioch, it was an integral part of Christianism. For Justin, the Eucharist was a major element in Christian philosophy. Like the rest of Christian philosophy, its reasonableness needed to be demonstrated.

As Christianity grew and became more prominent, rumors of its Eucharist, mostly sensational and scurrilous, spread through the population. Many discounted such rumors but did not understand what the Eucharist really was and what Christians did when they celebrated it. The Eucharist needed an apologist, one who could present it, describe it, and explain it. Justin, a lay person with philosophical credentials, took on the challenge.

Justin, Philospher and Apologist[1]

Justin was born in the reign of Trajan (98–117) between A.D. 100 and 110 at Flavia Neapolis, today's Nablus, in the heart of ancient Samaria.

As with Ignatius of Antioch, most of what we know about his life comes from his writings.

Justin was of mixed Greek and Roman ancestry. His family was not native to Samaria but settled there as colonists when Flavia Neapolis was established as a Roman colony in A.D. 72–73 in the aftermath of the First Jewish War (A.D. 66–73).[2] Like the city's other inhabitants, Justin's family received Roman citizenship.

As a young man, Justin pursued religious and philosophical truth, moving from teacher to teacher, beginning with a Stoic, transferring to a Peripatetic, going on to a Pythagorean, and finally settling with a Platonist whose teaching impressed him greatly. At the time, Justin thought he had reached the end of his quest.

Describing his philosophical journey in the *Dialogue with Trypho*, Justin dwelt at greater length on his experience as a Platonist: "Under him I forged ahead in philosophy and day by day I improved. The perception of incorporeal things quite overwhelmed me and the Platonic theory of ideas added wings to my mind, so that in a short time I imagined myself a wise man. So great was my folly that I fully expected immediately to gaze upon God, for this is the goal of Plato's philosophy."[3]

Justin was converted to Christianity during the reign of Hadrian (117–138) around the year 130, probably at Ephesus, as a result of a dialogue with an old man who told him about the ancient prophetic writings that "exalted God, the Father and Creator of all things, and made known Christ, His Son, who was sent by Him."[4] "My spirit," wrote Justin, "was immediately set on fire, and an affection for the prophets, and for those who are friends of Christ, took hold of me; while pondering on his words, I discovered that his was the only sure and useful philosophy."[5]

By A.D. 150, during the reign of Antoninus Pius (138–161), Justin had moved to Rome, where he founded a school of Christian philosophy. Using categories from Platonist philosophy, Justin presented the teaching of Jesus and Christianity as the fulfillment of Platonist philosophy as well as of Hebrew prophecy. In Justin's philosophical exposition on the *Logos*, the Platonist world of Ideas and the inspired word of God complemented one another, if not in a fully realized theology, at least in the beginnings of Christian thought.

Justin's most famous pupil was Tatian, who also took up Christian apologetics. Unlike his teacher, however, Tatian defended Christianity mainly by attacking Greek culture.

It was while at Rome that Justin wrote his three extant works, the *First Apology,* the *Second Apology,* written later but conceived as a supplement to the *First,* and the *Dialogue with Trypho,* all between 151 and 161.[6] Justin's teaching concerning the Eucharist is found in both the *First Apology* and the *Dialogue with Trypho.*

Justin was sentenced to death by Rusticus, the prefect of Rome, around A.D. 165 during the reign of Marcus Aurelius (161–180). According to the Acts of his martyrdom, Justin refused to sacrifice to the gods and was decapitated,[7] joining the growing list of martyrs for the faith.

The *First Apology*

Justin wrote the *First Apology* not long after he came to Rome (*circa* 150) and established his school of Christian philosophy. Like other philosophies, Christian philosophy was taught both as a system of thought and as a way of life.

In the Greco-Roman world, most philosophical systems, including the Platonist system from which Justin was converted, had a major religious component with implications for life and worship. For Justin, however, God was not just an idea, however exalted, but a personal being who revealed himself through the prophets and in the person of Jesus Christ, the definitive Word of God, God's *Logos* made flesh. Justin's philosophy was based on revelation. So was his *Apology.*

Justin addressed the *First Apology* "To the emperor Titus Aelius Adrianus Antoninus Pius Augustus Caesar," known to us as Antoninus Pius, "to his son Verissimus the philosopher," the future emperor Marcus Aurelius, whose original name was Verus, "to Lucius the philosopher, by birth son of Caesar and by adoption son of Pius, an admirer of learning," the future emperor Commodus, and "to the sacred Senate and to the whole Roman people."

Perhaps Justin hoped the *Apology* would reach the imperial family and obtain a favorable hearing, but as with most apologetics, the purpose was to bolster the faith of Christians who may have been wavering or confused by the arguments of others. It would also help them defend their faith against attacks in the public arena before civil authorities and other religious claims and philosophies. Addressing the petition to the emperor defined the context within which it would be read.

The *Apology* is a literary work but, as we expect from a teacher, its style remains close to an oral presentation. In this, the *Apology* resembles the letters of Paul, whose preaching remains just below the surface. Justin often has to provide a certain amount of background for his students. In part, this accounts for Justin's many digressions. Using Aristotle's standard, however, that "rhetoric is a counterpart of dialectic,"[8] Justin's dialectic or argumentative logic often overwhelms his rhetorical art of presentation.

Discerning even the general outline of the *First Apology* is no easy matter. The following attempt, however, may prove helpful.[9] Between the address (c. 1) and the close (c. 68) with the appended letter of Hadrian (c. 69), the *First Apology* unfolds in five sections, including

- an appeal for justice (c. 2),
- a response to slanders (cc. 3–12),
- arguments for the fundamental truth and value of Christianity (cc. 13–22),
- a more theological presentation (cc. 23–60),
- an account of the sacraments of baptism and the Eucharist (cc. 61–67).

It is in this fifth and last section that we find Justin's description of the Eucharist, first as a sacrament of initiation (c. 65) together with baptism (c. 61), then as celebrated in the weekly Sunday assembly (c. 67). He also provides some explanation regarding the food we call the Eucharist (c. 66).

The Eucharist in the *First Apology*

Justin's presentation concerning the Eucharist (cc. 65–67) is part of a larger section (cc. 61–67) introduced at the beginning of chapter 61: "Lest we be judged unfair in this exposition, we will not fail to explain how we consecrated ourselves to God when we were regenerated through Christ." The whole section (cc. 61–67) is thus added almost as an afterthought, or as an appendix, whose main purpose was to explain Christian religious practices that had been the object of gross accusations. Otherwise, Justin could have been accused of unfairness, avoiding matters that were problematic and embarrassing.

The Rites of Initiation

The section (cc. 61–67) describes the rites of Christian initiation (cc. 61, 65), provides explanatory comments regarding both baptism (c. 61) and the Eucharist (c. 66), shows their foundations in Scripture, the teaching of Christ and tradition (cc. 61, 66), distinguishes the Christian rites from pagan imitations (cc. 62–64), and speaks of practices that flow from Christian initiation, including the celebration of the Eucharist on the Day of the Sun (c. 67).

Like the *Didache*, Justin distinguishes the Sunday Eucharist (c. 67) from the special Eucharist celebrated after baptism as part of Christian initiation (cc. 65–66).[10] Unlike the *Didache*, he also shows how the two are related within the greater process of Christian life. To fully appreciate Justin's teaching on the Eucharist, it must be seen in the context of the whole section beginning with baptism (c. 61).

In the celebration of initiation, those who consecrate themselves to God are regenerated through Christ. The initiation thus has two complementary aspects: one active, consecration to God; and one passive, being regenerated through Christ.

To qualify for initiation, candidates had to be convinced and believe that "what we say and teach is the truth," and promise that they can live accordingly. Concretely, those to be initiated must have made the grade in a school of Christian philosophy, such as Justin's.

The purpose of Justin's school may consequently have been to prepare people for becoming Christians. If so, the content of the *First Apology* must reflect the teaching considered necessary for becoming a Christian in the mid-second century. Chapters 1 to 60 of the *First Apology* would thus parallel the *Didache*'s instruction on the two ways (cc. 1–6), which was transformed into a pre-baptismal instruction when the instruction on religious practices (cc. 7–10) was added.[11]

Justin's responsibility and that of his school was to instruct those inquiring or preparing to be Christians. It did not include their actual initiation. This could explain why Justin presented baptism and the Eucharist as a kind of appendix to the main part of the *Apology*.

Prayer and Fasting

The rites of initiation began with an instruction telling the candidates to prepare for baptism by prayer and fasting, asking God to forgive their past sins (c. 61). The length of this period of immediate preparation is not indicated, but we may assume it lasted at least one full day. The instruction in the *Didache* required a fast of one or two days (7:4). As in the *Didache* (7:4), the candidates were joined in their prayer and fasting by members of the community. From the beginning, the rites of initiation were a community event.

Baptism

For the actual baptism (c. 61), the candidates were led by members of the community to a place where there was water. On arriving, the candidates were brought to the water and baptized.[12] The baptismal regeneration took place in the same way those in the community had been baptized, that is, they were washed in the water *(to en to hudati tote loutron poiountai)* in the name of God, the Father and Lord of all, and of our Savior, Jesus Christ, and of the Holy Spirit.

The purpose of baptismal regeneration was to enter into the kingdom of God. For this, Justin refers to the teaching of Christ in John 3:3: "No one can see the kingdom of God without being born from above." The reason for baptizing with water was to be made clean of sins. For this, Justin refers to the prophetic exhortation and warning in Isaiah 1:16-20. The reason for the Trinitarian formula, with its reference to God as Father, was to indicate the source and nature of Christian regeneration. For this, Justin refers to apostolic teaching.

Justin viewed the central act of baptism as a symbolic washing away of sins (see 2 Pet 1:9), not as a drink of life-giving water (see John 4:7-15) or as a dying, being buried and rising with Christ (see Rom 6:3-11). "This washing," he says, "is called illumination *(photismos),*" since those who learn these things are spiritually illumined. By their first birth, Christians were children of necessity and ignorance. Baptismal regeneration made them children of free choice and knowledge. The baptismal experience was thus the climax of the teaching they received in their preparation for baptism.

The Eucharist

After the baptism, the newly baptized joined the community in a celebration of the Eucharist (c. 65). Members of the community had brought the candidates to a place where there was water (c. 61). After washing each one, they led the baptized to the place where those called "brothers and sisters" *(adelphoi)*[13] were assembled.

Those who were regenerated in the name of the Father, of the Son, and of the Holy Spirit were brothers and sisters to one another in the family of God, to whom they prayed as Father. The newly baptized were thus introduced into the community assembly of Christian brothers and sisters.

From Justin's description, it is clear that baptism and the Eucharist were celebrated in two different places. Baptism required water, normally flowing water. In Rome, this meant a pool or water from an aqueduct, such as the basin of a fountain with fresh, clean water. Dirty water would have been a poor symbol for cleansing. The baptismal area was not expected to accommodate the entire community. The

Eucharist, on the other hand, required a large reception room[14] or hall that was able to accommodate the whole assembly.

The purpose of the assembly was first to offer heartfelt prayer in common for the assembly and its members, for the newly baptized, who have now received illumination, and for all others, that is, for Christians everywhere. The baptismal assembly was thus aware of itself as a local community which is part of a larger, catholic, body of Christians.

The main intention of prayer was that those who had found the truth might by their actions earn recognition as good, law-abiding citizens and obtain eternal salvation. The ultimate concern of the Christians was for eternal salvation, but they also respected the temporal and social order of the Roman empire.

Once the prayers were completed, members of the assembly greeted one another with a kiss. After this, bread and a cup of water and wine *(poterion hudatos kai kramatos)* were brought to the president of the community *(to proestoti ton adelphon).* Justin refers to the president of the community with a very general term *(proestos)*, which in itself does not mean "presbyter" or "bishop" but can refer to one (see 1 Tim 5:17).

No mention is made of the reading of Scripture or of a homily by the president. The Eucharist, however, is very closely connected with baptism as part of a single celebration of initiation. It may be, therefore, that the opening instruction to the candidates and the subsequent period of prayer and fasting were viewed as a liturgy of the Word for the entire celebration.

Taking *(labon)* the bread and the cup of water and wine, the president "offers praise and glory to the Father of all, through the name of the Son and of the Holy Spirit" and offers lengthy thanksgiving *(eucharistian)* because the Father has found the community worthy of these gifts. Like the baptismal invocation over the candidates, the prayer offering the bread and the cup was Trinitarian, showing the close relationship between the Eucharist and baptism. Within this Trinitarian and general Eucharistic framework, the president enjoyed considerable latitude regarding the prayer's content, the wording, and length.

When the president completed the prayers and the thanksgiving *(tas euchas kai ten eucharistian)*, all the people present spoke their assent saying, "Amen." In an explanatory note, Justin indicates that the "Amen" is a Hebrew word meaning "So be it *(Genoito)*." Justin's description thus distinguishes between the role of the president, who alone speaks the Eucharistic prayer, and the rest of the assembly, who assent to the prayer with their "Amen."

After the president's prayer of thanksgiving and the people's assent, "they whom we call deacons *(diakonoi)*" give to each of those present to partake *(metalabein)* of the Eucharisticized bread *(apo tou eucharistethentos artou)* and the wine and water, and they bring them to those not present. The deacons represent a special office in the community. With regard to the Eucharist, it is they, not the president, who distributed Communion to the assembly,[15] now including the newly baptized, and who brought Communion to those who for some reason were prevented from being there.

Justin's reference to "Eucharisticized bread" represents a development in Eucharistic terminology, now focusing on the Eucharistic bread as well as on the Eucharistic prayer, Eucharistic acts, the Eucharistic event, and the Eucharistic assembly. This new focus allowed Christians to think of the Eucharist as intended for those also who were not able to be present at the celebration, and even as transcending the limited time of the celebration.

The Food Called Eucharist

Justin began by describing the Eucharist celebrated with baptism as a rite of initiation (c. 65). He now explains the meaning of Eucharistic food and how it came from Jesus (c. 66).

After describing "the washing" of those regenerated as Christians, Justin had indicated that "this washing *(loutron)* is called illumination *(photismos)*" (c. 61). After describing the baptismal meal with the Christian assembly, he indicates that "this food *(trophe)* is called by us Eucharist *(eucharistia)*" (c. 66). He had just said that "those called by us deacons *(diakonoi)*" distribute "the eucharisticized bread and wine and water" (c. 65).

"Food," like "washing," was an ordinary descriptive term understood by all. This food, however, and the washing were not ordinary food and washing, and those who distributed the food were not ordinary "servants." For that reason, Christians called the food "Eucharist," the washing "illumination," and gave special meaning to the term "servant," aptly rendered by the word "deacon."

Later, Justin would do the same for "the memoirs" of the apostles, "which are called Gospels *(euaggelia)*" (c. 66). "Memoirs" *(apomnemoneumata)*, like "food" and "washing," was an ordinary descriptive term understood by all. The apostolic memoirs, however, were not ordinary memoirs. To indicate their special nature, Christians called them "Gospels."

Among Christians, terms like "illumination," "deacon," "Eucharist," and "Gospels" could be taken for granted. Members of the community had personal experience of them and knew what they meant. Outside the community, however, such terms had to be explained. Granted that outsiders would not understand, at least they would not misunderstand them.

To understand, one had to join the Christian community in celebrating the Eucharist. But for that one would have to believe what Christians teach as true, be washed for the forgiveness of sins and regeneration, and live in the manner Christ handed down. The Eucharist, which was not received as common bread and common drink, was limited to those who fulfilled the conditions for baptism and were baptized.

To show the special nature of Eucharistic food, Justin offered the following comparison:

"We are taught that
    just as
        Jesus Christ,
        made flesh (*sarkapoietheis*)
        through the word of God (*dia logou theou*),
        took both flesh and blood
        for our salvation,
    so also
        the food,
        made Eucharist (*eucharistetheisan*)
        through the word of prayer (that comes) from him (Jesus)
            (*di' euches logou tou par' autou*)
        is the flesh and blood
            of that incarnate (*sarkopoiethentos*) Jesus
        from which our blood and flesh
            receive transforming nourishment (*kata metabolen trephontai*)."

The above translation and arrangement of the text highlight the parallel elements in Justin's five-point comparison. The food is parallel to the person of Jesus Christ, the Eucharist to the incarnation, the word of prayer coming from Jesus to the word of God, the Eucharistic flesh and blood to Jesus' incarnate flesh and blood, and our salvation to the transformation of our own flesh and blood.

The "word of prayer (coming) from him (Jesus)" is the liturgical prayer which came from Jesus through the apostles who were commanded to hand it down *(paredokan)* in memoirs that are called "Gospels." Continuing, Justin relates Jesus' "word of prayer" to the community's traditional liturgical formula:

"Jesus,
taking bread
and having given thanks,
said,
  'Do this for my memorial,
  this is my body';
and likewise
taking the cup
and giving thanks
he said,
  'This is my blood.'"

Very likely, the liturgical formula itself was more extensive. The only elements retained have a counterpart in Justin's comparison of the Eucharist with the incarnation. The bread and the cup refer to "the food," giving thanks to Jesus' "word of prayer," and the words "this is my body" and "this is my blood" to Jesus' flesh and blood. The command, "Do this for my memorial," shows the link between the words that came from Jesus and the "word of prayer" used in the liturgy.

Justin's comparison of the Eucharist with the incarnation was inspired by John 6, whose emphasis is on Jesus' flesh *(sarx)* and blood *(haima)*. The liturgical formula is a conflation of elements from the Synoptic Gospels, whose emphasis is on Jesus' body *(soma)* rather than flesh *(sarx)*.

The difference suggests that Justin and his school turned to the synoptics and the liturgy for historical questions regarding the origins and handing down of the Eucharist. For theological understanding, however, they turned to John and the Johannine tradition, as did Ignatius of Antioch.

Justin concludes the explanation, stating that Jesus gave this command exclusively to the apostles. What people did in the mysteries of Mithra was a demonic imitation, using bread and a cup of water in their rites of initiation and including invocations "which you either know or can learn."

Perhaps Justin's readers did know or could learn about the mysteries of Mithra. More likely they neither did nor could, not without being initiated in them. Justin's closing remark was thus a challenge. He had spoken openly, revealing and explaining what Christians did in their rites of initiation. Could the cult Mithra do the same?

The Sunday Eucharist

Justin's main presentation on the Eucharist was as a rite of initiation (cc. 65–66) accompanying baptism (c. 61). This special focus came from the apologetical need to distinguish the Eucharist from Mithraic rites of initiation. In the mid-second century, the cult of Mithra had become very popular. As a major rival for Christianity in the Roman world, it could not be ignored.[16]

Thanks to this apologetical concern, Justin's presentation highlighted not just the Eucharist, but its most important celebration. A baptismal Eucharist required a long preparation for the candidates. Together with the period of prayer and fasting, its celebration lasted at least two, perhaps three, days. Such a Eucharist was not celebrated very often, perhaps not more than once a year.

For those who were regenerated and introduced to the community, it was the event of a lifetime. For the community, it marked a high point on the Christian calendar. It comes as no surprise that such a Eucharist provided inspiration and a basic point of reference for other Christian events, including the weekly Sunday celebration of Eucharist, indeed for all of Christian life (c. 67).

Jesus commanded the apostles: "Do this in remembrance of me." Christians fulfilled his command in their baptismal Eucharist. From then on, they constantly reminded one another of these things, doing everything they did in remembrance of Jesus, the rich helping the poor, all living in unity, constantly blessing the maker of everything for everything received through his Son Jesus Christ and through the Holy Spirit. All, from city and countryside, assembled in common *(epi to auto)* on Sunday, the day called "Of the Sun" *(te tou heliou legomene hemera)*.

The whole of the Christian life was lived "in remembrance of him," which is done by the faithful by recalling the celebration in which they were regenerated and first joined the assembly to celebrate the Eucharist.

Justin indicates that for the most part the Sunday Eucharist was celebrated just like the baptismal Eucharist. Some things, however, were special to it. Notably, before the prayers were offered, someone read from the memoirs of the apostles or the writings of the prophets, "so long as there was time," and the president admonished and exhorted everyone to imitate the good things they heard. Besides these things, the Sunday celebration of the Eucharist included a collection, placed in the keeping of the president to help all those in need.

Justin's description of the celebration concludes by explaining why Christians hold their common assembly on the day of the Sun. Sunday is the first day of the week; the day on which God, transforming the darkness and matter, created the world. It is also the day our Savior Jesus Christ arose from the dead. They crucified him on the day before that of Saturn. The day after Sunday he appeared to his apostles and disciples and taught them "the things which we have passed on to you also for consideration" (c. 67).

The *Dialogue with Trypho*

Like Justin's *First Apology*, the *Dialogue with Trypho* is an apology. Its form, however, is different. The *First Apology* has the literary form of a discourse. The *Dialogue with Trypho* has the literary form of a dialogue, one which is well known especially from the *Dialogues* of Plato.

This difference between the *First Apology* and the *Dialogue with Trypho* should not be stressed. Reading the *First Apology*, one senses that it comes close to the form of a dialogue and could easily be transformed into one. Reading the *Dialogue with Trypho*, the reverse is true. The dialogue format seems artificial and could easily be transformed into a discourse.

The *Dialogue with Trypho* was written after the *First* and the *Second Apology*.[17] Addressed to a man named Marcus Pompeius,[18] it reports on a two-day dialogue with a Jew named Trypho[19] that had taken place some twenty-five years earlier, shortly after the Second Jewish War (132–135).[20] According to Eusebius, this two-day dialogue took place at Ephesus.[21]

As presented by Justin, the *Dialogue* is a literary dialogue, based on a real dialogue but benefitting no doubt from a number of other and more recent conversations and discussions with Jews as well as from Justin's repeated presentation of it in the course of his teaching. Justin himself must have been aware of this since at one point he has Trypho suggest, "You seem to have debated with many persons on every possible topic and consequently are ready to answer any of my questions" (c. 50). As a rhetorical work, we may consider the *Dialogue with Trypho* as summing up Justin's apologetical teaching regarding Jews and the interpretation of Scripture.

Like the *First Apology*, the *Dialogue* is filled with long digressions and is difficult to outline. This time, however, we do have the help of

Trypho's interventions, often indicating the transition from one section to another.

The introduction (cc. 1–10) shows how Justin met Trypho (c. 1) and told him about the philosophical journey that led him to Christianity (cc. 2–8). After Trypho's response, the subject of dialogue is determined (cc. 9–10). The conclusion speaks of their mutual satisfaction and amicable parting (c. 142).

The body of the dialogue (cc. 11–141) can be divided into three parts, showing

- how the Mosaic Law and the Jewish practices have been abrogated by the definitive Law of Christ, the gospel for all human beings (cc. 11–31);
- how Jesus is the Christ of God with divine and human origins (cc. 32–110);
- how the Gentiles were called to conversion, repented, and became part of the new covenant (cc. 111–141).

The *Dialogue* refers four times to the Eucharist, once in the introduction (c. 10), twice in Part II (cc. 41 and 70), and once in Part III (c. 117). While none of these approaches the historical value and theological reflection of the *First Apology,* each enlarges our understanding, especially concerning the Eucharist as sacrificial.

The Eucharist in the *Dialogue with Trypho*

The Eucharist is first referred to at the end of the introduction (cc. 9–10) where significant issues for dialogue are sorted out (c. 10). Justin asks Trypho and his friends what it is to which they object. Is it simply that Christians do not observe the Law, circumcise the flesh, and keep the Sabbath? Does it have to do with practices and morals? Justin brings this last up in case they were among those who think Christians eat human flesh and indulge their passions once they have eaten. Or is it that Christians hold doctrines and opinions that Trypho and his friends consider false?

Trypho dismisses the second charge, regarding the Eucharist and behavior at the Eucharistic assembly as coming from the rabble and too repulsive to be taken seriously. Bringing it up, however, does help to appreciate the popular prejudice regarding Christians and their Eucharistic assembly. For outsiders, the gospel of the word made flesh, liturgical expressions such as, "This is my body" and "This is my blood," the practice of Communion, the kiss of peace, and the openness of the Christians' assembly to women as well as men suggested infanticide, cannibalism, and debauchery.

In the *First Apology,* Justin referred to much the same accusations against the followers of Simon Magus of Samaria and Marcion of Pontus, saying, "We do not know whether they are guilty of sexual promiscuity and anthropophagy."

Such accusations say nothing about the Eucharist itself but do say a lot about the suspicions, fear, and hostility it could arouse among the many who had no personal contact with Christians and knew nothing of their actual practices. The fact that these accusations against Christians focused on the Eucharist reflects its central position in Christian life as well as its countercultural character.

In Part II of the *Dialogue* (cc. 32–110), Justin turns to the Eucharist on two occasions, first in a section devoted to showing that Jesus, who was crucified, was the Christ of God (cc. 40–47), second in one showing that Christ, who is both human and divine, is the eternal Son of God made man through a virgin (cc. 48–73).

Justin had just shown how, according to the prophets, the Messiah would suffer, die, ascend into heaven, and come again to reign eternally over all the nations (cc. 32–39). He then has to show that Jesus, whom Christians claim was crucified and ascended into heaven, is the Christ spoken of in the Scriptures as the Christ of God (cc. 39–47).

The reference to the Eucharist is in chapter 41. Just as the lamb sacrificed at Passover was a type of Christ (c. 40), the offering of fine flour for the purification of one who has been healed of leprosy (Lev 14:10) was a type of the Eucharistic bread (c. 41).

Christ had commanded them to offer this Eucharistic bread as a memorial of the passion he endured for all who are cleansed from sin and in thanksgiving to God for creating the world and all that is in it, for the human race and saving us from the sin in which we were born, and for the destruction of the powers of evil through him who suffered according to his will. These intentions for thanksgiving are typical of what could be expected as the Eucharistic prayer offered by the president of the assembly (see *First Apology,* cc. 65 and 67).

Referring to Malachi 1:10-12, he then shows how the Eucharist fulfills the prophet's announcement that God's name would be great among the Gentiles, who in every place would offer incense to his name, as well as a clean oblation. Malachi's announcement is fulfilled in the Eucharistic bread *(artos tes eucharistias)* and the Eucharistic cup (*poterion tes eucharistias*). The passage is important for focusing attention on the Eucharist as a sacrifice, an aspect that will be further developed in chapter 117.

The second reference to the Eucharist in Part II is in chapter 70, where again Justin dealt with Mithraic imitations of the Eucharist, this time by mimicking Isaiah's reference to bread in Isaiah 33:13-19. Justin responds: "It is quite evident that this prophecy also alludes to the bread which our Christ gave us to offer in remembrance of the body which he assumed for the sake of those who believe in Him, for whom he also suffered, and also to the cup which he taught us to offer in the Eucharist, in commemoration of his blood." The Eucharist is a memorial of Christ's incarnation as well as of his suffering and death.

Part III of the *Dialogue* (cc. 111–141) shows how the conversion of the Gentiles, like the new law (Part I) and Jesus Christ (Part II), was prefigured and announced in the Old Testament. In this new context, the *Dialogue* refers to the Eucharist for a fourth and last time (c. 117). The passage presents the Eucharist as a sacrifice of prayer and thanksgiving offered by people of every race and nation.

The argument begins in chapters 115 and 116 with two passages from Zechariah, an exhortation and a vision of Joshua the high priest. The exhortation is to rejoice. The Lord is coming to dwell in the midst of Zion. Many nations will join the Lord and they shall be his people (Zech 2:10-13). The vision then shows Joshua the high priest standing before the angel of the Lord with the devil at his right hand to oppose him. The angel speaks of Joshua as a brand snatched from the fire to rebuke the devil (Zech 3:1-2).

For Justin, the vision of Joshua the high priest, whose name in Greek was Jesus, announces what Jesus would do "as our priest and God and Christ, the Son of the universal Father."

As the vision continues, Joshua, who was dressed in dirty clothes, symbolic of his sins, has the dirty clothes removed and is clothed in splendid robes (Zech 3:3-5). Justin applies the event to all those who believe in Christ, the High Priest, the one who was crucified. Through grace conferred by Jesus, Gentiles have cast off their garments of sin and are dressed in new, Christian, garments.[22]

Like Joshua, Christians have been snatched from the fire of the devil's torment and have been set on fire by the word of Jesus' call, making them a true priestly family of God, that "in every place among the Gentiles pure and pleasing sacrifices might be offered to him."

With this reference to sacrifices, Justin returns to Malachi 1:10-12, the passage referred to in chapter 41 (c. 117). The Eucharist was indeed a

perfect and acceptable sacrifice, offered by Gentiles of every race —
"whether barbarians, or Greeks, or persons called by any other name,
nomads, or vagabonds, or herdsmen dwelling in tents" — who became
Christians in every part of the world (c. 117). Malachi's prophecy was
realized in the prayers Christians offer in thanksgiving for the food
commemorating the passion which the Son of God endured for us.

NOTES

1. For a brief synthesis of Justin's life and work, see Edward Rochie Hardy, "The First Apology of Justin, the Martyr," *Early Christian Fathers*, ed. Cyril C. Richardson (New York: Macmillan Publishing Company, 1970) 228–231; also L. W. Barnard, *Justin Martyr, His Life and Thought* (Cambridge: At the University Press, 1967) 1–13.

2. For the history of Flavia Neapolis, see Itzhak Magen, "Neapolis," *The New Encyclopedia of Archaeological Excavations in the Holy Land*, Vol. 4 (New York: Simon and Schuster, 1993) 1354–1359.

3. *Dialogue with Trypho*, 2. Here, as for other passages from the *Dialogue*, as well as from the *First Apology*, the translation is that of Thomas B. Falls, *Writings of Saint Justin Martyr* (New York: Christian Heritage, Inc., 1948).

4. *Dialogue with Trypho*, 7. Justin tells the story of his conversion as a dialogue within a dialogue in chapters 3–7.

5. *Dialogue with Trypho*, 8. Justin's report compresses the period of time it took to get to know the "friends of Christ" and to ponder his words.

6. See L. W. Barnard, *Justin Martyr, His Life and Thought* (Cambridge: At the University Press, 1967) 19–21, for the *First* and *Second Apology*, and 23–24, for the *Dialogue*.

7. Ibid., 5–6.

8. Aristotle, *The "Art" of Rhetoric*, i. 1. 1.

9. For an alternative outline, which may also prove helpful, see Edward Rochie Hardy, *Op. Cit.*, 236–237.

10. The *Didache* describes the initiation or baptismal Eucharist in cc. 9 and 10, and the Eucharist celebrated weekly on the Lord's Day in chapter 14.

11. See LaVerdiere, "On the Lord's Day: The Eucharist in the *Didache*," *Emmanuel* (October 1994) 458–459.

12. As Edward Rochie Hardy points out, later editors, influenced by the modern practice of individual baptism, emended some of the plurals in Justin's description to the singular. In the time of Justin, however, group baptism was the rule (*Op. Cit.*, 282–283, n. 71).

13. In Greek, as in many other languages, the masculine plural, in this case *adelphoi*, is inclusive when referring to a community of brothers (masculine) and sisters (feminine).

14. In a large Roman home or apartment, the principal reception room was a dining room, as it was in a Greek home. So long as the Eucharist was celebrated as a full meal, this is where it was celebrated. The Eucharist described by Justin, however, was no longer a full meal but a symbolic meal. It could therefore be cele-

brated in any convenient space where Christians could assemble undisturbed and the mystery of the Eucharist would be respected.

15. According to Acts, those selected and appointed to assure the service *(diakonia)* in the assembly at Jerusalem (6:1-7) fulfilled much the same function.

16. See Franz Cumont, *The Mysteries of Mithra* (New York: Dover Publications, Inc., 1903, 1956) and M. J. Vermaseren, *Mithriaca I, The Mithaeum at S. Maria Capua Vetere* (Leiden: E. J. Brill, 1971).

17. The *Dialogue with Trypho* refers to the *First* and *Second Apology* in c. 120: "'For I was not afraid either of any one of my people when I wrote an address to Caesar, and affirmed that they were mistaken in trusting Simon Magus in their nation, and in placing him above every principality, authority and power'" (see *I Apology*, c. 26; *II Apology*, c. 15).

18. The *Dialogue* must have begun by addressing the work to Marcus Pompeius and saying at least something about him. Unfortunately, the first page of the manuscript is lost. The extant text first refers to an addressee in c. 8 but does not name him until c. 141.

19. Nothing is known about the Jew named Trypho except Justin's presentation of him as a perfect gentleman, at once urbane and irenic, who conceded far more in argument than is realistically likely. Some suggest that Trypho is the same as Rabbi Tarphon, a prominent early second-century teacher mentioned in the Mishnah. Historically, that seems unlikely, but it would certainly have been to Justin's rhetorical advantage to evoke the prominent rabbi.

20. The War is referred to in cc. 1 and 9.

21. *Ecclesiastical History* 4, 18, 6.

22. In the ancient world, clothing was an apt symbol of a person's identity. Inspired by Paul, who spoke of baptism as putting on Christ (see Gal 3:27), the early Christians saw clothing, putting off old and soiled clothing, and putting on new, clean clothing, as a set of symbols for baptism.

Conclusion

We began by asking how Christians referred to the Eucharist before it had a name. We saw how names for the Eucharist came to be and how important they are. We continued by asking how the Eucharist was celebrated at the very beginning when there were no liturgical formulas relating it to Jesus' Last Supper. We reflected on how liturgical formulas came to be and what difference they make.

We then examined the Eucharist in the New Testament, in Paul's letters, primarily in 1 Corinthians, in the Gospels of Mark, Matthew, Luke, and John, and in the Acts of the Apostles. We also examined the Eucharist in the *Didache,* in the letters of Ignatius of Antioch, and in the work of Justin Martyr.

What then can we say about the Eucharist? What can we say about its place in the Church during the years we covered, from *circa* A.D. 30 to 155? Can we speak of a history of the Eucharist in the New Testament and the early Church? Or must we speak, rather, of histories of the Eucharist? And even then, do we have the data to put together any history at all, whether in the singular or in the plural?

Our texts from the New Testament and the early Church reveal a great "pluralism in Eucharistic thought and practice."[1] Each text comes from a particular community, with a setting, history, and tradition of its own. Each text witnesses to the history of the Eucharist in a particular Church. Even so, I believe it is possible to speak of the history of the Eucharist in the New Testament and the Early Church.

Much is at stake. As presented in the New Testament, the Eucharist is both a source of inspiration and guidance for today. Works from the early Church that are not part of the New Testament show how the New Testament heritage was understood and applied to new situations. Do the stories, traditions, and reflections from those early years witness only to diversity? Or do they also witness to unity? Do they then reveal unity in the midst of diversity? If so, it is possible to speak of the history of the Eucharist in the New Testament and the early Church.

At the very beginning, right after Jesus' passion and resurrection, there was but one community, and its Eucharistic meal was one. In that community, there must have been differences in attitude, participation and understanding of the Eucharist. In that context, however, the proper word to describe those differences is not "diversity" but "complementarity."

As, through the years, Christianity spread to new places and peoples, we do need to speak of diversity. From what we see in the New Testament and other early Christian works, however, the tendency was not centrifugal but centripetal. This is the tendency we see in the sharing of the Pauline letters among the communities, and their eventual collection into a body of letters. The same would be true for the Gospels and eventually for the entire New Testament. Very early on, each particular tradition became common property. In that context, it is more appropriate to speak of complementarity than mere diversity.

We also note a great respect for tradition, reflected, for example, in the liturgical formulas and the retelling of various Eucharistic stories. It is not in relation to tradition, however, that I speak of centripetal versus centrifugal, but in relation to the communities among themselves, in the way they adapted tradition and gave it life in new situations. In that context, noting the obvious diversity means recognizing that the diverse expressions of tradition complemented one another in the various communities. The *Didache* is a case apart. Here is a community that clung to its tradition so rigidly that it gradually drifted away from the others.

While respecting the diversity of texts, communities, and situations, therefore, a number of generalizations may contribute to the history of the Eucharist in the New Testament and the early Church. I shall focus on the Eucharist in relation to ecclesiology, Christology, and liturgy. Within those areas, it is also possible to account for various lines of development.

The Eucharist and the Church

From the very beginning, there was no separating the Eucharist from the Church and the local assembly. That is one of the most important things we learn from the Eucharist in the New Testament and the early

Church. The Eucharist, the sacrament of the body of Christ, makes and nourishes the Church as Christ's body. That was true from the beginning when Christ first appeared *(ophthe)* to the disciples at a meal, when the Eucharist did not yet have a name or a liturgical formula. Christ's presence transformed their gathering into an assembly *(ekklesia)* and their meal into the Eucharist *(eucharistia)*.

As long as Christians have assembled as a Church *(en ekklesia)*,[2] welcoming one another as children of God *(huioi tou theou)*, as brothers and sisters in Christ *(en Christo;* see Gal 3:26-28), the Eucharist has been part of their life. The Eucharist is the first and most distinctive expression of the Church *qua* Church. The proper adjective, *epiousios,* says as much about the distinctiveness of the Church as about its distinctive meal.

Conceived in Jesus' ministry and born in his passion and resurrection, the Eucharist and the Church were also one in every phase of their development. From the very beginning, the Eucharist was the primary sacrament of the Church's life in the world. And so it remains today. Consequently, to know the Eucharist in the New Testament and the early Church, one has only to look at the composition and actual life of the Church. Vice versa, to know the Church, one has only to look at the way it celebrates the Eucharist.

The Eucharist is like a mirror which images the life of the Church, and which reflects its qualities as well as its defects. At Corinth, the Christians assembled as a Church but did not act and relate to one another as a Church. Their supper made a mockery of the Lord's Supper (1 Cor 11:17-22).

The Eucharist is a constitutive aspect of the Church. That is why Luke was able to include the Eucharist, "the breaking of the bread," among the four visible marks of the Church: "They devoted themselves to the teaching of the apostles *(he didache ton apostolon)* and to the communal life *(he koinonia)*, to the breaking of the bread *(he klasis tou artou)*[3] and to the prayers *(hai proseuchai)*" (Acts 2:42).

That is also why the composition of a community and the circumstances in which it lives affects the community's celebration of the Eucharist. The community reflected and addressed in Matthew's Gospel had a strong Jewish background. It was very different from the Lukan communities, which were of Gentile background. This difference showed itself in the Matthean community's celebration of the Eucharist. Reporting Jesus' Eucharistic words at the Last Supper, Matthew related the Eucharist to the forgiveness of sins (Matt 26:29).

In the same way, the Johannine community was very different from the Markan communities, as was its celebration of the Eucharist.

That is also why any problems, disputes, and dissensions in the Church are reflected in its celebration of the Eucharist and its prophetic catechesis. Consider the way Paul wrote of the Eucharist in his admonition to the Corinthians (1 Cor 10:1–11:34). For Christians in the Pauline communities, a major challenge was transcending their ethnic origins and any differences in social status: "There is neither Jew nor Greek, there is neither slave nor free person, there is not male and female; for you are all one in Christ Jesus" (Gal 3:28). Being or not being Christian did not come from a person's birth; it came from baptism (Gal 3:27) at which time the convert died to their previous existence and they began "living for God in Christ Jesus" (Rom 6:1-11).

The same is true today at a time when the greatest challenges to being a Church are also those of celebrating the Eucharist, Christ's body given to form the body of Christ. At the same time, some of the differences among today's Christians, which must be transcended, are different. The differences that divide us today are related to a person's race, ethnic background, sex, culture, nationality, and economic class. They may result from a person's caste or tribal origin. But whatever our differences, the challenge to be one in Christ is the same. And the successfulness with which we meet that challenge shows when we assemble and celebrate the Eucharist.

The relationship between the Eucharist and the Church also helps account for the diversity in Eucharistic understanding and practice. At the very beginning, when the Church was basically a movement dedicated to Christ's mission, and as it developed into missionary communities, the Eucharist was bound to be an evangelical, missionary event, proclaiming "the death of the Lord until he comes" (1 Cor 11:26).

Later, when Church communities developed needs of their own, the Eucharistic assembly addressed those needs ministerially. In Jerusalem, this meant attending to widows who were of Greek-speaking background as well as those who were Hebrew-speaking (Acts 6:1-7). For Priscilla and Aquila, it meant offering hospitality to Paul (Acts 18:1-4) and instructing someone who had been formed in the Way of the Lord but knew nothing of Christian baptism (Acts 18:24-26).

When the Church understood itself as a communion of communities, transcending every local community, the Eucharist was understood as a celebration of the whole Church symbolically gathered for one large banquet. We see this, for example, in Mark's stories of Jesus breaking the bread for crowds of five thousand and four thousand (Mark 6:34-44; 8:1-9). As the Church moved beyond Judaism, becoming what Luke called "the Way" (*he hodos*, Acts 18:25-26; 24:14), the Eucharist was celebrated as a meal on "the Way." When, with Matthew, the community of disciples saw themselves as "the Church" (*he ekklesia*, Matt 16:18), the Eucharist was celebrated as the sacrament of "the Church."

When a community, such as that of the *Didache* was unable to transcend its origins in Judaism and became increasingly exclusive, it separated itself from other Christian communities. Its "Eucharist" ceased to celebrate its communion with all those who were in Christ.

Later, Ignatius of Antioch referred to the Church as "the catholic Church (*he katholike ekklesia*, Ephesians 3:2; Smyrnians 8:2). He also described the beliefs and way of life of the catholic Church as "Christianism" (*Christianismos*, Magnesians 10:3; Philadelphians 6:1). This new term, "Christianism," was inspired by an existing term, "Judaism" (*Ioudaismos*), describing the beliefs and the way of life of Jewish people at least from the end of the second century B.C. (1 Macc 2:21; Gal 1:13, 14). With Ignatius, the Eucharist was seen as an expression of unity with the catholic Church and as an essential element in Christianism.

Finally, "Christianism" gave rise to a Christian philosophy, in the school and work of Justin Martyr, challenging other religious philosophies in the Greco-Roman world. With Justin, the Eucharist became part of a way of life, one to be examined, reflected upon, and defended in the public forum. Justin was primarily an apologist. When the Eucharist was misunderstood or attacked, he became the first apologist of the Eucharist.

The Eucharist and Christology

Inseparable from the Church, the Eucharist is also inseparable from the person of Christ. That, too, was true from the very beginning, when Jesus the risen Lord appeared (*ophthe*) to the disciples shortly after his passion and resurrection. Every work we examined, save for the *Didache*, showed great Christological awareness and concern. The way people viewed Jesus and his mission determined their view of the Eucharist.

The early Christians associated the Eucharist with Jesus of Nazareth and his ministry in Galilee, with Jesus as risen Lord, living and present to them, and with Jesus, the Christ, who suffered and rose from the dead. This triple awareness led them to present the Eucharist as "the breaking of the bread," a sharing event inspired by Jesus, as "the Lord's Supper," a banquet at the table of the Lord, and as the memorial of Christ's passion and resurrection.

The memorial of Christ's death and resurrection forms the core of each liturgical formula, from the one Paul quoted in 1 Corinthians 11:23-25 to the one Justin referred to in his *First Apology* 66. From one point of view, the differences among the formulas are extremely important. They bring out the riches of the Eucharist and how it related to different pastoral situations. As such they provide an index of the Church's development. They show how the Church responded to local challenges and how various Churches related to one another. Churches that shared the same Eucharistic tradition were related to one another.

From another point of view, however, the similarities among the formulas are even more striking. All the Churches celebrated basically the same Eucharist. The early Churches had a great sense of apostolic tradition, nurturing in them fidelity to Jesus and what he did when he broke bread with his disciples, especially at the Last Supper. Jesus' command, "Do this in remembrance of me," whether expressed or implied, was part of the tradition guiding each local Church in its celebration of the Eucharist. However diverse the development of its Eucharistic practice, each Church sought to fulfill Jesus' command.

The one exception among the works we examined was the *Didache*, which associated its "Eucharist" with Jesus of Nazareth, but not with Jesus as the risen Lord who, as the Christ, suffered, died, and rose from the dead. The community of the *Didache* did not celebrate the Eucharist in memory of Christ's passion and resurrection. With this Christological deficiency it could not transcend its Jewish identity. There is no living as a Church or understanding the Church apart from the dying and rising of Christ. Nor is there celebrating and understanding the Eucharist apart from Christ's dying and rising.

There are situations, of course, where it was necessary to emphasize one Christological aspect more than another. Paul, for example, did not emphasize the historical Jesus save in relation to "the night he was handed over" (1 Cor 11:23). He emphasized the person of the Lord Jesus and Christ's passion and resurrection, achieving a remarkable synthesis of the two in 1 Corinthians 11:23-26.

To highlight the relationship between the Eucharist and the inclusive nature of the Church — Jew and Gentile, male and female — Mark situated his second story of Jesus breaking the bread after "three days," evoking Christ's resurrection and the source of the Church's universality (Mark 8:1-9). He thus showed how the invitation to Eucharist was meant for all.

Luke related the Eucharist to Jesus as a prophet, as the Christ and as the Lord. Through a history of meals with Jesus, he began by relating the Eucharist to the prophetic challenges of Jesus' mission and ministry. At the Last Supper he related it to the challenges of Jesus the Christ. In two post-Easter meals, he related the Eucharist to Jesus as risen Lord. The relation between the three, Jesus as prophet, the Christ and the Lord are shown in the story of the disciples of Emmaus (Luke 24:13-35).

John, the theologian of the Word made flesh, went further. While keeping his focus on Jesus' hour (John 2:4), that is the hour "to pass from this world to the Father" (John 13:1), John emphasized the identity of Jesus as the gift of God, indeed as "I AM," present to God's people, nourishing them sacramentally with his flesh and blood (John 6). John's Gospel responded to the tendencies some had to view Jesus merely as the awaited prophet Moses had announced.

Ignatius of Antioch would develop John's Christology even further, responding to those who denied that Jesus was truly human. If Jesus was not born, taking mortal, human flesh, neither did he die, and if he did not die, neither did he rise. If Jesus did not rise, there was no Eucharist. For Ignatius, therefore, the Eucharist was first the sacrament of the incarnation. Without the incarnation, the Eucharist would not have been the sacrament of redemption.

The Eucharist and the Liturgy

Examining the Eucharist as related to the Church and to the person of Jesus suggested a number of constants which enjoy a complementary relationship to each other in the midst of Eucharistic diversity. The Eucharist also enjoys a complementary relationship to its actual celebration in the liturgy. To better understand this we need to look at three areas: the liturgical formulas, the theological themes, and the actual shape of the liturgy.

The first and most important element uniting the Church's various celebrations of the Eucharist is found in the liturgical formulas (1 Cor 11:23-25; Mark 14:22-25; Matt 26:26-29; Luke 22:19-20; and Justin Martyr's *First Apology* 66). These formulas sprang from the earliest Eucharistic experience of the Church, before the Eucharist had a name.

Outside of the formulas themselves we find many references to them, especially in the accounts of Jesus breaking the bread for large crowds (Mark 6:41; 8:6; Matt 14:19; 15:36; Luke 9:16; John 6:11). Additional references to a Eucharistic, liturgical formula appear in the story of the disciples of Emmaus (Luke 24:30) and of Paul breaking the bread at the height of a great storm at sea (Acts 27:35).

There are many differences in these formulas and in the various references to them. Some of these differences come from liturgical tradition. For example, some show Jesus blessing *(eulogein)* God, while others show him thanking *(eucharistein)* God. To bless God is very biblical. We find it in Eucharistic accounts steeped in Jewish tradition (Mark 6:34-44). In relation to the Eucharist, thanking God reflects the new identity in which Jews and Gentiles are made one in Christ which we find in Eucharistic accounts conscious of the new Christian identity (Mark 8:1-9). Mark brought the two together in the liturgical formula used at the Last Supper (Mark 14:22-25).

More striking is the remarkable uniformity among the various traditions in which we find Jesus taking bread, blessing it, giving thanks, breaking it, and announcing this as his body. He does the same with the cup, which he declares the blood of the covenant, or new covenant, which would be poured out. The similarities extend even to the words of Jesus in John's Gospel: "The bread that I will give (this) is my flesh (body) for the life of the world (given for you)" (John 6:51c).

We also have some striking theological themes, notably that of the exodus, the manna, and the Passover. The oldest is that of the exodus, which may have been evoked even in the very beginnings when Christians first referred to the Eucharist as "our *epiousios* bread." Luke's tradition of the Lord's Prayer made the exodus theme even more prominent, asking not just for "the *epiousios* bread" but for "the bread of each day," a reference to the manna in the desert.

The exodus and manna theme is also found in 1 Corinthians 10, as in Mark's stories of Jesus breaking the bread in the desert for large crowds who had nothing to eat (Mark 6:34-44; 8:1-9). We find it also in John, contrasting the bread God gives in the person of Jesus with the bread obtained by their ancestors through the mediation of Moses (John 6:32-35).

The theme of the Passover, which was introduced later, was clearly related to that of the exodus and the manna. Paul did not refer to the Passover in relation to the Eucharist. Mark was the first to present Jesus' Last Supper as a Jewish Passover, but as announcing the new Passover Jesus would eat in the kingdom of God. In this he was followed by Matthew and Luke. Anticipating the new Passover, the synoptics present Jesus at the Last Supper speaking a liturgical formula for the Lord's Supper, showing the intimate link between the Last Supper and the Lord's Supper and how the new Passover replaced the old. John did not present the Last Supper as a Jewish Passover meal, but he did present it in a Passover atmosphere.

The early Christians did not celebrate the Eucharist as the Passover, which was a yearly feast. They celebrated it weekly, "on the first day of the week," the first day of the new creation. But since the Eucharist commemorated Christ's fulfillment of the Passover in his dying and rising, it had great Passover significance. Dying with Christ in baptism, the Christians were buried with him and entered into a new life with him. Participating in Christ's Passover by baptism, they celebrated his Passover, the Christian Passover, weekly. In the Synoptic Gospels, Christ's Passover was also the Christian Passover.

At the very beginning, right after Christ's passion and resurrection, the Eucharist had no special shape. When Jesus first appeared to his disciples, it was at a community meal. So it must have stayed a community meal for some time, the meal of a missionary community extending hospitality to new members. Eventually, however, the Eucharist seems to have taken the shape of a symposium, a meal followed by a discussion, a dialogue or a discourse, during which wine was served.

Celebrating the Eucharist as a symposium, however, may not have been the common practice. It presupposed that a member of the Christian community was able to host the entire community which presupposed considerable wealth. Ordinarily, Christians must have assembled as a Church in more humble circumstances. It may be that some communities never had a symposium at all. The interest in the symposium, a banquet provided by a *kurios*, lies in its emphasis on the Lordship of Christ. Regarding the shape of the liturgy, a symposium would have had "the liturgy of the word" not before but after "the liturgy of the Eucharist." In that setting, the liturgical formula consisted of two formulas, one spoken at the beginning of the meal, the other after the meal with the cup.

Little by little, the practice of celebrating the Eucharist as a full meal ceased, doing so earlier in some places than in others. Without a full meal, the Eucharistic symposium would also have ceased. Mark recalls a time when Christians celebrated the Eucharist as a symposium (Mark 6:34-44), and he presents Jesus' Last Supper as one. The fact, however, that he joins the two liturgical formulas into one formula suggests that the meal between the formulas had been dropped. If so, Mark would not have thought of the Eucharist, at least as celebrated in the Markan community, as a symposium.

By the time of Justin, the meal had become largely symbolic, as it is today. Several factors may have influenced this development, including the size of the community, the difficulty of providing the same hospitality for all, and the wealth it presupposed. Such factors seem already to have been at work when Paul wrote 1 Corinthians. They seem also to have been important issues in the Lukan communities (see Luke 14:1-25).

With the Eucharist no longer a full meal and the disappearance of the symposium format, "the liturgy of the word" now introduced the symbolic, ritual meal. This "liturgy of the word" may have been influenced by the practice of the synagogue. Justin's *First Apology*, however, suggests a different origin, that is, the close relationship between the Eucharist and baptismal catechesis.

When the Eucharist was celebrated as a rite of initiation, it did not include a special "liturgy of the word." Due to the baptismal catechesis, none was needed (*First Apology* 65). When the Eucharist was celebrated weekly on Sunday, however, "the liturgy of the word" was included (*First Apology* 66). It may be, therefore, that "the liturgy of the word," preceding rather than following the Eucharistic liturgy proper, may have been suggested by the community's initiation catechesis, which preceded baptism, rather than by the practice of the synagogue. Apart from baptism, the Sunday celebration of the Eucharist needed its own liturgical catechesis.

NOTES

1. Powers, *The Eucharistic Mystery*, 23.

2. The expression "as a Church" *(en ekklesia)* is from 1 Corinthians: "I hear that when you meet *(synerchomenon hymon)* as a church" (1 Cor 11:18). It was possible for Christians to meet without assembling "as a Church," not, however, for the Lord's Supper. For the Lord's Supper, they always assembled as a Church (1 Cor 11:20).

3. The oldest extant use of the name "the breaking of the bread" *(he klasis tou artou)* is in a summary of what the disciples of Emmaus reported to the assembled community on returning to Jerusalem: "Then the two recounted what had taken place on the way and how he was made known to them in the breaking of the bread" (Luke 24:35; see 24:30-31).

Index of Proper Names and Subjects

Index of Greek, Latin, and Hebrew Terms and Expressions

(ho) pais, 133
palin, 78 n. 7
panis quotidianus, 9
paradidomi, 31
  paradokan, 177
paradosis, 63 n. 4
paralambano, 31
paratheken trapezan, 108
pases tes ekklesias, 158
(to) pathein, 101
  tou pathous tou theou mou, 156
peri, 76
  peri de, 44 n. 7
peri de hon egrapsate, 44 n. 7
peri hemon, 76
(to) peri pollon, 76
peripsema hymon kai agnizomai hyper
  hymon, 158
phagein, 11 n. 9
pharmakon athanasia, 159
phileo
  ephilei, 117
philoi, 117
photismos, 173, 175
pleista chairein, 150
poterion kyriou pinein, 21
  hen poterion eis henosin tou
    haimatos autou, 160
  poterion hydatos kai kramatos, 174
presbyterion, 155, 160
proestos, 174
  to proestoti ton adelphon, 174
(he) proseuche, 106
  hai proseuchai, 103, 187
  eucharistias kai proseuches apechon-
    tai, 162
proton peri tou poteriou, 142

quotidianus, 9

sabbatizontes, 154
sarkopoietheis, 176

sarx, 156, 161, 177
  en sarki, 161
  hos sarkikos, 162
  mia sarx, 160
sectio panis, 51, 54, 69
sitos theou, 156
soma, 161, 162, 177
soteria, 109
spuris
  spurides, 57
syn, 11 n. 7, 101
synalizomai, 5, 11 n. 7
synalizomenos, 99, 101, 110 n. 6
synathroizestai, 153
syndoulos, 153
  tois syndoulois mou, 160
(te) syneidesei, 155
synerchomai, 45 n. 20
  koine synerchesthe, 158
  synerchomenon hymon, 189 n. 2
  synerchomenos hymon en ekklesia,
    xi n. 1
supersubstantialis, 9

tegos, 111 n. 16
teknon, 44 n. 17
  tekna, 44 nn. 16, 17
terminus a quo, 14
terminus ad quem, 14
thysia, 154, 156
  theo thysia, 156
  thysia hymon, 143
thysiasterion, 152, 154, 155, 156
  epi hen thysiasterion, 153
  ho ektos thysiasteriou, 155
  ho entos thysiasterion, 155, 157
trapezes kyriou metechein, 21
tris, 111 n. 16
tristegos, 111 n. 16
trophe, 175
  trophe phthoras, 156

Yahweh, 144